Nature, The Soul, and God

Nature, The Soul, and God

Jean W. Rioux
Benedictine College

Cascade Books
A division of *Wipf & Stock Publishers*
199 West 8th Avenue, Suite 3 • Eugene OR 97401

Cascade Books
199 W. 8th Avenue
Eugene, Oregon 97401
Www.wipfandstock.com

Nature, The Soul, and God
By Jean W. Rioux
Copyright © 2004 by Jean W. Rioux
ISBN: 1-59244-660-4

Contents

Contents

Preface

> *Man naturally desires to know.*
>
> *—Aristotle, Metaphysics—*

We are distinct among living things in that we can apply our minds, not only to life's mundane problems but also to questions which have no immediate practical consequence. We ask not only *how* or *what* but *why*, and it is the last question Aristotle has foremost in mind when he says that we have a natural desire to know. This distinctive trait is evident even in the very young, as evidenced by the persistent questioning of a child wanting to know *why* things are as they are.

We accordingly divide human knowing into *practical* and *speculative*, or *theoretical*. Most people (by far) are more familiar with practical knowing than with speculative, if only because it is of great importance in day-to-day life. As engineers, architects, surveyors, or craftsmen find the need to compute the length of the diagonal of a rectangle, they solve the problem by taking the square root of the sum of the squares on two adjacent sides, or, more familiarly, by applying the formula $a^2 + b^2 = c^2$ to the case at hand. Solving the problem in this way, even arriving at such a formula by trial-and-error, is a *practical* use of reason. But this is not what Aristotle intends when he says we naturally desire to know, since practical knowledge is itself directed to something else (to the building of a structure, or establishing property lines.) *Speculative* knowledge is not a *means*: here, one simply asks *why* it is that the sum of the squares on two adjacent sides of a rectangle is equal to the square on the diagonal. Asking *this* question assumes that one already knows the formula in question, (which is all that would be needed if one had solving some concrete problem in mind). What we desire here is to know, as such. Speculative inquiries are directed to the possession of knowledge itself, as to something desirable and good.

On the other hand, we know from history that even speculative uses of reason may have practical effects. The developments of our technological age, for example, are partially rooted in speculative disputes about how human beings come to know things. The point here, however, is that speculative reasoning is *good to do*, whether one gains in a practical way or not. In answer to a question from a student of his, who asked what was to be gained in a study of geometry, Euclid is supposed to have responded 'Give the man a coin, seeing that he feels he must profit in some way from what he learns.' The profit was in the learning itself—we can only hope that the student got the point.

Mathematics, literature, the arts, human history, natural science, all these and more present themselves as possible areas of a properly *speculative* study. Moreover, within these several areas, one might go about such a study in different ways. For example, one might ask the mathematical question: 'why are the angles of a triangle equal to two right angles?', which is to say: 'upon what basis is this true?' The solution to such a question would be a *mathematical* one. One might also look at the same subject and ask 'are there such things as triangles in reality?' or even 'how do we know the truth of the very starting-points of mathematics?' These latter questions are more properly *philosophical* ones, and resolving *such* questions is the work of philosophy, as we know it today.

To say the same thing somewhat differently, philosophy considers the more basic questions which arise in all areas of study. As we said, the mathematician would not ask whether triangles exist or not—the question is really not a *mathematical* one at all. *That* question is more like asking 'is there such a thing as a science of mathematics?' Rather, the mathematician assumes certain things within the study, and proceeds. The philosopher, in turn, asks questions about what is assumed by the mathematician.

In this book, we are concerned with the natural world. As you might expect, there are many ways in which one might study nature. Physics, biology, and chemistry study nature in a manner we call 'scientific'. They look at nature from a certain perspective, and they make assumptions about studying the natural world in this way. With these starting-points in mind, they proceed to deal with more specific questions about nature. In contrast, a *philosophical* study of nature is pre-scientific. It is more concerned with the *starting-points* of these sciences than with the detailed conclusions scientists are interested in. While the chemist would assume a certain table of elements, more or less well-established, and proceed to investigate the properties and various combinations of such elements, a philosopher would ask about the nature of elements and compounds themselves—what are they? is a compound merely a group of elements, or something different? While a classical physicist would assume that a body moving in a straight line would continue to do so unless impeded, a philosopher might ask: what is motion? does it really differ from rest, or is this only an apparent difference?

This book deals with philosophical questions about the natural world. Consequently, we have included readings from past philosophers to bring out these most basic questions, and most of the book is concerned directly with these. Further, in order to show what impact one's position on the natural world will have upon other things, we have included readings concerned with the immortality of the human soul and with the existence of God. As will become clear, there are definite and irreversible connections among our philosophical views—what we hold about some things has a real effect upon what we hold elsewhere. In particular, what we hold regarding the world of nature has a direct impact upon what we hold regarding human nature, as well as God. As one sees nature to be a certain way, so one sees human nature in a like vein. Insofar as one regards nature to be of this sort, so one defines what is beyond nature, or the 'supernatural'.

Acknowledgments

Excerpt from Anselm of Canterbury's *Proslogion*, translated by Jean W. Rioux. © 1996 Jean W. Rioux.

Selected chapters from Aristotle's *Physics*, translated by Jean W. Rioux. © 1992 Jean W. Rioux.

Passages from Democritus, translated by Jean W. Rioux. © 1995 Jean W. Rioux.

Excerpt from René Descartes' *Meditations on First Philosophy*, translated by John Veitch, 1901.

Excerpts from Jean Henri Fabre's *The Hunting Wasps*, translated by Alexander Reixiera de Mattos, 1915.

Excerpts from Lucretius's *On the Nature of Things*, translated by H. A. J. Munro. 1914.

Passages from Parmenides, Melissus, Zeno, Anaximander, Anaximenes, Empedocles, Anaxagoras, and Heraclitus, translated by John Burnett. 1892.

Excerpts from Plato's *Cratylus, Timaeus, Republic, and Laws*, translated by Benjamin Jowett, 1871.

Passages from Thales, translated by Jean W. Rioux. © 1995 Jean W. Rioux.

Thomas Aquinas' *On the Mixture of Elements*, translated by Jean W. Rioux. © 1991 Jean W. Rioux.

Excerpt from Thomas Aquinas' *On the Principles of Nature*, translated by Jean W. Rioux. © 1991 Jean W. Rioux.

Excerpt from Thomas Aquinas' *Summa Contra Gentiles*, translated by Jean W. Rioux. © 1991 Jean W. Rioux.

Excerpts from Thomas Aquinas' *Summa Theologica*, translated by Fathers of the English Dominican Province, 1947.

I. Nature

Unlike many of their modern counterparts, the earliest philosophers began their inquiries with questions about the natural world. While the principle of Descartes' philosophy (along with the dominant strains of all modern and contemporary philosophy) is the individual human person (the individual human *consciousness*, rather,) the first philosophers were philosophers of *nature*. Rather than attempting to discern what may be known outside of ourselves from what we know of ourselves, they began with a starting-point that was much more evident to them: that natural things change. It was the reality of change in the world about them that led the Pre-Socratic philosophers to speculate upon the origins of change, and even the origins of the natural world itself. There is much to be said in defense of the more ancient way of doing philosophy. After all, we are ourselves beings of nature, and are aware of things outside of ourselves long before we become self-aware. It is with basic philosophical accounts of nature itself, then, that we begin.

The Pre-Socratic Philosophers

The philosophers whom we shall first look at are called the *Pre-Socratics*, not only because they lived before Socrates, but also because their philosophical interests differ sharply from his. Socrates eventually despaired of coming to know the natural world and turned his attention to human affairs instead. The original writings of the Pre-Socratics have been lost, and these passages ('fragments') are quotations and paraphrases taken from other authors.

We will take up the Pre-Socratics in three groups. The first group contains Parmenides, Melissus, and Zeno, who are alike in holding that there are no natural principles, that being is one and unchangeable, and that we are deceived in thinking that there even is a natural world to explain. The position they hold is called *Eleaticism*. In the second group are found Thales, Anaximander, and Anaximenes. They are called the *Milesians* (from their native city of Milesia) and are alike in holding that there is a single natural principle: that nature is primarily known by reference to a single basic thing. The final group includes Empedocles, Anaxagoras, and Democritus. Not forming a single school of thought, they are yet similar in holding that nature is explained only by reference to several basic factors. We shall refer to them as the *Pluralists*.

The Eleatics

Parmenides of Elea

The Way of Truth

Come now, I will tell you—and do you hearken to my saying and carry it away—the only two ways of search that can be thought of. The first, namely, that *It is,* and that it is impossible for anything not
5 to be, is the way of conviction, for truth is its companion. The other, namely, that *It is not,* and that something must not be—that, I tell you, is a wholly untrustworthy path. For you cannot know what is not—that is impossible—nor utter it; for it is the same thing that can be thought and that can be.
10 It must be that what can be thought and spoken of is; for it is possible for it to be, and it is not possible for what is nothing to be. This is what I bid you ponder. I hold you back from this first way of inquiry, and from this other also, upon which mortals knowing nothing wander in two minds; for hesitation guides the wandering
15 thought in their breasts, so that they are borne along stupefied like men deaf and blind. Undiscerning crowds, in whose eyes the same thing and not the same is and is not, and all things travel in opposite directions!

For this shall never be proved, that the things that are not are;
20 and do you restrain your thought from this way of inquiry.

One path only is left for us to speak of, namely, that *It is.* In it are very many tokens that what is, is uncreated and indestructible, alone, complete, immovable and without end. Nor was it ever, nor will it be; for now *it is,* all at once, a continuous one. For what kind of origin for
25 it will you look for? In what way and from what source could it have drawn its increase? I shall not let you say nor think that it came from what is not; for it can neither be thought nor uttered that what is not is. And, if it came from nothing, what need could have made it arise later rather than sooner? Therefore must it either be altogether or be
30 not at all. Nor will the force of truth suffer anything to arise besides itself from that which in any way is. Wherefore, Justice does not loose

5

her fetters and let anything come into being or pass away, but holds it fast.

"*Is it* or *is it not?*" Surely it is judged, as it must be, that we are to
35 set aside the one way as unthinkable and nameless (for it is no true way), and that the other path is real and true. How, then, can what *is* be going to be in the future? Or how could it come into being? If it came into being, it is not; nor is it if it is going to be in the future. Thus is becoming extinguished and passing away not to be heard of.

40   Nor is it divisible, since it is all alike, and there is no more of it in one place than in another, to hinder it from holding together, nor less of it, but everything is full of what is. Wherefore all holds together; for what is, is in contact with what is.

Moreover, it is immovable in the bonds of mighty chains, without
45 beginning and without end; since coming into being and passing away have been driven afar, and true belief has cast them away. It is the same, and it rests in the self-same place, abiding in itself. And thus it remains constant in its place; for hard necessity keeps it in the bonds of the limit that holds it fast on every side. Wherefore it is not
50 permitted to what is to be infinite; for it is in need of nothing; while, if it were infinite, it would stand in need of everything.

Look steadfastly with your mind at things afar as though they were at hand. You cannot cut off what anywhere is from holding fast to what is anywhere; neither is it scattered abroad throughout the
55 universe, nor does it come together.

It is the same thing that can be thought and for the sake of which the thought exists; for you cannot find thought without something that is, to which it is betrothed. And there is not, and never shall be, any time other than that which is present, since fate has chained it so
60 as to be whole and immovable. Wherefore all these things are but the names which mortals have given, believing them to be true—coming into being and passing away, being and not being, change of place and alteration of bright color.

Where, then, it has a farthest boundary, it is complete on every
65 side, equally poised from the center in every direction, like the mass of a rounded sphere; for it cannot be greater or smaller in one place than in another. For there is nothing which is not that could keep it from reaching out equally, nor is it possible that there should be more

of what is in this place and less in that, since it is all inviolable. For,
70 since it is equal in all directions, it is equally confined within limits.

The Way of Opinion

Here shall I close my trustworthy speech and thought about the
truth. Henceforward learn the opinions of mortals, giving ear to the
deceptive ordering of my words.

75 Mortals have settled in their minds to speak of two forms, one of
which they should have left out, and that is where they go astray
from the truth. They have assigned an opposite substance to each,
and marks distinct from one another. To the one they allot the fire of
heaven, light, thin, in every direction the same as itself, but not the
80 same as the other. The other is opposite to it, dark night, a compact
and heavy body. Of these I tell you the whole arrangement as it
seems to men, in order that no mortal may surpass you in knowledge.

Thus, according to men's opinions, did things come into being,
and thus they are now. In time (they think) they will grow up and
85 pass away. To each of these things men have assigned a fixed name.

Questions To Consider

1 What is Parmenides' overall conclusion? How does he support this
conclusion?
2 Does Parmenides try to explain change and motion? Will he admit
to any sort of change at all? If so, to what sort does he admit? If
not, why not?
3 For Parmenides, what are the characteristics of what exists?
What does our experience of the world tell us about reality?
4 Distinguish between Parmenides' two *ways of inquiry*. Which is
the right way?
5 According to Parmenides, what "shall never be proved"? Does this
make sense?
6 How does Parmenides describe being (or *that which is*)?
7 If being is unchangeable, then what do the names 'coming into
being' and 'alteration' actually refer to?

Melissus of Samos

If nothing is, what can be said of it as of something real?

What was, was ever, and ever will be. For, if it had come into being, it needs must have been nothing before it came into being. Now, if it were nothing, in no wise could anything have arisen out of 5 nothing.

Since, then, it has not come into being, and since it is, was ever, and ever shall be, it has no beginning or end, but is without limit. For, if it had come into being, it would have had a beginning (for it would have begun to come into being at some time or other) and an 10 end (for it would have ceased to come into being at some time or other); but, if it neither began nor ended, and ever was and ever will be, it has no beginning or end; for it is not possible for anything to be ever without all being.

Further, just as it ever is, so it must ever be infinite in 15 magnitude.

But nothing which has a beginning or end is either eternal or infinite.

If it were not one, it would be bounded by something else.

For if it is infinite, it must be one; for if it were two, it could not 20 be infinite; for then they would be bounded by one another.

And, since it is one, it is alike throughout; for if it were unlike, it would be many and not one.

So then it is eternal and infinite and one and all alike. And it cannot perish nor become greater, nor does it suffer pain or grief. For, 25 if any of these things happened to it, it would no longer be one. For if it is altered, then the real must needs not be all alike, but what was before must pass away, and what was not must come into being. Now, if it changed by so much as a single hair in ten thousand years, it would all perish in the whole of time.

30 Further, it is not possible either that its order should be changed; for the order which it had before does not perish, nor does that which was not come into being. But, since nothing is either added to it or passes away or is altered, how can any real thing have had its order changed? For if anything became different, that would amount to a 35 change in its order.

8

Nor does it suffer pain; for a thing in pain could not all be. For a thing in pain could not be ever, nor has it the same power as what is whole. Nor would it be alike, if it were in pain; for it is only from the addition or subtraction of something that it could feel pain, and then
40 it would no longer be alike. Nor could what is whole feel pain; for then what was whole and what was real would pass away, and what was not would, come into being. And the same argument applies to grief as to pain.

Nor is anything empty. For what is empty is nothing. What is
45 nothing cannot be.

Nor does it move; for it has nowhere to bring itself to, but is full. For if there were anything empty, it would bring itself to the empty. But, since there is nothing empty, it has nowhere to bring itself to.

And it cannot be dense and rare; for it is not possible for what is
50 rare to be as full as what is dense, but what is rare is at once emptier than what is dense.

This is the way in which we must distinguish between what is full and what is not full. If a thing has room for anything else, and takes it in, it is not full; but if it has no room for anything and does not take
55 it in, it is full.

Now, it must needs be full if there is nothing empty, and if it is full, it-does not move.

This argument, then, is the greatest proof that it is one alone; but the following are proofs of it also. If there were a many, these would
60 have to be of the same kind as I say that the one is. For if there is earth and water, and air and iron, and gold and fire, and if one thing is living and another dead, and if things are black and white and all that people say they really are,-if that is so, and if we see and hear aright, each one of these must be such as we first decided, and they
65 cannot be changed or altered, but each must be just as it is. But, as it is, we say that we see and hear and understand aright, and yet we believe that what is warm becomes cold, and what is cold warm; that what is hard turns soft, and what is soft hard; that what is living dies, and that things are born from what lives not; and that all those
70 things are changed, and that what they were and what they are now are in no way alike. We think that iron, which is hard, is rubbed away by contact with the finger; and so with gold and stone and everything which we fancy to be strong, and that earth and stone are made out of

water; so that it turns out that we neither see nor know realities.
75 Now these things do not agree with one another. We said that there
were many things that were eternal and had forms and strength of
their own, and yet we fancy that they all suffer alteration, and that
they change from what we see each time. It is clear, then, that we did
not see aright after all, nor are we right in believing that all these
80 things are many. They would not change if they were real, but each
thing would be just what we believed it to be; for nothing is stronger
than true reality. But if it has changed, what was has passed away,
and what was not is come into being. So then, if there were many
things, they would have to be just of the same nature as the one.

85   Now, if it were to exist, it must needs be one; but if it is one, it
cannot have body; for, if it had body it would have parts, and would
no longer be one.

If what is real is divided, it moves; but if it moves, it cannot be.

Questions To Consider

1   For Melissus, what are the characteristics of what exists?
     Compare his position with that of Parmenides. To what extent
     are the positions similar? To what extent are they dissimilar?
2   According to Melissus, is any sort of change possible? If so, what
     sort is possible? If not, why not?
3   Analyze Melissus' argument that being is ungenerated and
     cannot be corrupted. What is his conclusion, and what reasons
     does he give in support of this conclusion? In your judgment, is
     this a good argument?

Zeno of Elea

You cannot traverse an infinite number of points in a finite time. You must traverse the half of any given distance before you traverse the whole, and the half of that again before you can traverse it. This goes on *ad infinitum*, so that there are an infinite number in any
5   given space, and it cannot be traversed in a finite time.

A   C   D   E   B

Achilles must first reach the place from which the tortoise started. By that time the tortoise will have got on a little way. Achilles must then traverse that, and still the tortoise will be ahead.
10   He is always coming nearer, but he never makes up to it.

A Question To Consider

What is a *paradox*? Why would each of these three arguments be called *paradoxes*?

The Milesians

Thales

All things come from water.
The earth rests on water.
A magnet has a soul, since it moves iron.
All things are full of gods.
5   The wet nature, easily reformed into each thing, is shaped in various ways: for [the part] of it which turns into vapor becomes like air, and what is thinned out of the air becomes ether, and, as water settles and changes into mud, it becomes earth. Therefore Thales claimed that, among the four elements, water was *the* element, as
10 being more of a cause [than the others].
   —*Taken from Heraclitus Homericus*

Questions To Consider

1   For Thales, is being one, or many? What, for him, is the principle of all things? In your judgment, is this claim plausible in any way?

2   Does Thales admit any sort of change? If so, what kind does he admit? If not, why not?

3   What kind of a principle is water, for Thales? That is, does it bring about change in some way, or is it merely required in order for change to occur?

4   In your judgment, is the difference between water and other things which exist (such as air, and earth) real, or merely apparent for Thales?

5   What makes the difference, say, between air and earth for Thales? Would it be fair to Thales to assert that air and earth are different kinds of thing?

Anaximander

Anaximander of Miletus, son of Praxiades, a fellow-citizen and associate of Thales, said that the material cause and first element of things was the Infinite, he being the first to introduce this name of the material cause. He says that it is neither water nor any other of
5 what are now called the elements, but a substance different from them which is infinite, from which arise all the heavens and the worlds within them.

He says that this is eternal and ageless, and that it encompasses all the worlds.

10 And into that from which things take their rise they pass away once more, "as is ordained; for they make reparation and satisfaction to one another for their injustice according to the appointed," as he says in these somewhat poetical terms.

And besides this, there was an eternal motion, in which was
15 brought about the origin of the worlds.

He did not ascribe the origin of things to any alteration in matter, but said that the oppositions in the substratum, which was a boundless body, were separated out.

[He holds] that this (i.e., a body over and above the elements) is
20 what is infinite, and not air or water, in order that the other things may not be destroyed by their infinity. They are in opposition to one another—air is cold, water moist, and fire hot.—and therefore if any one of them were infinite, the rest would have ceased to be by this time. Accordingly [he says] that what is infinite is something other
25 than the elements, and that from it the elements arise.

Questions To Consider

1 For Anaximander, is being one or many? What is his first principle? Is this claim at all probable?

2 How does Anaximander's principle differ from those of Thales and Anaximenes? How would you describe his principle?

3 Why, claims Anaximander, can the principle of all things **not** be earth, or air, or fire, or water?

Anaximenes

Anaximenes of Miletus, son of Eurystratos, who had been an associate of Anaximander, said, like him, that the underlying substance was one and infinite. He did not, however, say it was indeterminate, like Anaximander, but determinate; for he said it was
5   Air.

From it, he said, the things that are, and have been, and shall be, the gods and things divine, took their rise, while other things come from its offspring.

"Just as," he said, "our soul, being air, holds us together, so do
10   breath and air encompass the whole world."

And the form of the air is as follows. Where it is most even, it is invisible to our sight; but cold and heat, moisture and motion, make it visible. It is always in motion; for, if it were not, it would not change so much as it does.

15   It differs in different substances in virtue of its rarefaction and condensation.

When it is dilated so as to be rarer, it becomes fire; while winds, on the other hand, are condensed Air. Cloud is formed from air by compression; and this, still further condensed, becomes water. Water,
20   condensed still more, turns to earth; and when condensed as much as it can be, to stones.

Questions To Consider

1   For Anaximenes, is being one or many? What is his first principle? Is this claim at all probable?

2   Does Anaximenes admit change of any sort?

3   Is "infinite air" the same sort of principle as Thales' "water"?

4   How do things other than air (such as fire, water, and earth) differ from one another, for Anaximander?

5   In your judgment, is the difference between infinite air and the other things which exist (such as fire, water, and earth) real, or merely apparent, for Anaximenes?

6   Taking the Milesians as a group, is there a difficulty in saying that all things come to be out of a single sort of thing, whatever that might be? What about the *differences* among things?

The Pluralists

Empedocles of Acragas

Fools!—for they have no far-reaching thoughts—who think that what before was not comes into being, or that anything can perish and be utterly destroyed. For it cannot be that anything can arise from what in no way is, and it is impossible and unheard of that what
5 is should perish; for it will always be, wherever one may keep putting it.

A man who is wise in such matters would never surmise in his heart that, as long as mortals live what men choose to call their life, [so long] they are, and suffer good and ill; while before they were
10 formed and after they have been dissolved they are, it seems, nothing at all.

There is no coming into being of anything that perishes, nor any end for it in baneful death.; but only mingling and separation of what has been mingled. 'Coming into being' is but a name given to these by
15 men.

But, when the elements have been mingled in the fashion of a man and come to the light of day, or in the fashion of the race of wild beasts or plants or birds, then men say that these come into being; and when they are separated, they call that, as is the custom, woeful
20 death. I too follow the custom, and call it so myself.

Come, I shall now tell you first of all the beginning of the sun, and the sources from which have sprung all the things we now behold, the earth and the billowy sea, the damp mist and the Titan air that binds his circle fast round all things.

25 Hear first the four roots of all things: shining Zeus [fire], life-bringing Hera [air], Aidoneus [earth], and Nestis [water] dripping with tears, the well-spring of mortals.

Behold the sun, everywhere bright and warm, and all the immortal things that are bathed in its heat and bright radiance.
30 Behold the rain, everywhere dark and cold; and from the earth issue forth things close-pressed and solid. When they are in strife all these

17

are different in form and separated; but they come together in love,
and are desired by one another.

For out of these have sprung all things that were and are and
35 shall be—trees and men and women, beasts and birds and the fishes
that dwell in the waters, yes, and the gods that live long lives and are
exalted in honor.

For these things are what they are; but, running through one
another, they take different shapes—so much does mixture change
40 them.

Just as when painters are elaborating temple-offerings, men
whom Metus has well-taught their art—they, when they have taken
pigments of many colors with their hands, mix them in a harmony,
more of some and less of others, and from them produce shapes like
45 all things, making trees and men and women, beasts and fishes that
dwell in the waters, yes, and gods, that live long lives, and are exalted
in honor—so let not the error prevail over your mind, that there is
any other source of all the perishable creatures that appear in
countless numbers. Know this for sure, for you have heard the tale
50 from a goddess.

And the kindly earth in its well-wrought ovens received two parts
of shining Nestis out of the eight, and four of Hephaistos; and they
became white bones, divinely fitted together by the cements of
Harmony.

55 And the earth meets with these in nearly equal proportions, with
Hephaistos and Water and shining Air, anchoring in the perfect
havens of Kypris—either a little more of it, or less of it and more of
them. From these did blood arise and the various forms of flesh.

At one time things grew together to be one only out of many, at
60 another they parted asunder so as to be many instead of one—Fire
and Water and Earth and the mighty height of Air; dread Strife, too,
apart from these, and balancing every one of them, and Love among
them, their equal in length and breadth. Contemplate her with your
mind, nor sit with dazed eyes. It is she that is thought to be
65 implanted in the frame of mortals. It is she that makes them have
kindly thoughts and work the works of peace. They call her by the
names of Joy and Aphrodite.

For all these are equal and alike in age, yet each has a different
prerogative and its own peculiar nature. And nothing comes into

70 being besides these, nor do they pass away; for, if they had been passing away continually, they would not be now.

Nor is any part of the whole empty. From where, then, could anything come to increase it? Where, too, could these things perish, since no place is empty of them? They are what they are, but, running 75 through one another, different things continually come into being from different sources, yet ever alike.

I shall you a twofold tale. At one time things grew to be one only out of many; at another, that divided up to be many instead of one. There is a double becoming of perishable things and a double passing 80 away. The coming together of all things brings one generation into being and destroys it; the other grows up and is scattered as things become divided. And these things never cease, continually changing places, at one time all uniting in one through Love, at another each carried in different directions by the repulsion of Strife. Thus, as far 85 as it is their nature to grow into one out of many, and to become many once more when the one is parted asunder, so far they come into being and their life abides not. But, inasmuch as they never cease changing their places continually, so far they are immovably as they go round the circle of existence.

90 But, as divinity was mingled still further with divinity, these things joined together as each might chance, and many other things beside them continually arose.

Questions To Consider

1 What do fools think, and why is it foolish?
2 Does Empedocles have the same sort of principle as the Milesians? What are his principles?
3 For Empedocles, can there be more than four kinds of thing? (For example, would he agree that horses, trees, bone, blood, and so on, even exist?) If so, how? If not, why not?
4 Does Empedocles have any principles other than the four elements? If so, what are these principles? If not, how does he explain motion and change?
5 Are *love* and *hatred* a different sort of principle from those we have already seen? If so, how do they differ? If not, how are they related to change?
6 Are coming-to-be and passing away real, for Empedocles?

7 How would Empedocles explain regularity in nature, for example, that cattle normally have the heads of cattle and men the heads of men? Is there any *reason* why things should be as they are, for Empedocles?

8 In your judgment, is it probable in any way that things are made up of earth, air, fire, and water? Is his explanation of *how* compounds are formed altogether unreasonable, or does it even resemble a current view?

9 Are earth, air, fire, and water destructible, by Empedocles' account?

10 Is change real, for Empedocles? Is his account of change (leaving aside, for the moment, his choice of elements) an unreasonable one?

Anaxagoras of Clazomenae

All things were together, infinite both in number and in smallness—for the small too was infinite. And, when all things were together, none of them could be distinguished because of their smallness. For air and ether prevailed over all things, being both of
5   them infinite; for among all things these are the greatest both in quantity and size.

Nor is there a least of what is small, but there is always a smaller; for it is impossible that what *is* should cease to be by being divided. But there is always something greater than what is great,
10   and it is equal to the small in amount, and, compared with itself, each thing is both great and small.

And since these things are so, we must suppose that there are contained many things and of all sorts in all (the things) that are brought together, seeds of all things, with all sorts of shapes and
15   colors and flavors.

But before they were separated off, when all things were together, not even was any color distinguishable; for the mixture of all things prevented it—of the moist and the dry, and the warm and the cold, and the light and the dark [and much earth being in it], and of a
20   multitude of innumerable seeds in no way like each other. For none of the other things either is like any other.

For how can hair come from not-hair, or flesh from not-flesh?

And since the portions of the great and of the small are equal in amount, for this reason, too, all things will be in everything; nor is it
25   possible for them to be apart, but all things have a portion of everything. Since it is impossible for there to be a least thing, they cannot be separated, nor come to be by themselves; but they must be now, just as they were in the beginning, all together. And in all things many things are contained, and an equal number both in the greater
30   and in the smaller of the things that are separated off.

Nor are the things that are in one world divided nor cut off from one another with a hatchet, neither the warm from the cold nor the cold from the warm.

And when those things are being distinguished in this way, we
35   must know that all of them are neither more nor less; for it is not possible for them to be more than all, and all are always equal.

The Hellenes are wrong in using the expressions 'coming into being' and 'passing away'; for nothing comes into being or passes away, but there is a mingling and separation of the things that are.
40 So they would be right to call coming into being 'mixture', and passing away 'separation'.

Because of the weakness of our senses we cannot judge the truth.

In everything there is a portion of everything except Nous [Mind], and there are some things in which there is Nous also.

45 And when Nous began to move things, separating off took place from all that was moved, and so far as Nous set in motion all was separated. And as things were set in motion and separated, the revolution caused them to be separated much more.

[Things] revolve and are separated off by the force and speed. And
50 the speed makes the force. And their speed is not like the speed of any of the things that are now among men, but in every way many times as quick.

The dense and the moist and the cold and the dark came together where the earth is now, while the rare and the warm and the dry
55 [and the bright] went out towards the further part of the ether.

From these as they are separated off earth is solidified; for from mists water is separated off, and from water earth. From the earth stones are solidified by the cold, and these rush outwards more than water.

60 All other things partake in a portion of everything, while Nous is infinite and self-ruled, and is mixed with nothing, but is alone, itself by itself. For if it were not by itself, but were mixed with anything else, it would partake in all things if it were mixed with any; for in everything there is a portion of everything, as has been said by me in
65 what went before, and the things mixed with it would hinder it, so that it would have power over nothing in the same way that it has now being alone by itself. For it is the thinnest of all things and the purest, and it has all knowledge about everything and the greatest strength; and Nous has power over all things, both greater and
70 smaller, that have life. And Nous had power over the whole revolution, so that it began to revolve in the beginning. And it began to revolve first from a small beginning; but the revolution now extends over a larger space, and will extend over a larger still. And all the things that are mingled together and separated off and

75 distinguished are known by Nous. And Nous set in order all things
that were to be and that were, and all things that are not now and
that are, and this revolution in which now revolve the stars and the
sun and the moon, and the air and the ether that are separated off.
And this revolution caused the separating off, and the rare is
80 separated off from the dense, the warm from the cold, the light from
the dark, and the dry from the moist. And there are many portions in
many things. But no thing is altogether separated off nor
distinguished from everything else except Nous. And all Nous is
alike, both the greater and the smaller; while nothing else is like
85 anything else, but each single thing is and was most manifestly those
things of which it has most in it.

Questions To Consider

1   Anaxagoras' position is unlike any we have encountered so far.
How does he propose to explain change, for example, how,
according to him, is it possible for wood to become fire when it
burns?

2   Does Anaxagoras' view really explain change? If so, what sort of
change? If not, why not?

3   Is there anything in Anaxagoras' explanation of change which is
similar to Empedocles' own notion? If so, where is the similarity?
If not, how does change come about for Anaxagoras?

4   Given that everything is in everything, how does Anaxagoras
explain the differences among things, for example, what would
make calcium different from iron, assuming that each contains
infinitely small parts of everything?

5   Is real change possible, according to Anaxagoras?

6   How does Anaxagoras use the word "infinite" in his explanation of
nature and change (there are at least two senses of the word as he
uses it)?

7   What is the basic argument that all things must be in all things?
With what basic data does this argument begin? Would this
argument be reasonable in the context of the other positions we
have considered so far?

8   How many *first principles* does Anaxagoras suppose?

9   What is the point of the fifth paragraph?

10 Does anything ever come into existence or cease to be, for Anaxagoras?

11 What is *Nous*, and what function does it have in a change?

12 How is it that one thing even *appears* to differ from another, given Anaxagoras' position that everything is in everything else?

Democritus of Abdera

The elements [of all things] are the full and the empty—being and non-being; being is full and solid, non-being is empty and rare: being exists no more than non-being, because the void exists [no less] than body: and these are the causes of things as matter.

5　[These] principles are infinite in number—and they are atoms, undivided bodies, which are unchangeable due to their solidity, and which have no void within them.

It is impossible that many things come from one or one from many.

Things are divisible because of the void in them.

10　The differences [among the atoms] are the causes of other things—and there are three such differences: shape, arrangement, and position... for A differs from N in shape, AN from NA in arrangement, I from H in position.

The number of shapes [of atoms] is infinite, since there is no 15　reason why they should be one shape rather than another.

The atoms move in the infinite void, and are separate from one another, and they differ in shape, size, position, and arrangement. Overtaking one another, they come together, and some are cast away in a chance direction, while others, having become intertwined with 20　each other on account of the symmetry of their shapes, sizes, positions, and arrangement, hold fast, and in this way compound bodies come into being.

And [the atoms] cling to one another and stay together until such time as a stronger necessity from the outside shakes them and 25　scatters them apart.

The first bodies are always in motion in the infinite void.

[Atoms] move in the infinite void as the result of mutual impact.

Sweet and bitter exist by convention, hot and cold exist by convention, color exists by convention—but in reality only atoms and 30　void. (It is thought and imagined that the things we sense do exist, but there is no such thing as it is sensed—only atoms and the void.)

Bitter taste comes from small, smooth, round [atoms], which have a winding surface: so they are sticky and viscous; salt taste comes from large [atoms which are] not round, but sometimes uneven.

35　Nothing occurs by chance, but all happens for a reason and of necessity.

Necessity is the resistance and motion and impact of matter.

In compound bodies, the lighter is what has more void, while the heavier is what has less void.

Questions To Consider

1   What is Democritus' first basic point? Of the Pre-Socratics, who would agree with this point and who would disagree?

2   Democritus says "it is impossible that one thing come from two or two things from one." Does his explanation of the world support this? Would Empedocles agree? Would Anaxagoras?

3   Why is empty space needed for change to occur? Given this, what sort of change does Democritus admit? Does he admit any other sorts of change?

4   How does Democritus explain color, taste, and, in general, all the sensible qualities?

5   Do the atoms themselves have any characteristics? If so, describe them. If not, why not?

6   Does Democritus have anything in his explanation of nature and change which is similar to Empedocles' love and hatred and to Anaxagoras' mind? If so, what is it? If not, how does change come about?

7   Do the atoms differ from one another in any way? If so, how?

8   Would Democritus admit that a cactus differs essentially from a pig? If he would, how would they differ? If he would not, what follows with respect to our knowledge of the world?

9   In your judgment, is Democritus more, or less, consistent with common experience than Empedocles, Anaxagoras, or the Milesians?

10 What are Democritus' *first principles*? What is it which makes the motion of the atoms even possible?

11 *Why* do the atoms combine in various ways?

12 Are colors and flavors *real*, by Democritus' account? If the atoms have no color or flavor, then how might one explain these things?

13 Given Democritus' system, why is it impossible for one thing to come from two or two from one?

Epicurus and Lucretius

After the conquests of Alexander the Great, the Hellenistic era of philosophy began, producing two prominent philosophical views: stoicism and epicureanism. Of the two, the philosophy of Epicurus represents a development of Pre-Socratic thought (his basic assumptions are those of Democritus.) A later, Roman proponent of epicureanism was Titus Lucretius Carus (or simply *Lucretius*). His own contribution to philosophy, *On The Nature of Things*, is, in fact, a single long poem dealing with physical theory and ethics. Though Lucretius was born 300 years after the death of Socrates, the Pre-Socratic way of looking at nature remains strong.

Epicurus

Letter to Herodotus

Nothing is created out of that which does not exist: for if it were, everything would be created out of everything with no need of seeds. And again, if that which disappears were destroyed into that which did not exist, all things would have perished, since that into which
5 they were dissolved would not exist.

Furthermore, the universe always was such as it is now, and always will be the same. For there is nothing into which it changes: for outside the universe there is nothing which could come into it and bring about the change.

10 Moreover, the universe is bodies and space: for that bodies exist, sense itself witnesses in the experience of all men, and in accordance with the evidence of sense we must of necessity judge of the imperceptible by reasoning, as I have already said. And if there were not that which we term void and place and intangible existence,

27

15 bodies would have nowhere to exist and nothing through which to
move, as they are seen to move.

And besides these two nothing can even be thought of either by
conception or on the analogy of things conceivable such as could be
grasped as whole existences and not spoken of as the accidents or
20 properties of such existences. Furthermore, among bodies some are
compounds, and others those of which compounds are formed. And
these latter are indivisible and unalterable (if, that is, all things are
not to be destroyed into the non-existent, but something permanent is
to remain behind at the dissolution of compounds): they are
25 completely solid in nature, and can by no means be dissolved in any
part. So it must needs be that the first-beginnings are indivisible
corporeal existences.

Moreover, the universe is boundless. For that which is bounded
has an extreme point: and the extreme point is seen against
30 something else. So that as it has no extreme point, it has no limit;
and as it has no limit, it must be boundless and not bounded.
Furthermore, the infinite is boundless both in the number of the
bodies and in the extent of the void. For if on the one hand the void
were boundless, and the bodies limited in number, the bodies could
35 not stay anywhere, but would be carried about and scattered through
the infinite void, not having other bodies to support them and keep
them in place by means of collisions. But if, on the other hand, the
void were limited, the infinite bodies would not have room wherein to
take their place.
40 Besides this the indivisible and solid bodies, out of which too the
compounds are created and into which they are dissolved, have an
incomprehensible number of varieties in shape: for it is not possible
that such great varieties of things should arise from the same atomic
shapes, if they are limited in number. And so in each shape the atoms
45 are quite infinite in number, but their differences of shape are not
quite infinite, but only incomprehensible in number.
And the atoms move continuously for all time, some of them
falling straight down, others swerving, and others recoiling from their
collisions. And of the latter, some are borne on, separating to a long
50 distance from one another, while others again recoil and recoil,
whenever they chance to be checked by the interlacing with others, or

else shut in by atoms interlaced around them. For on the one hand
the nature of the void which separates each atom by itself brings this
about, as it is not able to afford resistance, and on the other hand the
55 hardness which belongs to the atoms makes them recoil after collision
to as great a distance as the interlacing permits separation after the
collision. And these motions have no beginning, since the atoms and
the void are the cause.

    These brief sayings, if all these points are borne in mind, afford a
60 sufficient outline for our understanding of the nature of existing
things.

    Moreover, we must suppose that the atoms do not possess any of
the qualities belonging to perceptible things, except shape, weight,
and size, and all that necessarily goes with shape. For every quality
65 changes; but the atoms do not change at all, since there must needs
be something which remains solid and indissoluble at the dissolution
of compounds, which can cause changes; not changes into the non-
existent or from the non-existent, but changes effected by the shifting
of position of some particles, and by the addition or departure of
70 others.

    For this reason it is essential that the bodies which shift their
position should be imperishable and should not possess the nature of
what changes, but parts and configuration of their own. For thus
much must needs remain constant. For even in things perceptible to
75 us which change their shape by the withdrawal of matter it is seen
that shape remains to them, whereas the qualities do not remain in
the changing object, in the way in which shape is left behind, but are
lost from the entire body. Now these particles which are left behind
are sufficient to cause the differences in compound bodies, since it is
80 essential that some things should be left behind and not be destroyed
into the non-existent.

    Moreover, we must not either suppose that every size exists
among the atoms, in order that the evidence of phenomena may not
contradict us, but we must suppose that there are some variations of
85 size. For if this be the case, we can give a better account of what
occurs in our feelings and sensations. But the existence of atoms of
every size is not required to explain the differences of qualities in

things, and at the same time some atoms would be bound to come within our ken and be visible; but this is never seen to be the case, nor is it possible to imagine how an atom could become visible.

Besides this we must not suppose that in a limited body there can be infinite parts or parts of every degree of smallness. Therefore, we must not only do away with division into smaller and smaller parts to infinity, in order that we may not make all things weak, and so in the composition of aggregate bodies be compelled to crush and squander the things that exist into the non-existent, but we must not either suppose that in limited bodies there is a possibility of continuing to infinity in passing ever to smaller and smaller parts. For if once one says that there are infinite parts in a body or parts of any degree of smallness, it is not possible to conceive how this should be, and indeed how could the body any longer be limited in size? (For it is obvious that these infinite particles must be of some size or other; and however small they may be, the size of the body too would be infinite.)

And again, since the limited body has an extreme point, which is distinguishable, even though not perceptible by itself, you cannot conceive that the succeeding point to it is not similar in character, or that if you go on in this way from one point to another, it should be possible for you to proceed to infinity marking such points in your mind.

We must notice also that the least thing in sensation is neither exactly like that which admits of progression from one part to another, nor again is it in every respect wholly unlike it, but it has a certain affinity with such bodies, yet cannot be divided into parts. But when on the analogy of this resemblance we think to divide off parts of it, one on the one side and another on the other, it must needs be that another point like the first meets our view. And we look at these points in succession starting from the first, not within the limits of the same point nor in contact part with part, but yet by means of their own proper characteristics measuring the size of bodies, more in a greater body and fewer in a smaller.

Now we must suppose that the least part in the atom too bears the same relation to the whole; for though in smallness it is obvious that it exceeds that which is seen by sensation, yet it has the same relation to sensible bodies that the atom has size, only we placed it far below them in smallness. Further we must consider these least

indivisible points as boundary-marks, providing in themselves as primary units the measure of size for the atoms, both for the smaller and the greater, in our contemplation of these unseen bodies by means of thought. For the affinity which the least parts of the atom
130 have to the homogeneous parts of sensible things is sufficient to justify our conclusion to this extent: but that they should ever come together as bodies with motion is quite impossible.

Furthermore, in the infinite we must not speak of 'up' or 'down,' as though with reference to an absolute highest or lowest - and indeed
135 we must say that, though it is possible to proceed to infinity in the direction above our heads from wherever we take our stand, the absolute highest point will never appear to us - nor yet can that which passes beneath the point thought of to infinity be at the same time both up and down in reference to the same thing: for it is
140 impossible to think this. So that it is possible to consider as one single motion that which is thought of as the upward motion to infinity and as another the downward motion, even though that which passes from us into the regions above our heads arrives countless times at the feet of beings above and that which passes downwards from us at
145 the head of beings below; for none the less the whole motions are thought of as opposed, the one to the other, to infinity.

Moreover, the atoms must move with equal speed, when they are
· borne onwards through the void, nothing colliding with them. For neither will the heavy move more quickly than the small and light,
150 when, that is, nothing meets them: nor again the small more quickly than the great, having their whole course uniform, when nothing collides with them either: nor is the motion upwards or sideways owing to blows quicker, nor again that downwards owing to their own weight. For as long as either of the two motions prevails, so long will
155 it have a course as quick as thought, until something checks it either from outside or from its own weight counteracting the force of that which dealt the blow.

Moreover, their passage through the void, when it takes place without meeting any bodies which might collide, accomplishes every
160 comprehensible distance in an inconceivably short time. For it is collision and its absence which take the outward appearance of slowness and quickness. Moreover, it will be said that in compound bodies too one atom is faster than another, though as a matter of fact

all are equal in speed: this will be said because even in the least
165 period of continuous time all the atoms in aggregate bodies move
towards one place, even though in moments of time perceptible only
by thought they do not move towards one place but are constantly
jostling one against another, until the continuity of their movement
comes under the ken of sensation.

170   For the addition of opinion with regard to the unseen, that the
moments perceptible only by thought will also contain continuity of
motion, is not true in such cases; for we must remember that it is
what we observe with the senses or grasp with the mind by an
apprehension that is true. Nor must it either be supposed that in
175 moments perceptible only by thought the moving body too passes to
the several places to which its component atoms move (for this too is
unthinkable, and in that case, when it arrives all together in a
sensible period of time from any point that may be in the infinite
void, it would not be taking its departure from the place from which
180 we apprehend its motion); for the motion of the whole body will be the
outward expression of its internal collisions, even though up to the
limits of perception we suppose the speed of its motion not to be
retarded by collision. It is of advantage to grasp this first principle as
well.

Questions To Consider

1   With whose philosophical position is Epicurus' own most in
agreement?
2   What two basic principles does Epicurus enunciate at the outset?
Have we seen them before. Apart from their differences, would
the Pre-Socratics agree with these principles?
3   Epicurus gives arguments for the existence of atoms and void.
What would Parmenides say of his argument for the existence of
bodies? What type of argument (categorical, conditional) does he
offer for the existence of void?
4   How does Epicurus argue that the universe is boundless?
5   In what condition are the atoms throughout all of time? What
sorts of motion do they undergo?
6   What are the characteristics of the atoms (speed, direction,
composition, divisibility, size) and the space (void) they exist in?

Lucretius

<u>De Rerum Natura</u> (On the Nature of Things)

Selections from Books I and II

This terror and darkness of mind must be dispelled, not by the rays of the sun and glittering shafts of day, but by the aspect and the law of nature, the warp of whose design we shall begin with this first principle, nothing is ever gotten out of nothing by divine power. Fear, in truth, holds in check all mortals in this way, because they see many operations go on in earth and heaven, the causes of which they can in no way understand, believing them therefore to be done by divine power. For these reasons, when we shall have seen that nothing can be produced from nothing, we shall then more correctly ascertain that which we are seeking, both the elements out of which everything can be produced and the manner in which all things are done without the hand of the gods.

If things came from nothing, any kind might be born of anything, and nothing would require seed. Men, for instance, might rise out of the sea, the scaly race out of the earth, and birds might burst out of the sky, horned and other herds, every kind of wild beasts would haunt with changing brood tilth and wilderness alike. Nor would the same fruits keep constant to trees, but would change; any tree might bear any fruit. For if there were not begetting bodies for each, how could things have a fixed unvarying mother? But in fact because things are all produced from fixed seeds, each thing is born and goes forth into the borders of light out of that in which resides its matter and first bodies; and for this reason all things cannot be gotten out of all things, because in particular things resides a distinct power. Nor would time be required for the growth of things after the meeting of the seed, if they could increase out of nothing. Little babies would at once grow into men and trees in a moment would rise and spring out of the ground. But clearly none of these events ever comes to pass, since all things grow step by step at a fixed time, as is natural, since they all grow from a fixed seed and in growing preserve their kind; so

that you may be sure that all things increase in size and are fed out of
their own matter. Why could not nature have produced men of such a
size and strength as to be able to wade on foot across the sea and rend
great mountains with their hands and outlive many generations of
35 living men, if not because an unchanging matter has been assigned
for begetting things and what can arise out of the matter is fixed? We
must admit therefore that nothing can come from nothing, since
things require seed before they can severally be born and be brought
out into the buxom fields of air.
40   Moreover nature dissolves every thing back into its first bodies
and does not annihilate things. For if anything were mortal in all its
parts alike, the thing in a moment would be snatched away to
destruction from before our eyes, since no force would be needed to
produce disruption among its parts and undo their fastenings.
45 Whereas, in fact, as all things consist of an imperishable seed, nature
suffers the destruction of nothing to be seen, until a force has
encountered it sufficient to dash things to pieces by a blow or to
pierce through the void places within them and break them up. Again
if time, whenever it makes away with things through age, utterly
50 destroys them eating up all their matter, out of what does Venus
bring back into the light of life the race of living things each after its
kind, or, when they are brought back, out of what does earth manifold
in works give them nourishment and increase, furnishing them with
food each after its kind? Out of what do its own native fountains and
55 extraneous rivers from far and wide keep full the sea? Out of what
does ether feed the stars? For infinite time gone by and lapse of days
must have eaten up all things which are of mortal body. Now if in
that period of time gone by those things have existed, of which this
sum of things is composed and recruited, they are possessed no doubt
60 of an imperishable body, and cannot therefore any of them return to
nothing. A thing therefore never returns to nothing, but all things
after disruption go back into the first bodies of matter. None of the
things therefore which seem to be lost is utterly lost, since nature
replenishes one thing out of another and does not suffer any thing to
65 be begotten, before she has been recruited by the death of some other.
     Now mark me: since I have taught that things cannot be born
from nothing, cannot when begotten be brought back to nothing, that
you may not haply yet begin in any shape to mistrust my words,

because the first-beginnings of things cannot be seen by the eyes,
70 take moreover this list of bodies which you must yourself admit are in
the number of things and cannot be seen. First of all the force of the
wind when aroused beats on the harbors and whelms huge ships and
scatters clouds; sometimes in swift whirling eddy it scours the plains
and straws them with large trees and scourges the mountain
75 summits with forest-rending blasts: so fiercely does the wind rave
with a shrill howling and rage with threatening roar. Winds therefore
sure enough are unseen bodies which sweep the seas, the lands, and
even the clouds of heaven, tormenting them and catching them up in
sudden whirls. Then again, we perceive the different smells of things,
80 yet never see them coming to our nostrils; nor do we behold heats nor
can we observe cold with the eyes nor are we used to seeing voices.
Yet all these things must consist of a bodily nature, since they are
able to move the senses: for nothing but body can touch and be
touched. Further, after the revolution of many of the sun's years a
85 ring on the finger is thinned on the under side by wearing, the
dripping from the eaves hollows a stone, the bent plowshare of iron
imperceptibly decreases in the fields, and we behold the stone-paved
streets worn down by the feet of the multitude, the brass statues too
at the gates show their right hands to be wasted by the touch of the
90 numerous passers by who greet them. These things then we see are
lessened, since they have been thus worn down; but what bodies
depart at any given time the nature of vision has jealously shut out
our seeing. Nature therefore works by unseen bodies.

And yet all things are not on all sides jammed together and kept
95 in by body: there is also void in things. To have learned this will be
good for you on many accounts; it will not allow you to wander in
doubt and seeking the sum of things and distrustful of our words. If
there were not void, things could not move at all: for that which is the
property of body, to stand firm and hinder, would be present to all
100 things at all times; nothing therefore could go on, since no other thing
would be the first to give way. But in fact throughout seas and lands
and the heights of heaven we see before our eyes many things move
in many ways for various reasons, which things, if there were no void,
I need not say would lack restless motion: they never would have
105 been begotten at all, since matter, jammed on all sides, would have
been at rest. Again, however solid things are thought to be, you may

yet learn from this that they are of porous body: in rocks and caverns
the moisture of water oozes through and all things weep with
abundant drops, food distributes itself through the whole body of
110 living things, trees grow and yield fruit in season, because food is
diffused through the whole from the very roots over the stem and all
the boughs. Voices pass through walls and fly through houses shut,
stiffening frost pierces to the bones. Now if there are no void parts, by
what way can the bodies severally pass? You would see it to be quite
115 impossible. Once more, why do we see one thing surpass another in
weight though not larger in size? For if there is just as much body in
a ball of wool as there is in a lump of lead, it is natural it should
weigh the same, since the property of body is to weigh all things
downwards, while on the contrary the nature of void is ever without
120 weight. Therefore when a thing is just as large, yet is found to be
lighter, it proves sure enough that it has more of void in it, while on
the other hand that which is heavier shows that there is in it more of
body and that it contains within it much less of void. Therefore that
which we are seeking with keen reason exists sure enough, mixed up
125 in things: and we call it void.

First-beginnings [atoms] therefore are of solid singleness, massed
together and cohering closely by means of least parts, not
compounded out of a union of those parts, but, rather, strong in
everlasting singleness. From them nature allows nothing to be torn,
130 nothing further to be worn away, reserving them as seeds for things.

They who have held fire to be the matter of things and the sum to
be formed out of fire alone, are seen to have strayed most widely from
true reason. At the head of whom enters Heraclitus to do battle,
famous for obscurity more among the frivolous than the earnest
135 Greeks who seek the truth. For fools admire and like all things the
more which they perceive to be concealed under involved language,
and determine things to be true which can prettily tickle the ears and
are varnished over with finely sounding phrase.

I want to know how things can be so various, if they are formed
140 out of fire one and unmixed: it would avail nothing for hot fire to be
condensed or rarefied, if the same nature which the whole fire has
belonged to the parts of fire as well. The heat would be more intense
by compression of parts, more faint by their severance and dispersion.
More than this you cannot think it in the power of such causes to

145 effect, far less could so great a diversity of things come from mere
rarity and density of fires. Observe also, if they suppose void to be
mixed up in things, fire may then be condensed and left rare; but
because they see many things rise up in contradiction to them and
shrink from leaving unmixed void in things, fearing the steep, they
150 lose the true road, and do not perceive on the other hand that if void
is taken from things, all things are condensed and out of all things is
formed one single body, which cannot briskly radiate anything from
it, in the way heat-giving fire emits light and warmth, letting you see
that it is not of closely compressed parts. But if they happen to think
155 that in some other way fires may be quenched in the union and
change their body, you are to know that if they shall scruple on no
side to do this, all heat sure enough will be utterly brought to
nothing, and all things that are produced will be formed out of
nothing. For whenever a thing changes and quits its proper limits, at
160 once this change of state is the death of that which was before.
Therefore something or other must needs be left to those fires of
theirs undestroyed.

For these reasons they who have held that fire is the matter of
things and that the sum can be formed out of fire, and they who have
165 determined air to be the first-beginning in begetting things, and all
who have held that water by itself alone forms things, or that earth
produces all things and changes into all the different natures of
things, appear to have strayed exceedingly wide of the truth, as well
as they who make the first-beginnings of things twofold, coupling air
170 with fire and earth with water, and they who believe that all things
grow out of four things, fire, earth, air, and water, chief of whom is
Agrigentine Empedocles.

He and those whom we have mentioned above immeasurably
inferior and far beneath him, although the authors of many excellent
175 and godlike discoveries, who have given responses from, so to say,
their hearts' holy of holies with more sanctity and on much more
unerring grounds than the Pythia who speaks out from the tripod and
laurel of Phoebus, have yet gone to ruin in the first-beginnings of
things: it is there they have fallen, and, great themselves, great and
180 heavy has been that fall, first because they have banished void from
things and yet assign to them motions, and allow things soft and rare,
air, sun, fire, earth, living things and corn, and yet mix not up void

with their body, next because they suppose that there is no limit to
the division of bodies and no stop set to their breaking and that there
185   exists no least of all [indivisible atoms] in things.

'But plain matter of fact clearly proves' you say 'that all things
grow up into the air and are fed out of the earth; and unless the
season at the propitious period send such abundant showers that the
trees reel beneath the soaking storms of rain, and unless the sun on
190   its part foster them and supply heat, corn, trees, and living things
could not grow.' Quite true, and unless solid food and soft water
should recruit us, our substance would waste away and life break
wholly up out of all the sinews and bones; for we beyond doubt are
recruited and fed by certain things, this and that other thing by
195   certain other things. Because many first-beginnings common to many
things in many ways are mixed up in things, therefore sure enough
different things are fed by different things. And it often makes a great
difference with what things and in what position the same first-
beginnings are held in union and what motions they mutually impart
200   and receive; for the same make up heaven, sea, lands, rivers, sun, the
same make up corn, trees, and living things, but they are mixed up
with different things and in different ways as they move. No, you see
throughout even in these verses of ours many elements common to
many words, though you must admit that the lines and words differ
205   one from the other both in meaning and in sound, so much can
elements effect by a mere change of order. But those elements which
are the first-beginnings of things can bring with them more
combinations out of which different things can severally be produced.

Let us now examine the *homoeomeria* of Anaxagoras, as the
210   Greeks term it, which the poverty of our native speech [Latin] does
not allow us to name in our own tongue, though it is easy enough to
set forth in words the thing itself. First of all then, when he speaks of
the 'homoeomeria' of things, you must know he supposes bones to be
formed out of very small and minute fleshes and blood by the coming
215   together of many drops of blood, and gold he thinks can be composed
of grains of gold and earth be a concretion of small portions of earth,
and fire can come from fire and water from water, and everything else
he fancies and supposes to be produced on a like principle. And yet at
the same time he does not allow that void exists anywhere in things,
220   or that there is a limit to the division of things. Wherefore he appears

to me on both these grounds to be as much mistaken as those whom
we have already spoken of above. Moreover, the first-beginnings he
assumes are too frail, if those things which are possessed of a nature
like to the things themselves and are just as liable to suffering and
225 death and which nothing reins back from destruction even are first-
beginnings. For which of them will hold out, so as to escape death,
beneath so strong a pressure within the very jaws of destruction? Fire
or water or air? Which of these? Blood or bones? Not one, I think,
where everything will be just as essentially mortal as those things
230 which we see with the senses perish before our eyes, vanquished by
some force. But I appeal to facts demonstrated above for proof that
things cannot fall away to nothing nor on the other hand grow from
nothing.

Here some slight opening is left for evasion, which Anaxagoras
235 avails himself of, choosing to suppose that all things though latent
are mixed up in things, and that alone is visible of which there are
the largest number of bodies in the mixture and these more ready to
hand and stationed in the first rank. This however is far banished
from true reason. For then it were natural that corn too should often,
240 when crushed by the formidable force of the stone, show some mark of
blood or some other of the things which have their nourishment in
our body. For like reasons it were fitting that from grasses too, when
we rub them between two stones, blood should ooze out, that waters
should yield sweet drops, in flavor like to the udder of milk in sheep,
245 and that often, when clods of earth have been crumbled, kinds of
grasses and corn and leaves should be found to lurk distributed
among the earth in minute quantities, and lastly that ash and smoke
and minute particles of fire should be found latent in branches when
they are broken off. Now since plain matter of fact teaches that none
250 of these results follow, you are to know that things are not so mixed
up in things, rather, seeds common to many things must in many
ways be mixed up and latent in things.

'But it often comes to pass on high mountains' you say 'that
contiguous tops of tall trees rub together, the strong south winds
255 constraining them to do so, until the flower of flame has broken out
and they have burst into a blaze.' Quite true and yet fire is not innate
in woods, but there are many seeds of heat, and when they, by
rubbing, have streamed together, they produce conflagrations in the

forests. But if the flame was stored up ready made in the forests, the
260   fire could not be concealed for any length of time, but would destroy
forests, burn up trees indiscriminately. Do you now see, as we said a
little before, that it often makes a very great difference with what
things and in what position the same first-beginnings are held in
union and what motions they mutually impart and receive, and that
265   the same may when a little changed in arrangement produce say fires
and a fir, just as the words too consist of elements only a little
changed in arrangement, though we denote firs and fires with two
quite distinct names?

This point too herein we wish you to apprehend: when bodies are
270   borne downwards sheer through void by their own weights, at quite
uncertain times and uncertain spots they push themselves a little
from their course: you just and only just can call it a change of
inclination. If they were not used to swerve, they would all fall down,
like drops of rain, through the deep void, and no clashing would have
275   been begotten nor blow produced among the first-beginnings: thus
nature never would have produced anything.
But if perhaps someone believes that heavier bodies, as they are
carried more quickly sheer through space, can fall from above on the
lighter and so beget blows able to produce begetting motions, he goes
280   most widely astray from true reason. For whenever bodies fall
through water and thin air, they must quicken their descents in
proportion to their weights, because the body of water and subtle
nature of air cannot retard everything in equal degree, but more
readily give way, overpowered by the heavier: on the other hand
285   empty void cannot offer resistance to anything in any direction at any
time, but must, as its nature craves, continually give way; and for
this reason all things must be moved and borne along with equal
velocity though of unequal weights through the unresisting void.
Therefore heavier things will never be able to fall from above on
290   lighter nor of themselves to beget blows sufficient to produce the
varied motions by which nature carries on things. Wherefore again
and again I say bodies must swerve a little; and yet not more than the
least possible; lest we be found to be imagining oblique motions and
this the reality should refute. For this we see to be plain and evident,

295 that weights, so far as in them is, cannot travel obliquely, when they fall from above, at least so far as you can perceive; but that nothing swerves in any case from the straight course, who is there that can perceive?

Questions To Consider

1   How does Lucretius argue that nothing comes from nothing?

2   What are Lucretius' *first principles*? How does he argue for the existence of these things?

3   What is Lucretius' objection to fire as the *first principle* of everything?

4   Summarize Lucretius' view of Empedocles' account of natural things.

5   What does Lucretius criticize in Anaxagoras' explanation of nature? In your judgment, are Lucretius' arguments against the early pre-Socratics good ones? What of his *own* account of the first principles of nature?

6   The last two paragraphs explain the need for something in order to 'get things going' among the atoms. Explain what this is, and how Lucretius arrives at the need for such a thing.

Heraclitus and Plato

Without a doubt, Plato was one of the greatest philosophers who ever lived. A student of Socrates, he was 28 years old when Socrates was brought up on charges of impiety and corrupting the youth (399 B.C.) As we discover through Plato's own works, his teacher was convicted and sentenced to death by drinking poison.

Most of Plato's writings have been passed on to us in the form of dialogues, many with Socrates as the principal speaker. Through the medium of his teacher, Plato addressed many important and vexing questions which confront us even to this day.

Although Socrates (and Plato) tended to shy away from discussions about nature and our understanding of it, there is one dialogue which takes up such questions in detail: the *Timaeus*. As an account of the creation of the natural world itself, this work exerted a tremendous influence upon the thinkers of those times and later ones. Along with these passages from the Timaeus we have included key selections from Plato's most famous dialogue, the *Republic*, in which Plato elaborates upon his doctrine of Forms.

We have included fragments from another Pre-Socratic philosopher of note, *Heraclitus*, as a fitting introduction to Plato's own writings. Assuming the general Heraclitean account of nature, Plato sought a basis for human knowledge—for if we could not depend upon Heraclitus' ever-changing world for truth, upon what could we depend? The problem is brought out well in the short selection we have included from Plato's *Cratylus*, while the passages from the *Timaeus* and *Republic* provide Plato's solution.

Heraclitus of Ephesos

It is wise to hearken not to me but to my argument, and to confess that all things are one.

This order, which is the same in all things, no one of gods or men has made; but it was ever, is now, and ever shall be an ever-living
5 Fire, fixed measures of it kindling and fixed measures going out.

The transformations of Fire are, first of all, sea (and half of the sea is earth, half fiery storm-cloud).

All things are exchanged for Fire, and Fire for all things, as wares are exchanged for gold and gold for wares.
10 Fire is want and satiety.

Fire lives the death of earth, and air lives the death of fire; water lives the death of air, earth that of water.

The sun is new every day.

Hesiod is most men's teacher. Men think he knew very many
15 things, a man who did not know day and night! They are one.

It is cold things that become warm, and what is warm that cools; what is wet dries, and the parched is moistened.

You cannot step twice into the same rivers; for fresh waters are ever flowing in upon you.
20 Homer was wrong in saying: "Would that strife might perish from among gods and men!" He did not see that he was praying for the destruction of the universe; for, if his prayer were heard, all things would pass away.

War is the father of all and the king of all; and some he has made
25 gods and some men, some bond and some free.

Men do not know how that which is drawn in different directions harmonizes with itself. The harmonious structure of the world depends upon opposite tension, like that of the bow and lyre.

It is opposition that brings things together.
30 Good and ill are the same.

You must couple together things whole and things not whole, what is drawn together and what is drawn asunder, the harmonious and the discordant. The one is made up of all things, and all things issue from the one.
35 We must know that war is the common and justice is strife, and that all things come into being and pass away through strife.

The way up and the way down is one and the same.

The quick and the dead, the waking and the sleeping, the young and the old, are the same; the former are changed and become the
40 latter, and the latter are changed into the former.

We step and do not step into the same rivers; we are and are not.

It finds rest in change.

It is not good for men to get all they wish to get. It is disease that makes health pleasant and good; hunger, plenty and weariness, rest.
45   One day is equal to another.

Questions To Consider

1   As you can tell from reading Heraclitus, he wrote in a poetical manner, not unlike Parmenides, and it is quite difficult to decipher just what it is he is trying to say. First, what are your rough impressions of Heraclitus' philosophical position? If we were to speak of the basic 'stuff' out of which all things are made, what would this be, for Heraclitus?

2   Parmenides and Zeno tended to emphasize the unity and immovability of what exists. Would Heraclitus be inclined to agree with them?

3   One of Heraclitus' most famous remarks is what he says about stepping into the same river twice (lines 18-19). What is Heraclitus getting at here?

4   Compare what Heraclitus says at line 41 to what he says at lines 18-19. Strictly speaking, how do these two claims relate to one another?

5   Further, Heraclitus has another curious statement (which is also inconsistent with itself, at least to all appearances,) at line 42. What do you believe he means by this statement?

6   Consider what place the many contrasts Heraclitus includes in his account of nature have in his overall argument. (Such contrasts are, for example, life and death, day and night, good and evil, up and down, and so on.)

Plato

The Cratylus

439c-440e

There is a matter, master Cratylus, about which I often dream, and should like to ask your opinion: Tell me whether there is, or is not, any absolute beauty or good, or any other absolute existence?

Certainly, Socrates, I think that there is.

5   Then let us seek the true beauty: not asking whether a face is fair, or anything of that sort, or whether all this is in a flux; but let us ask whether the true beauty is not always beautiful.

Certainly.

And can we rightly speak of a beauty which is always passing

10 away, and is first this and then that; must not the same thing be born and retire and vanish while the word is in our mouths?

Undoubtedly.

Then how can that be a real thing which is never in the same state? for obviously things which are the same cannot change while

15 they remain the same; and if they are always in the same state and the same, then, without losing their original form, they can never change or be moved.

Certainly they cannot.

Nor yet can they be known by anyone; for at the moment that the

20 observer approaches, then they become other and of another nature, so that you cannot get any further in knowing their nature and state, for you cannot know that which has no state.

That is true.

Nor can we reasonably say, Cratylus, that there is knowledge at

25 all, if everything is in a state of transition and there is nothing abiding; for if knowledge did not change or cease to be knowledge, then knowledge would ever abide and exist. But if the very nature of knowledge changes, at the time when the change occurs, there will be no knowledge; and if the transition is always going on, there will

30 always be no knowledge, and, according to this view, there will be no one to know and nothing to be known: but if that which knows and that which is known exists ever, and the beautiful and the good and

every other thing also exist, then I do not think that they can be like
a flux or progress, as we were just now supposing. Whether there is
35   this eternal nature in things, or whether the truth is what Heraclitus
and his followers and many others say, is a question hard to
determine; and no man of sense will like to put himself or the
education of his mind in the power of names; neither will he so far
trust names or the givers of names as to be confident in any
40   knowledge which condemns himself and other existences to an
unhealthy state of unreality; he will not believe that everything is in
a flux like leaky vessels, or that the world is a sick man who has a
running at the nose. This doctrine, Cratylus, may indeed, perhaps, be
true, but is also very likely to be untrue; and therefore I would have
45   you reflect well and manfully, and not allow yourself to be too easily
persuaded now in the days of our youth, which is the time of learning;
but search, and when you have found the truth, come and tell me.

I will do as you say, though I can assure you, Socrates, that I have
been considering the matter already, and the result of a great deal of
50   trouble and consideration is that I incline to Heraclitus.

Then, another day, my friend, when you come back, you shall give
me a lesson; but at present, go into the country, as you are intending,
and Hermogenes shall set you on your way.

Very good, Socrates; and I hope that you will not cease to think
55   about these things yourself.

Questions To Consider

1   Historically, Cratylus was a student of Heraclitus. Does Cratylus
    initially support his teacher's view of things? Does he ultimately
    do so?
2   What problem does Socrates discover when he considers the view
    that all things change up against the claim that there is an
    absolute beauty, goodness, and so on?
3   What position does Socrates favor by the end of this selection:
    that there are absolutes, or that all things constantly change?
    What about Cratylus?

Plato

The Timaeus

49c-52c

In the first place, we see that what we just now called water, by condensation, I suppose, becomes stone and earth, and this same element, when melted and dispersed, passes into vapor and air. Air, again, when inflamed, becomes fire, and again, fire, when condensed
5 and extinguished, passes once more into the form of air, and once more, air, when collected and condensed, produces cloud and mist—and from these, when still more compressed, comes flowing water, and from water comes earth and stones once more—and thus generation appears to be transmitted from one to the other in a circle.
10 Thus, then, as the several elements never present themselves in the same form, how can anyone have the assurance to assert positively that any of them, whatever it may be, is one thing rather than another? No one can. But much the safest plan is to speak of them as follows. Anything which we see to be continually changing,
15 as, for example, fire, we must not call *this* or *that*, but rather say that it is *of such a nature*, nor let us speak of water as *this*, but always as *such*, nor must we imply that there is any stability in any of those things which we indicate by the use of the words *this* and *that*, supposing ourselves to signify something thereby, for they are too
20 volatile to be detained in any such expressions as *this*, or *that*, or *relative to this*, or any other mode of speaking which represents them as permanent. We ought not to apply *this* to any of them but rather the word *such*, which expresses the similar principle circulating in each and all of them; for example, that should be called *fire* which is
25 of such a nature always, and so of everything that has generation. That in which the elements severally grow up, and appear, and decay, is alone to be called by the name *this* or *that*, but that which is of a certain nature, hot or white, or anything which admits of opposite qualities, and all things that are compounded of them, ought
30 not to be so denominated.
Let me make another attempt to explain my meaning more clearly. Suppose a person to make all kinds of figures of gold and to be always remodeling each form into all the rest; somebody points to one of them and asks what it is. By far the safest and truest answer
35 is, *That is gold,* and not to call the triangle or any other figures which

are formed in the gold *these*, as though they had existence, since they
are in process of change while he is making the assertion, but if the
questioner be willing to take the safe and the indefinite expression,
such, we should be satisfied. And the same argument applies to the
40   universal nature which receives all bodies—that must be always
called the same, for, inasmuch as she always receives all things, she
never departs at all from her own nature and never, in any way or at
any time, assumes a form like that of any of the things which enter
into her; she is the natural recipient of all impressions, and is stirred
45   and informed by them, and appears different from time to time by
reason of them. But the forms which enter into and go out of her are
the likenesses of eternal realities modeled after their patterns in a
wonderful   and   mysterious   manner,   which   we   will   hereafter
investigate. For the present we have only to conceive of three
50   natures: first, that which is in process of generation; secondly, that in
which the generation takes place; and thirdly, that of which the thing
generated is a resemblance naturally produced. And we may liken
the receiving principle to a mother, and the source or spring to a
father, and the intermediate nature to a child, and may remark
55   further that if the model is to take every variety of form, then the
matter in which the model is fashioned will not be duly prepared
unless it is formless and free from the impress of any of those shapes
which it is hereafter to receive from without. For if the matter were
like any of the supervening form, then whenever any opposite or
60   entirely different nature was stamped upon its surface, it would take
the impression badly, because it would intrude its own shape.
Wherefore that which is to receive all forms should have no form, as
in making perfumes they first contrive that the liquid substance
which is to receive the scent shall be as inodorous as possible, or as
65   those who wish to impress figures on soft substances do not allow any
previous impression to remain, but begin by making the surface as
even and smooth as possible. In the same way that which is to receive
perpetually and through its whole extent the resemblances of all
external beings ought to be devoid of any particular form. Wherefore
70   the mother and the receptacle of all created and visible and in any
way sensible things is not to be termed earth or air or fire or water,
or any of their compounds, or any of the elements from which these
are derived, but is an invisible and formless being which receives all
things and in some mysterious way partakes of the intelligible, and is
75   most incomprehensible. In saying this we shall not be far wrong; as
far, however, as we can attain to a knowledge of her from the
previous considerations, we may truly say that fire is that part of her

nature which from time to time is inflamed, and water that which is moistened, and that the mother substance becomes earth and air, 80 insofar as she receives the impressions of them.

Let us consider this question more precisely. Is there any self-existent fire, and do all those things which we call self-existent exist, or are only those things which we see or in some way perceive through the bodily organs truly existent, and nothing whatever 85 besides them? And are those intelligible forms, of which we are accustomed to speak, nothing at all, and only a name? Here is a question which we must not leave unexamined or undetermined, nor must we affirm too confidently that there can be no decision; neither must we interpolate in our present long discourse a digression 90 equally long, but if it is possible to set forth a great principle in a few words, that is just what we want.

Wherefore also we must acknowledge that one kind of being is the form which is always the same, uncreated and indestructible, never receiving anything into itself from without, nor itself going out 95 to any other, but invisible and imperceptible by any sense, and of which the contemplation is granted to intelligence only. And there is another nature of the same name with it, and like to it, perceived by sense, created, always in motion, becoming in place and again vanishing out of place, which is apprehended by opinion jointly with 100 sense. And there is a third nature, which is space and is eternal, and admits not of destruction and provides a home for all created things, and is apprehended, when all sense is absent, by a kind of spurious reason, and is hardly real—which we, beholding as in a dream, say of all existence that it must of necessity be in some place and occupy a 105 space, but that what is neither in heaven nor in earth has no existence. Of these and other things of the same kind, relating to the true and walking reality of nature, we have only this dreamlike sense, and we are unable to cast off sleep and determine the truth about them. For an image since the reality after which it is modeled 110 does not belong to it, and it exists ever as the fleeting shadow of some other, must be inferred to be in another (that is, in space), grasping existence in some way or other, or it could not be at all. But true and exact reason, vindicating the nature of true being, maintains that while two things (that is, the image and space) are different they 115 cannot exist one of them in the other and so be one and also two at the same time.

Questions To Consider

1   What three principles come out of this discussion of natural changes?
2   What is the function of matter, "that in which generation (or change) takes place"? How does Plato describe matter? To what does he compare matter?
1   How does Plato argue that matter can contain no form of its own?
2   What is the function of the forms which are constantly changing, coming into and going out of the matter? What is their relation to the third principle mentioned, the eternal forms?
3   Bearing in mind the discussion found in the Cratylus, why would Plato be inclined to insist that, beyond any changeable form, there must be "the form which is always the same, uncreated and indestructible, never receiving anything into itself from without, nor itself going out to any other, but invisible and imperceptible by any sense, and of which the contemplation is granted to intelligence only"? Are such forms found in the world of matter?

Plato

The Republic

509d-518b

You have to imagine, then, that there are two ruling powers, and
that one of them is set over the intellectual world, the other over the
visible. I do not say heaven, lest you should fancy that I am playing
upon the name. May I suppose that you have this distinction of the
5 visible and intelligible fixed in your mind?

I have.

Now take a line which has been cut into two unequal parts, and
divide each of them again in the same proportion, and suppose the
two main divisions to answer, one to the visible and the other to the
10 intelligible, and then compare the subdivisions in respect of their
clearness and want of clearness, and you will find that the first
section in the sphere of the visible consists of images. And by images I
mean, in the first place, shadows, and in the second place, reflections
in water and in solid, smooth and polished bodies and the like: Do you
15 understand?

Yes, I understand.

Imagine, now, the other section, of which this is only the
resemblance, to include the animals which we see, and everything
that grows or is made.

20 Very good.

Would you not admit that both the sections of this division have
different degrees of truth, and that the copy is to the original as the
sphere of opinion is to the sphere of knowledge?

Most undoubtedly.

25 Next proceed to consider the manner in which the sphere of the
intellectual is to be divided.

In what manner?

Thus—There are two subdivisions, in the lower of which the
should uses the figures given by the former division as images; the
30 enquiry can only be hypothetical, and instead of going upwards to a
principle descends to the other end; in the higher of the two, the soul
passes out of hypotheses, and goes up to a principle which is above

hypotheses, making no use of images as in the former case, but proceeding only in and through the ideas themselves.

35   I do not quite understand your meaning, he said.

Then I will try again; you will understand me better when I have made some preliminary remarks. You are aware that students of geometry, arithmetic, and the kindred sciences assume the odd and the even and the figures and three kinds of angles and the like in
40   their several branches of science; these are their hypotheses, which they and everybody are supposed to know, and therefore they do not deign to give any account of them either to themselves or others; but they begin with them, and go on until they arrive at last, and in a consistent manner, at their conclusion?

45   Yes, he said, I know.

And do you not know also that although they make use of the visible forms and reason about them, they are thinking not of these, but of the ideals which they resemble; not of the figures which they draw, but of the absolute square and the absolute diameter, and so
50   on—the forms which they draw or make, and which have shadows and reflections in water of their own, are converted by them into images, but they are really seeking to behold the things themselves, which can only be seen with the eye of the mind?

That is true.

55   And of this kind I spoke as the intelligible, although in the search after it the soul is compelled to use hypotheses; not ascending to a first principle, because she is unable to rise above the region of hypothesis, but employing the objects of which the shadows below are resemblances in their turn as images, they having in relation to the
60   shadows and reflections of them a greater distinctness, and therefore a higher value.

I understand, he said, that you are speaking of the province of geometry and the sister arts.

And when I speak of the other division of the intelligible, you will
65   understand me to speak of that other sort of knowledge which reason herself attains by the power of dialectic, using the hypotheses not as first principles, but only as hypotheses—that is to say, as steps and points of departure into a world which is above hypotheses, in order that she may soar beyond them to the first principle of the whole; and
70   clinging to this and then to that which depends on this, by successive

steps she descends again without the aid of any sensible object, from ideas, through ideas, and in ideas she ends.

I understand you, he replied; not perfectly, for you seem to me to be describing a task which is really tremendous; but, at any rate, I
75 understand you to say that knowledge and being, which the science of dialectic contemplates, are clearer than the notions of the arts, as they are termed, which proceed from hypotheses only: these are also contemplated by the understanding, and not by the senses: yet, because they start from hypotheses and do not ascend to a principle,
80 those who contemplate them appear to you not to exercise the higher reason upon them, although when a first principle is added to them they are cognizable by the higher reason. And the habit which is concerned with geometry and the cognate sciences I suppose that you would term understanding and not reason, as being intermediate
85 between opinion and reason.

You have quite conceived my meaning, I said; and now, corresponding to these four divisions, let there be four faculties in the soul—reason answering to the highest, understanding to the second, faith (or conviction) to the third, and perception of shadows to the
90 last—and let there be a scale of them, and let us suppose that the several faculties have clearness in the same degree that their objects have truth.

I understand, he replied, and give my assent, and accept your arrangement.

BOOK VII

95 And now, I said, let me show in a figure how far our nature is enlightened or unenlightened—Behold! human beings living in an underground den, which has a mouth open towards the light and reaching all along the den; here they have been from their childhood, and have their legs and necks chained so that they cannot move, and
100 can only see before them, being prevented by the chains from turning round their heads. Above and behind them a fire is blazing at a distance, and between the fire and the prisoners there is a raised way, like the screen which marionette players have in from of them, over which they show the puppets.
105 I see.

And do you see, I said, men passing along the wall carrying all sorts of vessels, and statues and figures of animals made of wood and stone and various materials, which appear over the wall? Some of them are talking, others silent.

110   You have shown me a strange image, and they are strange prisoners.

Like ourselves, I replied; and they see only their own shadows, or the shadows of one another, which the fire throws on the opposite wall of the cave?

115   True, he said; how could they see anything but the shadows if they were never allowed to move their heads?

And of the objects which are being carried in like manner they would only see the shadows?

Yes, he said.

120   And if they were able to converse with one another, would they not suppose that they were naming what was actually before them?

Very true.

And suppose further that the prison had an echo which came from the other side, would they not be sure to fancy when one of the 125   passers-by spoke that the voice which they heard came from the passing shadow?

No question, he replied.

To them, I said, the truth would be literally nothing but the shadows of the images.

130   That is certain.

And now look again, and see what will naturally follow if the prisoners are released and disabused of their error. At first, when any of them is liberated and compelled suddenly to stand up and turn his neck round and walk and look towards the light, he will suffer sharp 135   pains; the glare will distress him, and he will be unable to see the realities of which in his former state he had seen the shadows; and then conceive some one saying to him, that what he saw before was an illusion, but that now, when he is approaching nearer to being and his eye is turned towards more real existence, he has a clearer vision, 140   —what will be his reply? And you may further imagine that his instructor is pointing to the objects as they pass and requiring him to name them,—will he not be perplexed? Will he not fancy that the shadows which he formerly saw are truer than the objects which are now shown to him?

145   Far truer.

And if he is compelled to look straight at the light, will he not have a pain in his eyes which will make him turn away to take refuge in the objects of vision which he can see, and which he will conceive to be in reality clearer than the things which are now being shown to

150 him?

True, he said.

And suppose once more, that he is reluctantly dragged up a steep and rugged ascent, and held fast until he is forced into the presence of the sun himself, is he not likely to be pained and irritated? When he

155 approaches the light his eyes will be dazzled, and he will not be able to see anything at all of what are now called realities.

Not all in a moment, he said.

He will require to grow accustomed to the sight of the upper world. And first he will see the shadows best, next the reflections of

160 men and other objects in the water, and then the objects themselves; then he will gaze upon the light of the moon and the stars and the spangled heaven; and he will see the sky and the stars by night better than the sun or the light of the sun by day?

Certainly.

165 Last of all he will be able to see the sun, and not mere reflections of him in the water, but he will see him in his own proper place, and not in another; and he will contemplate him as he is.

Certainly.

He will then proceed to argue that this is he who gives the season

170 and the years, and is the guardian of all that is in the visible world, and in a certain way the cause of all things which he and his fellows have been accustomed to behold?

Clearly, he said, he would first see the use and then reason about him.

175 And when he remembered his old habitation, and the wisdom of the den and his fellow-prisoners, do you not suppose that he would felicitate himself on the change, and pity them?

Certainly, he would.

And if they were in the habit of conferring honors among

180 themselves on those who were quickest to observe the passing

shadows and to remark which of them went before, and which
followed after, and which were together; and who were therefore best
able to draw conclusions as to the future, do you think that he would
care for such honors and glories, or envy the possessors of them?
185   Would he not say with Homer,

> 'Better to be the poor servant of a poor master,'

and to endure anything, rather than think as they do and live
after their manner?

Yes, he said, I think that he would rather suffer anything than
190   entertain these false notions and live in this miserable manner.

Imagine once more, I said, such an one coming suddenly out of
the sun to be replaced in his old situation; would he not be certain to
have his eyes full of darkness?

To be sure, he said.

195   And if there were a contest, and he had to compete in measuring
the shadows with the prisoners who had never moved out of the den,
while his sight was still weak, and before his eyes had become steady
(and the time which would be needed to acquire this new habit of
sight might be very considerable), would he not be ridiculous? Men
200   would say of him that up he went and down he came without his eyes;
and that it was better not even to think of ascending; and if any one
tried to loose another and lead him up to the light, let them only
catch the offender, and they would put him to death.

No question, he said.

205   This entire allegory, I said, you may now append, dear Glaucon,
to the previous argument; the prison-house is the world of sight, the
light of the fire is the sun, and you will not misapprehend me if you
interpret the journey upwards to be the ascent of the soul your desire,
I have expressed—whether rightly or wrongly God knows. But,
210   whether true or false, my opinion is that in the world of knowledge
the idea of good appears last of all, and is seen only with an effort;
and, when seen is also inferred to be the universal author of all things
beautiful and right, parent of light and of the lord of light in this
visible world, and the immediate source of reason and truth in the
215   intellectual; and that this is the power upon which he who would act
rationally either in public or private life must have his eye fixed.

I agree, he said, as far as I am able to understand you.

Moreover, I said, you must not wonder that those who attain to this beatific vision are unwilling to descend to human affairs; for
220 their souls are ever hastening into the upper world where they desire to dwell; which desire of theirs is very natural, if our allegory may be trusted.

Yes, very natural.

And is there anything surprising in one who passes from divine
225 contemplations to the evil state of man, misbehaving himself in a ridiculous manner; if, while his eyes are blinking and before he has become accustomed to the surrounding darkness, he is compelled to fight in courts of law, or in other places, about the images or the shadows of images of justice, and is endeavoring to meet the
230 conceptions of those who have never yet seen absolute justice?

Anything but surprising, he replied.

Any one who has common sense will remember that the bewilderments of the eyes are of two kinds, and arise from two causes, either from coming out of the light or from going into the
235 light, which is true of the mind's eye, quite as much as of the bodily eye; and he who remembers this when he sees any one whose vision is perplexed and weak, will not be too ready to laugh; he will first ask whether that soul of man has come out of the brighter life, and is unable to see because unaccustomed to the dark, or having turned
240 form darkness to the day is dazzled by excess of light. And he will count the one happy in his condition and state of being, and he will pity the other; or, if he have a mind to laugh at the soul which comes from below into the light, there will be more reason in this than in the laugh which greets him who returns from above out of the light into
245 the den.

Questions To Consider

1 Draw the image that Plato describes here, of the "divided line". What does each portion of this four-part line represent?

2 Notice that the ratio of the major parts of the line is the same as that of the lesser pairs to one another. What does this suggest about the relation between shadows and reflections of natural images to natural things, hypotheses to truth itself, and the whole visible order to the whole intelligible order?

3   Describe Plato's cave. Who do the cave's prisoner's represent? What is the function of the fire burning within the cave, compared to that of the sun, burning outside it?

4   What would the passage from the cave correspond to, in our lives? What would existence outside the cave signify, then?

5   If the cave signifies the state of human ignorance, our present life, then why would a freed prisoner ever want to return? Through what successive stages would such a person go in their journey? Do you think Plato (who wrote the dialogue) has anyone especially in mind when he says "Men would say of him [the returning prisoner] that up he went and down he came without his eyes; and that it was better not even to think of ascending; and if any one tried to loose another and lead him up to the light, let them only catch the offender, and they would put him to death"?

Aristotle

Aristotle was born in Stagira some fifteen years after Socrates' death. He was educated in Athens and entered Plato's school, where he studied for about twenty years. He eventually took a position to teach Philip II's son, Alexander (the Great). When he returned to Athens he opened his own school, the Lyceum. Upon the death of Alexander he fled, fearing a fate like Socrates'. He is reported to have remarked that he was doing so 'lest Athens sin twice against philosophy.'

Many of Aristotle's writings have come down to us. He wrote works in biology, astronomy, logic, philosophical psychology, ethics, politics, natural philosophy, and metaphysics. No area of thought was too lowly, or too lofty, for his interest. As he says in his *Ethics*:

> We ought not to follow the advice of those who say that we, being human, ought to think of human things, and being mortal, ought to think of mortal things, rather we ought, as much as we can, to make ourselves immortal, and to do all things in our lives in accordance with what is best in us: for though it be small in size, yet in power and worth it exceeds all others by far.

Aristotle's *Physics*, the first of his writings on nature, was his starting point for a study of the natural world. The *Physics* came to exert a great influence on philosophy, even to the modern era and the development of the scientific method and the assumptions of modern-day science. The *Physics* raises many questions which it is well for our sciences to take into account. It is wholly within the spirit of the passage quoted from the *Ethics*, above, that Aristotle would treat of the First Unmoved Mover at the end of his *Physics*.

Taking matter and form as principles of all natural things had implications for Aristotle's psychology, ethics, and natural theology, as well as various branches of study within these areas.

Aristotle

Physics I

Chapter 1

Since understanding and scientific knowledge come about from a knowledge of principles, causes, and elements in all inquiries in which there are such things, (for we think that we know some thing when we know its first causes and first principles, all the way down
5 to its primary elements), it is clear that we should first try to define those things which concern the principles in the science of nature also.

The natural way to proceed is from things which are more known and clearer to us to things which are clearer and more known by
10 nature: for what is known *to us* and what is known *simply* [by nature] are not the same. And so it is necessary to proceed in this way, from things which are less clear by nature (but which are clearer to us) to things which are clearer and more known by nature.

But what are at first clear and evident to us are things that are
15 more confused: later, the elements and principles become known from these by dividing them. And so one ought to proceed from universals to singulars: for the whole is more known according to the senses, and the universal is a kind of whole: for it includes many things as parts within itself. Names also have a similar relation to a definition: for
20 they signify some whole in an indefinite way, (for example, 'circle',) whereas the definition distinguishes it into particulars. Also, children at first call all men fathers and all women mothers, but later identify each of them.

Questions To Consider

1   As one would expect, the first chapter of Aristotle's *Physics* is an introduction to the general study of natural things. Here

Aristotle tells us where we ought to begin in this science and why
we must begin there.

2   What is the conclusion of the first paragraph in this chapter?
What evidence does Aristotle give to support this conclusion? (We
shall refine the distinction between principles, causes, and
elements later on in the course.)

3   What is the 'natural way to proceed' in learning? Does Aristotle
take this method to apply to all learning, or merely to learning in
this science?

4   In learning, from what sorts of thing and to what sorts of thing
ought we to proceed? What is meant by 'what is by nature clearer
and more known'?

5   Aristotle gives three examples to support his claim that, in
learning, we naturally proceed from what is more known to us to
what is more known by nature. Given this, what sorts of thing,
generally, are more known to us?

Chapter 2

Now it is necessary that there be either one principle or more
than one, and if one, that it be either immovable, as Parmenides and
Melissus say, or moved, as the natural philosophers, some saying that
the first principle is air, others that it is water: but if there is more
5   than one [principle], they must be either finite or infinite [in number],
and if finite, (but more than one,) either two, or three, or four, or
some other number, but if infinite [in number], either one in kind, as
Democritus holds, but different, or even contrary, in figure or species,
[or even different in kind]. And those who ask how many beings there
10   are do a similar thing: for they ask whether the basic elements of
things are one or many, and if there is more than one, whether they
are finite or infinite [in number], so that they too are asking whether
the principle and the element is one or many.

A Question To Consider

How does what Aristotle says at the beginning of chapter two
relate to what he concluded in chapter one? What is the basis of
the first division he makes of the principles of nature? Is this
basis familiar?

Chapter 5

Everyone, then, makes the principles contraries, both those who say that the universe is one and unmoved, (for even Parmenides makes his principles the hot and the cold, and these he names *fire* and *earth*) and those who introduce as principles *the rare* and *the*
5 *dense*. And Democritus makes his principles *the solid* and *the void*, of which the former, he says, is being, while the latter is non-being. Besides this, he distinguishes the solid by position, figure, and order (for these are the genera of contraries:) by position, as up, down, behind, and before, by figure, as angular and without angles,
10 straight, and circular.

That everyone makes the principles contraries in some way, then, is clear. And this is reasonable: for it is necessary both that principles should not be produced from each other nor from other things, and that from these [principles] all other things should come about. And
15 the first contraries have these [characteristics:] for, because they are first, they do not come about from other things, and, because they are contraries, they do not come about from each other. But it is necessary to inquire how this comes about by reason.

First, then, it must be assumed that nothing by nature acts upon,
20 or is acted upon by, just any chance thing, nor does any thing come from just any thing, unless one regards this as happening *per accidens*: for how can the white come from the musical, unless the musical happened to be not-white or black? Rather, white comes from what is not white, and not from just anything which is not white, but
25 from black, or some one of the intermediate colors. The musical also comes from what is not musical, yet not from just any thing which is not [musical,] but from that which lacks music, or something, if there be such a thing, between these.

Nor is a thing corrupted into just any chance thing, as the white
30 is not corrupted into the musical, (unless, perhaps, *per accidens*,) but into what is not white, and not into just any thing which is not white, but into black, or some intermediate color. Similarly, the musical, is corrupted into what is not musical, not into just any thing unmusical, but into that which lacks music, or into something between these, if
35 there be any such thing.

This also occurs in other things, since things which are not simple, but composite, occur according to similar reasoning, but, since

the opposite states are not named, we do not know that this happens:
for every thing which is harmonized must come from that what lacks
40   harmony, and what lacks harmony from what is harmonized. And
what is harmonized must also be corrupted into what lacks harmony;
and not into just any thing [which does not have harmony,] but into
its opposite [the inharmonious.] And there is no difference whether
we say this of harmony, or order, or composition: for clearly the same
45   reasoning will apply to all these. A house also, and a statue, and any
thing else, come about in the same way: a house comes about from
things which are not joined together but separated in some way, and
a statue, (and any other thing which is shaped,) comes about from
what lacks shape: and each of these is partly order and partly a
50   certain composition.

   If, then, this is true, whatever comes about does so from, and
whatever is destroyed is destroyed into, contraries or what is
intermediate. And the intermediates come from contraries: as, for
instance, intermediate colors come from white and black. And so all
55   things which come about by nature either *are* contraries or *come from*
contraries.

   So far, then, nearly all the ancient philosophers have advanced
together with us, as we have said: for all of them say that the
elements, and those things which they call principles, are contraries,
60   though they assume them without argument, as if they were
compelled by truth itself. They differ, however, from each other in
that some of them assume prior principles, while others posit
posterior principles, and some of them assume things more known
according to reason, while others posit principles more known
65   according to sense: for some make the hot and the cold, others the
moist and the dry, the causes of generation, while others assume the
odd and the even, and still others strife and friendship. And these
differ from each other in the way mentioned above.

   And so, in a certain respect they say the same things, yet they
70   speak differently from each other. They say different things, indeed,
as is clear to most men, but the same things, insofar as they speak
analogously. For they take their principles from the same pairs of
contraries, some of them being more general, others more specific.
And so they say both the same and different things, some worse and
75   some better. And some assume things more known according to

reason, as we have before observed, while others take things more known according to sense. (For the universal is more known according to reason, while that which is particular is more known according to sense, for reason is concerned with universals, but sense
80 with particulars.) For instance, the great and the small are more known according to reason, but the rare and the dense according to sense.

It is clear, then, that the principles must be contraries.

Questions To Consider

1   Beginning with this chapter, Aristotle proceeds to give his own account of the principles of natural things.
2   What is the conclusion of this chapter?
3   What is the first evidence Aristotle gives of the conclusion of this chapter? Is this evidence sufficient? If so, how? If not, why not?
4   What two conditions must the principles of nature fulfill, according to Aristotle? Are these reasonable criteria? How would change become impossible if either of these criteria were not met? What, in general, does meet these criteria?
5   Strictly speaking, does change take place from non-being, that is, in heating food, does the food begin by being non-hot (that is, everything which is not the quality of being hot?) Similarly with destruction. When the hot food cools, does the food change from hot to non-hot, strictly speaking? Summarize Aristotle's distinctions with respect to this question.
6   From the arguments just given, why must it follow that the principles are contraries? How do contraries differ from contradictories (recall the distinctions we made in the section on logic)? What difference does this make in this case?
7   Does Aristotle's conclusion have the support (at least implicit,) more or less, of the pre-Socratic philosophers?

Chapter 6

Next, we should say whether there are two, or three, or more principles.

Now there cannot be one principle only, since there cannot be one contrary, nor can there be an infinite number of principles since being
5   could not be known then.

Also, there is a single contrariety in each genus, and substance is one genus.

Also, it is possible [to explain generation] using finite principles, and it is better [if things come about] from a finite number, as
10   Empedocles says, than from an infinite number: for Empedocles thinks that he explains all things [using finite principles] just as Anaxagoras does using infinite principles.

Further, some contraries are prior to others, and some are generated from others, as, for example, the sweet and the bitter, or
15   the white and the black. But the principles must always remain.

From these things, therefore, it is evident that there is neither one principle, nor an infinite number of principles.

Yet, though they are finite in number, there is some reason why there could not be only two. For someone, may doubt how density is
20   naturally adapted to cause rarity, or rarity density, and so it is with respect to any other contrariety: for friendship does not conjoin strife, or produce anything from it, nor does strife make any thing from friendship; rather, both produce some other third thing. And some assume even more principles, from which they construct all of nature.

25   Further, someone might object if another nature is not a subject to the contraries: for we see that the contraries are not the substance of things, and a principle ought not to be predicated of some subject, for if it were, there would be a principle of a principle: for the subject is a principle, and appears to be prior to what is predicated of it.

30   Further, we say that a substance is not contrary to a substance. How, then, will substance come from things which are not substance? or how will what is not substance be prior to substance?

Hence, if someone thinks that what was said before is true, and also admits the truth of what was just said, if he wishes to keep both
35   assertions he must assume a third thing as a subject to the contraries, as they say who affirm that the universe is of one nature, as water or fire, or what is intermediate between these. Yet it

appears that the subject is *more* what is intermediate between the elements: for fire and earth, air and water, are themselves composed
40 of contraries. And so those who make the underlying subject something different from [the elements] are not absurd. And of the rest, [they think more rightly] who make air the subject: for air has fewer sensible differences than the rest. And water follows air. All, however, give form to this one thing by means of contraries, as, for
45 example, by means of density and rarity, or by means of the more and the less. And these things, in general, are excess and defect, as was said above.

This teaching, too, appears to be an old one: I mean, that *the one, excess, and defect,* are the principles of things, except that early
50 thinkers did not consider these principles in the same way as later ones: for the ancients said that two of these principles are active, while the one is acted upon, whereas some of the more recent thinkers say, on the contrary, that the one is active, while the two are acted upon.

55 The claim that there are three elements, therefore, appears to have some weight from these and other such consideration, as said above. It is not likely, however, that there are more than three principles: for one principle is sufficient for the purpose of being acted upon, and if there were four principles and two contrarieties, some
60 other intermediate nature would have to be assumed as a subject separate from both, and if, being two, they are able to come from each other, one of the contrarieties will be superfluous. Further, there cannot be more than one first contrariety: for substance is a single genus of being: so that the principles will differ from each other in
65 prior and posterior alone, but not in genus: for in one genus there is always one contrariety, and all contrarieties appear to be referred to one.

Clearly, then, there cannot be a single element nor more than two or three: but whether there are two, or three, is a matter of some
70 difficulty.

Questions To Consider

1   Having determined that the principles of change must be contraries of some sort, with what question does Aristotle

continue his discussion of these matters? What are the possibilities in trying to give an answer to this question?

2 Why can there not be a single principle of nature (or change?) Why can the principles of nature not be infinite in kind? (Be specific in your answers.)

3 If there is more than one but less than an infinite number of principles, what must follow? Why might we say that the principles must be more than two? (Two major arguments are given. Summarize them in your own words.)

4 If there were three principles, two contraries and some third thing, could the third principle also be a contrary? If so, how? If not, why not? Describe this underlying subject in your own words.

5 Why are there not four, or more, kinds of principle? With what difficulty is Aristotle left at the end of this chapter?

Chapter 7

We, therefore, shall speak as follows: first discussing generation as a whole: for it is according to nature first to consider what is common and then what is proper to each species.

Now we say that one thing comes from another, and one sort of
5 thing from another sort, in speaking either of simple things, or of those which are composite. My meaning is this. A man may become a musician, or what is not musical may become a musician, or a man who is not musical may become a musical man. Now I call what is becoming [something,] man, and what is not musical, simple, and
10 what is coming about, the musical, I also call simple. But [I call] composite both what is becoming [something] and what is coming about, as when we say that a man who is not musical becomes a musical man.

Now of these, one is not only said to have *become* this, but also to
15 have *come from* this, as for example, the musical from what is not musical, but the reverse is not said of all things: for a musician does not come from a man, whereas a man becomes a musician.

Some of the simple things which become [something,] however, remain, while others do not remain: for the man remains, and is a
20 man still in becoming a musician, but what is not musical and the unmusical do not remain, whether simply or in a composite way.

Now these things being set out, from every thing which comes about this may be concluded by any one who directs his attention to it, that there must always be something which is the subject of
25 generation, as we have said. And this, though it is one in number, yet is not one in form: (for by one in form, I mean the same thing as one in definition: for to be a man and to be unmusical are not the same.) And one [principle,] indeed, remains, but the other does not remain: what is not opposed remains, for man remains, but the musical and
30 the unmusical do not remain. Nor does that which is composed of the two remain, as, for example, an unmusical man.

Now that a thing should *come from* something, rather than that a thing *becomes* another, is said more of things which do not remain, as, for example, the musical is said to come about from the
35 unmusical, but not from man. Even so, this is sometimes said of things which remain: for we say that a statue comes from bronze and not that the bronze becomes a statue. The coming about from the opposite, which does not remain, however, is described in both ways, namely: this thing is said to come from that, and that thing is said to
40 become this: for the musical comes from the unmusical, and the unmusical becomes musical. The like also takes place with the composite: for both one becomes musical from being an unmusical man, and an unmusical man is said to have become musical.

Since, however, the term 'coming to be' is said in many ways,
45 some things are said not to come about *simply*, but to become *this*, and to come about *simply* belongs only to substances.

Now with things other [than substance,] there clearly must be something which is the subject of what is coming about: for quantity, quality, relation, when, and where come about through a subject, for
50 substance alone is said of no other subject, whereas all other things are said of substance.

But that substances, and other simple things, come about from a subject will become clear to one who considers the matter. For there is always some subject from which the thing produced comes about,
55 as, for example, plants and animals from seed.

But of the simple things which come into being, some come about by a change of shape, as a statue from bronze, some by addition, as things which are increased, some by separation, as Mercury from a

stone, others by composition, as a house, and still others by a change
60   in quality, as things which are changed according to their matter.

Clearly, then, all the things which come into being come about
from an underlying subject. From what has been said, then, it is clear
that whatever comes into being is always something composite.

And there is something, indeed, which comes about, but there is
65   also something which becomes this thing, and this is twofold: for it is
either the subject or the opposite. I mean, for example, that the
unmusical is the opposite, and that man is the subject, or that the
lack of shape, form, or order, are opposites, and that the bronze, the
stone, or the gold, are underlying subjects.

70   Clearly, therefore, if natural things have causes and principles
from which primarily they are and come to be, not accidentally, but
what each is said to be according to its essence: then every thing
comes about from subject and form: for a musical man is composed, in
a certain way, from man and the musical: for you resolve the
75   definition [of musical man] into the definitions of these things.
Clearly, then, things which come about come from these [subject and
form.]

The subject, however, is one in number, but two in kind: (for man
and gold, and in short matter, can be numbered: for it is more a 'this',
80   and what comes about is not generated from it according to accident,
whereas the privation, or contrary, is accidental:) and form, however,
is one principle, as, for example, order, or music, or one of other
things which are predicated in this way.

And so, in one way there are two principles, but in another there
85   are three, and in one way the contraries are the principles as if
someone should speak of the musical and the unmusical, or of the hot
and the cold, or the harmonized and the unharmonized, whereas in
another way they are not contraries: for it is impossible for contraries
to be acted upon by each other. This [problem], however, is solved
90   because the subject is something [entirely] different: for it is not a
contrary. So that, in a way, the principles are no more than the
contraries, but two in number, as it were, nor again are they simply
two, because their essence is different, but three: for the essence of
man differs from the essence of the unmusical, and also the essence of
95   shapelessness differs from that of bronze.

We have declared how many are the principles of natural things which are concerned with coming into being and how they are just so many. It is also clear that something must subsist as a subject to the contraries and that the contraries are two; yet in a way this is not 100 necessary: for one of the contraries is sufficient to produce change by its absence and presence.

And the underlying nature may be scientifically known by analogy. For just as the bronze is to the statue, or the wood to the bed, or matter (before it receives form) and the lack of form to 105 anything which has form, so is this subject nature to substance, or to a 'this', or to a being.

This, then, is one of the principles, though it is not one, nor a being, in the same way as a 'this', another principle is form, and, further, there is what is contrary [to form,] the privation.

110 Now how there are two principles, and how there are more than two, has been declared above. First , then, it was said that the principles are contraries only, then, that something else must be admitted as a subject and that there are three principles. Yet, from what we have just said, it is evident how the contraries differ, how 115 the principles are related to each other, and what their subject is. It is not yet clear, however, whether the form, or the subject, is the essence of a thing. But that the principles are three, and how they are three, and what the mode is of their existence, is clear.

How many principles there are, then, and what they are, can be 120 seen from what has been said.

Questions To Consider

1 Why does Aristotle consider generation (coming to be) in general before he considers each type of generation in detail?

2 Explain the distinction between a simple thing and a composite thing using an original example. Taking our example of food becoming hot, what is the simple thing which persists throughout this change? What simple thing does not persist throughout the change? Is what persists one of the contraries? Is what does not persist one of the contraries?

3 What, then, are the three kinds of principle involved in any change? Is there anything in our language which reflects this distinction among principles?

4   What are the two types of generation (or becoming) to which
    Aristotle refers?   In the case of something becoming this, for
    example, food becoming hot, is it obvious what the underlying
    subject is? Suppose, however, we consider the change involved in
    digesting the food.   Whereas before, we could say the food
    changed from being cold to being hot, is it apparent what the
    underlying subject is in the food becoming part of an animal?
    According to Aristotle, is there an underlying principle in this
    second type of change?

5   How does Aristotle show that what is involved in a change must
    be a composite thing?   What does Aristotle call the underlying
    principle?   What does he call that principle which is no longer
    present at the end of the change?

6   Considering the state of things before a change, how might we say
    that there is a single principle? How might we say that there are
    two principles?   Considering the whole change, then, does
    Aristotle's claim that, in one respect there must be two principles
    of change and in another respect there must be three, make any
    more sense?

7   In what manner are we aware of the underlying principle in a
    change in substance (as in the case of digesting food?)   What
    names does Aristotle give to the three types of principle involved
    in change?

8   Summarize what Aristotle has done from chapter five through
    this chapter.

Chapter 8

Next, we shall show that the problems of the early [philosophers]
can be solved in this way alone.

For the first philosophers, in investigating the truth and the
nature of things, erred, led by their lack of understanding into
5   another path, and they said that nothing is either generated or
destroyed, because what is generated must be generated either from
being or from non-being, yet both of these are impossible: for being
cannot come into being, since it is already, nor can something come
from non-being, since there must [already] be a subject. And so,
10 exaggerating the implications of this, they denied many things [even]

exist, and said that being itself is one, and they held this opinion for the above-mentioned reasons.

But *we* say that for a thing to come into being from being or non-being, or for non-being or being to do or undergo any thing, or for this
15 particular individual thing to become any thing whatever, in one way does not differ in any respect from asserting that a doctor does or suffers any thing, or that any thing is, or comes about from, a doctor. So that, since this is said in two ways, it is clear that this will also be the case with the phrases 'from being,' and 'being either acts or is
20 acted upon.' A doctor builds a house, not insofar as he is a doctor, but insofar as he is a builder, and he becomes white [white-haired] not insofar as he is a doctor, but insofar as he is black [dark-haired.] But he heals, or loses his medical skill, insofar as he is a doctor. Since, however, we say that a doctor does or suffers any thing, or something
25 comes from a doctor most properly when he suffers or does these things *insofar as he is a doctor*, it is also clear that to claim that something comes from non-being [most properly] means *insofar as it is non-being*.

But the early philosophers did not make this distinction, and they
30 went astray, and because of their lack of understanding they came to understand even less, going so far as to believe that nothing else came about or even existed, and they did away with all coming into being.

We ourselves claim that nothing comes from non-being simply, [or
35 as such,] but that at the same time something may come from non-being accidentally, as it were: (for a thing comes about from a privation, which is non-being in itself yet does not remain in the thing which is generated. But this is remarkable, and it is thought impossible that any thing should come about in this way from non-
40 being.) Similarly, we say that nothing comes about from being, nor does being come about, except accidentally. And we likewise say that this takes place in the same way, as if animal should come about from animal, and a certain animal from a certain animal: as, for example, a dog from a horse. For the dog would come about, not only from a
45 certain animal, but also from animal, though not insofar as it is animal, because it is this already. But if it happened that something became an animal not accidentally, it would not be from animal [that it did so,] and if something came to exist, it would not have come

about from being, nor from non-being: for we have observed that the
50   expression *from non-being* signifies, *insofar as it is non-being.*

Nor do we subvert the claim that every thing either is or is not.

This, then, is one way of solving the doubt. Another way is this:
that we may speak of the same things according to potency and
according to actuality. But we have more accurately discussed this
55   elsewhere.

So that, as we have said, the doubts are solved, on account of
which the early thinkers were compelled to deny some of the things
mentioned above: for it is because of these [problems] that they
wandered so far from the way which leads to coming into being and
60   corruption, and, in short, to all change, since this [underlying] nature,
if they had perceived it, would have dispelled all their lack of
understanding.

Questions To Consider

1   What, in summary, was Parmenides' chief error, as it is related in
     this section?
2   What distinction, according to Aristotle, avoids Parmenides'
     error?
3   Would Aristotle maintain that 'nothing is generated from
     unqualified non-being?' Would he maintain that 'nothing is
     generated from qualified non-being?' Summarize Aristotle's
     answer to Parmenides' difficulty, namely, that 'nothing can come
     to be from non-being.'

Chapter 9

Now some others also grasped this [underlying nature], but not
sufficiently. For, in the first place, they agree that something can be
generated from non-being simply, so that Parmenides spoke truly:
further, it seems to them that if [this nature] is one in number, it is
5   also only one in potency. Yet there is a great difference [between
these.]

For we assert that matter and privation are different and that, of
these, matter is non-being accidentally, whereas privation is non-
being in itself, and matter is nearly, and in a certain way is,
10   substance, whereas the privation is not [substance] at all: and some

claim that the great and the small are alike non-being, either together or separate from one another. So that this triad differs entirely from that. For they have gone so far as to see that there must be an underlying nature, and they made this one: (for though one
15 person makes it a dyad, calling it the great and the small, nevertheless it comes to the same thing, since he neglects the other [principle].

Now the underlying matter is a joint cause, with form, of what comes to be—somewhat like a mother: but the other part of the
20 contrariety might often seem, to one who concentrates upon its evil character, not to exist at all. For, since there is something divine, good, and desirable, we assert that there is one [principle] contrary to that, and another which naturally desires and extends itself toward it.

25 But, according to these men, it happens that the contrary desires its own corruption. But the form can neither desire itself, since it does not lack [itself,] nor what is contrary to itself, for contraries are destructive of each other, rather, what desires [the form] is matter, just as the female desires the male and the ugly desires the beautiful:
30 except that the ugly does not of itself (desire the beautiful,) nor does the female of itself desire the male, but accidentally.

In one way matter itself is generated and corrupted, in another way it is not. Insofar as it is that *in which* [the privation is found], it is corrupted in itself (for that which is corrupted, the privation, is in
35 it): but insofar as it in potency it is not generated and corrupted in itself, rather it must be incorruptible and ungenerated. For if it were generated, there would have to be some first subject from which it came: but this is its own nature, so that it would exist before it came into being (for I call matter the first subject of a thing from which, as
40 something which remains in it, something comes into being, and not accidentally): and if it [matter] were destroyed, it would ultimately arrive at this, so that it would be destroyed before it is destroyed.

Now concerning the principle according to form, whether it be one or many, and what it is or what they are, it is the business of first
45 philosophy [metaphysics] to accurately determine: so that it must be set aside until then. We shall speak of natural and corruptible forms, however, later in this work.

We have determined, then, that there are principles, what they are, and how many there are. Let us now proceed from another
50   beginning.

Questions To Consider

1   What is matter? How does it differ from privation? In things which come to be, which two principles are found together at the end of the change?   Which two are found together at the beginning of the change?

2   Why might someone think that privation is unimportant? Can change take place without privation? Aristotle refers to the good (form) and its contrary (privation,) but to what does he refer as desiring the form? Why might this be so?

3   Taking the matter and privation together before a change takes place, for example, food and cold, what is, and what is not, destroyed in the change? Is the composite of the two destroyed? Is the matter (or subject) destroyed? Ultimately, can matter be generated or destroyed through a change? If so, how? If not, why not?

Physics II

Chapter 1

Of things that exist, some exist by nature, and others through other causes. Animals and their parts, as well as plants and simple bodies, such as earth and fire, air and water, exist by nature: for we say that these and similar things exist by nature—yet all these things
5 seem to differ from those which do not exist by nature. For each of them has within itself a principle of motion and rest, whether according to place, or according to increase and decrease, or according to alteration [change in quality], whereas a bed, a garment, and any other thing of this sort, insofar as they receive these names, and
10 insofar as they are produced by art, have no innate tendency to change. *Yet*, insofar as such things happen to be made of stone or earth, or a mixture of these, to that extent they do have [such a principle]. So that nature is a certain principle and cause of motion and rest in that to which it primarily belongs essentially, not
15 accidentally (and I say *not accidentally*, because a man being a doctor, might be a cause of his own health: yet it is not insofar as he is healed that he possesses [the art of] medicine, rather it happens that the physician and the one healed are the same: it is also the case that these are sometimes separated from each other.) And so it is with
20 everything else which is made: for none of them has in itself a principle of [its own] making, rather for some this principle] is in other things external to themselves, for example, a house, and everything else which is made by hand, while others have it in themselves, yet not essentially—such things as are causes of
25 themselves accidentally. 'Nature', then, is what we have said.

Those things 'have a nature' which have this sort of principle. And these are all substances: for [a substance] is a subject, and nature always exists in a subject. These [substances] are also 'according to nature', as well as those things which are found in them
30 in virtue of what they are, as that fire tends upwards: for this [property] is not 'a nature,' nor does it 'have a nature', rather it is 'by nature' or 'according to nature'. *What* nature is, then, and what 'by

nature' and 'according to nature' [mean], has been stated. And to try
to prove that nature *exists* would be absurd: for it is clear that there
35 are many such things, but to show things which are clear through
such as are unclear is characteristic of one who cannot distinguish
between what is known through itself and what is not known through
itself (and it is clear that this could happen: for one who was blind
from birth might reason about colors), so that for such men the
40 discussion would be about mere words, and they would understand
nothing.

Now to some, the nature and substance of things which exist by
nature seems to be the first constituent of a thing and what is
essentially without order. For example, wood is the nature of a bed,
45 and brass of a statue.

A sign of this, says Antiphon, is that if some one were to bury a
bed, and the rotted wood acquired the power to germinate, it would
not be a bed that would come up, but wood, so that the arrangement,
according to rule and art, belonged to it [only] accidentally, whereas
50 the substance is what remains, which is continually acted upon. And
if each of these is related to something else in the same way (as, for
example, brass and gold to water, or bones and wood to earth, and so
on,) that thing, then, would be their nature and substance. And so
some say that fire, others earth, others air, others water, others some
55 of these, and still others all of them, is the nature of things. For
whatever one of them thought to be of this kind, whether one or
many, this, or these, they said, is the whole of substance, and all
other things are the passions, habits, and dispositions of these, and
any one of them is eternal (since there is no change among
60 themselves,) whereas other things are generated and corrupted over
and over again.

In one way, then, nature is said to be the first subject matter in
everything which has in itself a principle of motion and change. Yet
in another way it is said to be the shape or form which is according to
65 the definition. For just as what is according to art or artistic is called
'art', so also that which is according to nature or natural is called
'nature'. We should not say that something exists by art if it is a bed
(for example) only in potency and does not have the form of a bed yet,
nor should we say that it is a work of art. The same holds true for
70 things which exist by nature: for what is flesh or bone in potency does

not have its own nature, nor does it exist by nature, until it receives the form which is according to the definition, and it is in defining this that we say what flesh is, or bone. So that, in another way, the nature of things which contain in themselves a principle of motion is the
75 form or species, which is separable [from the thing] only in definition. (And what is composed of these, for example, a man, is not a nature, but is natural.)

And this [form] is the nature [of a thing] more than matter: for a thing is said to exist more when it is actual than when it is potential.
80 Further: man is generated from man, but a bed is not generated from a bed: and so they say that it is not the arrangement that is the nature [of that thing], but the wood, since, if it were to germinate, it would not become a bed, but wood. If, then, this [matter] is art, form is also nature: for man is generated from man.
85 Again, nature, when considered as the process of coming into being, is said to be the way to nature [as a form]. For it is not the same as healing, which is said to be the way not to the art of medicine but to health: for healing must come from the art of medicine, and not lead to it. Nature [as the process of generation], however, is not
90 related to nature [as form] in this way, rather that which is born proceeds or grows *from* something *to* something. Into what, then, does it grow? Not into that from which [it came], but into that to which [it tends]. Form, then, is also nature. But form and nature are said in two ways: for the privation is also a form, in some way. And whether
95 there is a privation or a contrary [involved] in simple generation or not will be taken up later.

Questions To Consider

1 According to Aristotle, in what two ways do things exist? What seems to be common to those things which exist by nature?
2 How do artifacts differ from natural things? Given this preliminary difference, how does Aristotle define nature?
3 Why does Aristotle add the qualification 'but not accidentally' to his definition of nature? What does accidentally mean in this context? What examples does Aristotle give of accidental things?

4   If nature is a principle, what sorts of thing have natures?[1] What
     sorts of thing are according to nature? Give examples of each.
     How do having a nature and being according to nature differ from
     nature itself?

5   Does Aristotle prove that there are natures? If so, how? If not,
     why not?

6   In trying to render the definition of nature more precise, Aristotle
     refers to what sort of principle? Have we seen this principle
     before? If so, where? What evidence is there that the nature of a
     thing is its matter?

7   To what principle does Aristotle next make reference in rendering
     his definition of nature more specific? Have we seen this
     principle before? If so, where? Why might someone think that
     the nature of something is its form? Is the form of a thing
     something existing separately from it?

8   Is what is composed of matter and form a nature? If so, why? If
     not, why not? Can a principle exist by itself?

9   Of the two, matter and form, which is more the nature of
     something? Why?

10   Summarize the third sense of nature which Aristotle gives here.
     If matter and form are nature, in some way, what of privation? Is
     privation the nature of a thing in any way?

---

[1]   That nature *is* a principle in a thing and *is not* the thing itself is of
       extreme importance. Accordingly, the distinctions among natures, things
       which have natures, and things which are according to nature come
       immediately after the definition of nature.

Chapter 3

Having defined these things, let us consider the causes: both what they are and how many: for since this inquiry is for the sake of knowledge, and we do not think that we know anything until we understand 'why' it is so (and this is to have a grasp of its first cause,)
5 we must do the same as regards generation and corruption and every sort of physical change, so that, knowing their principles, we may try to refer each of those things that we seek to them.

In one way, then, a cause is said to be that from which something comes into being, and which remains, for example, bronze is the cause
10 of the statue, silver of the bowl, as well as the *genera* of these.

In another way, cause is the form or the paradigm, that is, the definition of the essence [of a thing] and its genus (for example, the form of the octave is two to one, and in general, number), as well as the parts which are contained in the definition.

15 Further, cause is said to be the first principle of change or of coming to rest, for example, an advisor is [such] a cause, a father is a cause of his child, and, in general, the maker is the cause of that which is made and that which brings about a change is the cause of that which is changed.

20 Again, cause is the end, that is, that for the sake of which, for example, health is a cause of walking: for *why* does he walk? We answer, 'in order to be healthy', and having said this, we think that we have given the cause. So it is among such things as are for the sake of the end but are intermediate, for example, losing weight, or
25 purging, or medicines, or instruments, are for the sake of health: for all these are for the sake of the end, yet they differ from each other insofar as some of them are activities, while others are instruments. 'Cause', then, has about this many meanings.

Yet, since 'cause' has many meanings, it happens that there may
30 be several non-accidental causes of the same thing, for example, the art of the sculptor and bronze are both causes of the statue *as a statue* (and not as something else) but not in the same way: one is a cause as matter, while the other as that from which the change began.

And some things are causes of each other, for example, work is
35 the cause of good bodily condition, and good bodily condition is a cause of work, yet not in the same way: one is the end, while the other is the principle of motion.

Again, the same thing can be the cause of contraries: for that
which when present is the cause of some effect is sometimes said by
40   us to be the cause of a contrary effect when it is absent, for example,
we say that the cause of the shipwreck is the absence of the pilot,
whose presence is the cause of its safety.

And all the causes just mentioned fall into four clear groups. For
letters are the causes of syllables, the material of artificial things, fire
45   and such things of bodies, parts of the whole, and premises of the
conclusion as *that from which* something comes. And of these, some
are causes as subjects, for example, parts, while others are causes as
 -essences: the whole, and composition, and form. But seed, a
physician, an advisor, and in general the maker, are all causes as a
50   principle of change, or of coming to rest, or of motion. Still others are
causes as the end, or what is good for other things: for *that for the*
sake of which is what is best, and the end of the other things; and it
makes no difference here whether we say the end is *the good itself* or
the apparent good. Such, then, and so many are the types of cause.

55   The modes of the causes, however, are many, though they are
fewer when summarized. For 'cause' is said in many ways, and one of
those which are of a similar type may be prior or posterior to another,
for example, the physician and the artist are causes of health, the
double and number are causes of the octave, and whatever contains is
60   related to the particulars in this way. Causes, as well as their genera,
are also said accidentally, for example, in one way Polyclitus is the
cause of the statue and in another way the sculptor is the cause, since
the sculptor happens to be Polyclitus. Similarly, those things which
contain what is accidental are said to be causes [in this way], as if
65   man, or, in general, animal, were the cause of the statue. And some of
these accidents are more or less remote than others, as if the white or
the musician were said to be the cause of the statue.

But all the causes, both proper and accidental, are also said to be
either potential or actual, for example, the builder who is about to
70   build a house, or the builder who is building one now.

The like may also be said about the effects brought about by these
causes, for example, about this particular statue, or about a statue,
or, in general, about an image, or about this brass, or about brass, or,
in general, about matter; and this holds for accidents also. And all

75 these may be said in combination, for example, not Polyclitus, nor a
sculptor, but Polyclitus the sculptor.

All these [modes], however, are six in number, and each is said in
two ways: for [they are said] either as a particular or as a genus, as
accidental or as the genus of an accident, or in combination or
80 singly—and all these either as actual or as potential. And the
difference is this: that causes which are actual and particular exist or
do not exist at the same time as their effects, for example, this man
who heals exists at the same time as the one who is being healed, and
this builder exists at the same time as the building which is being
85 built. But this is not always so for potential causes: for the house and
the builder do not cease to exist at the same time.

Now one ought always to consider the highest cause here, as with
other things, (for example, a man builds because he is a builder, but
he is a builder according to the art of building: this, then, is the prior
90 cause; and so it is with every other thing.)

Further, one ought to consider general [causes] of general
[effects], and particular [causes] of particular [effects], for example, a
sculptor is the cause of a statue, and this sculptor is the cause of this
statue. And one ought also to consider potential [causes] of potential
95 [effects], and actual [causes] of actual [effects].

Let this be a sufficient description, then, of how many causes
there are and in what ways they are causes.

Questions To Consider

1   Why does Aristotle take up causes next? What is the relation
between the question why is it so? and a cause?
2   List and describe the four causes. Give examples of each. Which
of the four causes are also principles of nature? Which cause is
matter? Which might be called an agent (acting) cause? What do
we call that which brings about an end?
3   Can a single effect have more than one cause? If so, give an
example. If not, why not? Can causes cause each other? Can the
same thing be a cause of contrary effects?
4   Summarize, in your own words, what has been noted about the
four causes.

5   Having considered the four causes in themselves, Aristotle next
    turns to how something might be a cause: this is called the mode
    of a cause.

6   How does a prior cause differ from a posterior cause? Give an
    example of each.

7   How does a proper cause differ from an accidental cause? Give
    examples of each.

8   How do single causes differ from causes taken in combination?
    Give examples of each.

9   Aristotle notes that there are six distinct modes, each of which
    can be taken in two ways. What are the six modes, and what are
    the two ways in which each mode can be taken (yielding twelve
    modes?) Are these modes of causes alone, or also of the effects of
    causes?

10 When one is speaking of an actual mode, must both cause and
    effect be present simultaneously? If so, why? If not, why not?
    When one is speaking of a potential mode, must both cause and
    effect be present simultaneously? If so, why? If not, why not?

Chapter 4

    Luck and chance are also said to be causes, and many things are
said both to be and to come about by luck or chance. Let us consider,
then, in what way fortune and chance may be included among the
causes, and whether luck is the same as chance or different, and, in
5   general, what luck and chance are. For some have a problem whether
they even exist or not: for they say that nothing comes about by luck,
rather there is some *definite* cause of everything which we say comes
about by luck or chance, for example, the cause of a man's coming to
the market and, by luck, finding someone whom he wished, but did
10 not expect, to find, is really his desire to buy something when he came
to the market. And so it is with other things which are said to come
about by luck, that one may always find some cause, but not luck,
because if luck *were* something, it would seem strange that none of
the ancient wise men, in speaking of the causes of generation and
15 destruction, has ever said anything about it; so it would seem that
they did not believe anything comes about by luck either. But this
would be remarkable: for many things both come about and exist by
reason of luck and chance, and, though everyone knows that all these

things may be explained through some definite cause (just as the old
20 argument which denies chance claims), yet at the same time they say
that some of them are by chance and others are not: and so they
should have brought it to mind in some way.

But none of them thought that luck was something like friendship
or strife or fire or mind, or any other such thing. And this is strange,
25 whether they supposed that it did not exist, or, believing that it did,
simply omitted it—especially those who used it, as Empedocles, when
he says that air is not always separated into the highest place, but as
it may chance: anyway, he does say in his Cosmogony:

It happened to run this way at that time, but it often ran
30 otherwise.

He also says that most of the parts of animals came about by
chance.

There are some who say that chance is the cause both of the
heavens and of all the things of this world: for they say that the
35 vortex, the motion which separated and arranged everything in order,
was due to chance. And this is quite remarkable, that they should say
that animals and plants neither exist nor come about by chance, but
that either nature, or intellect, or some other such thing is their cause
(for it is not just any chance thing which comes from a seed, but an
40 olive from this seed, and a man from that), but that the heavens and
the most divine of the things that we see should come about by
chance, and that there is no cause of these things like what they say
is the cause of plants and animals. Indeed, if it were so, this is itself
worthy of consideration, and it would have been well to say
45 something concerning it. For beside the absurdity of the statement
itself, to affirm it is even more absurd when we see that nothing in
the heavens happens by chance, whereas many things do come about
by chance among those things which [they say] are not due to chance,
though the exact opposite should occur.

50 And to some, chance seems to be a cause, but one which cannot be
comprehended by the human mind—something divine and godlike.

And so let us consider what each of them is, and whether luck
and chance are the same or different, and how they fit into the causes
already given.

Questions To Consider

1   Why does Aristotle consider luck and chance next? What three
    questions does he ask about these things?
2   What is the argument that luck and chance do not exist? Does
    Aristotle accept this argument?
3   Did any of the ancient philosophers (prior to Aristotle) ever use
    luck or chance in their explanations of nature? Did they ever
    explain what luck and chance were in themselves?
4   According to some, our world was brought about reasonably,
    while the heavens were brought about by chance. How does
    Aristotle argue against this position?
5   If some thought chance was a cause, how did they tend to regard
    it?

Chapter 5

   First, then, since we see that some things always come about in
the same way and others for the most part, it is clear that neither
chance nor what comes from chance can be said to be the cause of
these: neither of that which comes about of necessity, and always, nor
5 of that which happens for the most part. But since there are other
things which come about besides these, which all men say are due to
chance, it is clear that both luck and chance exist: for we know that
things of this sort are due to chance and that things due to chance are
of this sort.
10   Further, of things which come about, some come about for the
sake of something and others do not (and some of these come about
through deliberate choice and others do not, yet both come about for
the sake of something). Clearly, then, apart from those things which
come about of necessity or for the most part, there are some which
15 can come about for the sake of something. Those things which come
about for the sake of something occur as a result either of thought or
of nature. We assert that things of this sort, when they come about
accidentally, are by chance (for just as one being may be essential and
another accidental, so it is with causes, for example, the essential
20 cause of a house is the builder, while accidental causes could be the
white or the musical; and the essential cause is definite, whereas the

accidental cause is indefinite: for an infinite number of characteristics may happen to belong to a single thing.

As we have said, then, when this happens among things which
25 come about for the sake of something they are said to be due to chance or luck (we shall explain later how these differ—at present it is clear that both are found among things which come about for the sake of something). For example, a man collecting money would have come [to a certain place] to receive it if he had known that he could:
30 but he did not come for this, rather it merely happened that he came, and that he collected it, nor did this usually (or always) occur when he went there: and the end result, receiving the money, is not one of those things which are causes in themselves, yet is included among things which are deliberately chosen and due to thought, and so it is
35 said to have come about by luck, whereas if he had gone by choice for the sake of [receiving the money], whether always or in most cases, this would not have occurred by luck.

Clearly, then, luck is an accidental cause among those things which are done by choice and for the sake of something. And so
40 thought and luck are concerned with the same thing: for there is no deliberate choice without thought.

And the causes of what comes about by luck must be indefinite. So it may seem that luck is something indefinite and incomprehensible to us, and even that nothing really does come about
45 by luck. For all these things are rightly said because they are reasonable. For in a certain way something *does* come about by luck, for it comes about accidentally, and luck is an accidental cause; but simply speaking it is not the cause of anything, for example, a builder is the cause of a house, but a flute-player is also the cause [of the
50 house] accidentally, and the causes of a man's coming to the market and receiving money (when he did not come for the sake of this) are infinite—for the cause might be the desire to see someone, or to follow someone, or to avoid someone, or to see a play. It is rightly said, then, that luck is something beyond reason: for reason is about things
55 which are either always or usually so, whereas luck is found among things which come about in a different way. Consequently, since things which are causes in this way are indefinite, luck also is indefinite.

Yet at the same time, someone may wonder whether just
60 anything can become a cause of luck, for example, wind or heat is the
cause of health, but not having one's head shaved. For some
accidental causes are closer [to the effect] than others.

And luck is said to be good when something good occurs and bad
when something bad occurs, and they are called 'good fortune' or
65 'misfortune' when [the effect] is great: and so, when we come very
close to some great evil or good, we are said to be 'fortunate' or
'unfortunate', because the mind asserts this as if it were so: and the
small difference seems insignificant.

Further, it is reasonable to say that good fortune is unstable: for
70 fortune itself is unstable: since none of the things which come about
by chance happen either always or usually so.

As has been said, then, both luck and chance are accidental
causes among those things which come about neither simply nor
usually so [but rarely], and which happen for the sake of something.

Questions To Consider

1   Aristotle begins this chapter with a division based upon the way
     in which things come about. What is the distinction? Could luck
     or chance be associated with either of these? If so, how? If not,
     why not?
2   Aristotle proceeds to make another division of the way in which
     things come about. What is this division? Do things which
     happen by luck or by chance pertain in any way to either of these?
3   Explain, in your own words, Aristotle's example of a lucky
     incident.
4   Explain Aristotle's definition of luck. Is luck a cause? If so, of
     what sort? If not, how does it bring things about? In what sphere
     of things will luck be found?
5   How does Aristotle explain why luck is unpredictable and
     seemingly irrational? What does luck's being an accidental cause
     have to do with this?

Chapter 6

They differ in that 'chance' is more general: for everything which comes about by luck comes about by chance, but not everything which comes about by chance also comes about by luck.

For luck, and what comes about by luck, belong to those things
5 which can be fortunate and which can *act*. And so luck must be found among things which are *done* (and a sign of this is that good fortune seems to be either the same as happiness or very close to it, and happiness is an activity, since it is doing well), so that whatever cannot act in this way can do nothing by luck. Consequently, neither
10 inanimate things nor brute animals nor infants can do anything by luck, since they do not have deliberate choice: nor are they either fortunate or unfortunate, except by virtue of a similitude, as Protarchus saying that the stones used for the altar are fortunate since they are honored, while others of the same sort are trampled on.
15 Yet these things can be affected by luck, in some way, insofar as someone who does something with them is acting by luck, but not otherwise.

Chance, however, is found among the other animals and even among many inanimate things, for example, we say that the horse
20 came by chance because his coming saved him, though he did not come for the sake of being saved, or that the tripod fell by chance, for it stands for the sake of being sat upon, yet it did not fall for the sake of being sat upon.

And so it is clear that among things which come about, generally,
25 for the sake of something, when they do not come about for the sake of what actually happens and also have an external cause, then we say that they come about by chance. And of these, those things occur by luck which come about by chance and are chosen by those who have deliberate choice.

30 A sign of this is 'in vain'; a thing is said to be done 'in vain', when that for the sake of which it is done does not come about, but something else, for example, when walking is for the sake of evacuation, if this does not occur to him who walks we say that he walked in vain, and that his walking was vain; so that, what is
35 naturally for the sake of something else is *in vain* when it does not bring about that for the sake of which it *naturally* was done: for if someone were to say that he washed in vain because the sun did not

set he would be ridiculous: since [his washing] was not for the sake of
that. So that chance, even according to its name, is when a thing is
40   done in vain: for the stone fell not for the sake of striking any one,
therefore it fell by chance, because it might have been thrown by
someone for the sake of striking.

Now chance differs from luck mostly among things which are
produced by nature: for when anything is made contrary to nature,
45   we do not say that it came about by luck, rather we say that it was
due to chance. There is also this difference: for the cause of one is
external, but of the other it is internal.

Thus we have shown what chance and luck are and how they
differ from each other.

50   As to *how* they are causes, each of them is a principle of change:
for the causes of such things are always either nature or mind, and
these are infinite in number.

Now chance and luck are causes of things which the mind or
nature bring about, when something accidentally becomes the actual
55   cause of these things. And since nothing which is accidental is prior
to what is essential, it is clear that an accidental cause cannot be
prior to an essential one. Chance and luck, therefore, are posterior
both to the mind and to nature. Consequently, even if chance were
truly the cause of the heavens, nevertheless intelligence and nature
60   would necessarily be prior causes of many other things, as well as of
the universe itself.

Questions To Consider

1   How do luck and chance differ? Must there be a choice in order
for some event to be a lucky one? Must there be a choice in order
for some event to come about by chance?
2   How is what occurs by chance like what occurs *in vain*?
3   Explain the parts of the final definitions of luck and chance.
4   When is chance most obvious? Why might this be so?
5   We have seen that luck and chance are accidental causes, which
is, as we have seen, one of the modes of causality. But, of the four
causes, of what sort are luck and chance?
6   Could luck or chance be the source of all that is (as, for example,
Empedocles seems to have held?) If so, how? If not, why not?

Chapter 7

That there *are* causes, then, and that they are as many in number as we have said, is clear: for the question 'why is it?' is asked in as many ways: for this question is either finally referred, among immovable things, to 'what' something is, (as in mathematics, for it is
5 finally referred to the definition of a straight line, or of the commensurate, or of some other such thing), or it is referred to the first mover (for example, why did they fight?—because they were robbed), or, for the sake of what? (that they might govern), or, among those things which are generated, matter.
10 That these are the causes, then, and that they are just so many, is clear.

But since there are four causes, it belongs to the natural philosopher to know them all, and, referring back to all these, he will give the reason why in a way proper to natural philosophy: the
15 matter, the form, the mover, and 'that for the sake of which'. Frequently, though, three of these causes come down to one: for what a thing is and 'that for the sake of which' are one, whereas the first principle of motion is the same in kind as these: for man generates man—and, in general, things which are moved cause motion (and
20 such things as are not moved no longer belong to the study of nature: for they cause motion, not by having motion or a principle of motion in themselves, but are themselves immovable: whence there are three types of treatment: one dealing with what is immovable, another dealing with what is moved, yet is incorruptible, and a third dealing
25 with corruptible things).

So that 'why something is' is answered by referring to matter, to what it is, and to the first mover. For, when considering coming-into-being, they usually consider causes in this way: 'what came to be after what?' and 'what acted first, or was acted upon?', and always
30 what follows in this way.

And there are two principles which cause motion in a physical way, one of which is not physical, since it has no principle of motion in itself. And that which causes motion without being moved is of this kind, as is that which is entirely unmoved, the first of all things, as
35 well as the *whatness* and form: for this is the end and 'that for the sake of which'. Hence, since nature is for the sake of something, one must also know this cause, and 'why is it?' must be entirely answered:

for example, that such a thing comes from this (whether it be always from this, or usually so), and if this is to be then that must be (for
40 example, if the conclusion [is to be then] the premises [must be]), and that this is the essence, and because it is better in this way, not simply, but in relation to the substance of each thing.

Questions To Consider

1   Which of the four causes ought the philosopher of nature to consider? If the philosopher of nature considers nature, which is a principle of change, then why would he consider the agent and final causes in addition to matter and form? Are the agent and final causes the same as matter or form in any given case of change?
2   Will the philosopher of nature consider all agent causes (or movers?) If so, why? If not, why not?
3   How does Aristotle show that a consideration of all four causes will pertain to the philosophy of nature? (What sorts of question are asked concerning a given change, or generation?) To which cause does the phrase 'because it is better in this way' correspond? Why might this be so?
4   To what sort of mover is Aristotle alluding at the end of this Chapter?

Chapter 8

First, then, we must say why nature is one of the causes which [act] for the sake of something, then how necessity is found in physical things: for all come back to this cause, saying that since what is hot is naturally a thing of this kind, as is what is cold, and so
5 on, certain things *necessarily* are and will *necessarily* come about: for even though they refer to another cause (one [speaking of] friendship and strife, another, mind), yet they merely mention it, and then dismiss it.
     There is a doubt: what prevents nature from operating, not for
10 the sake of something and because it is better to do so, but just as it rains, not that corn may grow, but of necessity (for what is drawn up must be cooled; and what has been cooled, upon becoming water, must fall, and it happens that the corn grows as a consequence of

this), and similarly, if the corn on the ground were spoiled, it does not
15 rain in order that it might be spoiled, but this is accidental—so that
what prevents the parts in nature also coming about in this way, for
example, that our teeth should come up of necessity, the front ones
sharp and able to tear, and the back teeth broad and able to grind the
food—since they did not come about for the sake of this, but it merely
20 happened? And similarly for the other parts of the body which seem
to be for the sake of something. And whenever all such things came
about *as if* for the sake of something, they survived, being suitably
put together by chance, whereas the things which were not put
together in this way died off, and continue to die off, as Empedocles
25 says of the 'man-faced offspring of oxen'.

Æ This, then, (and any other such), is the argument which might
cause someone difficulties. Yet it is impossible that things should be
in this way. For these things, and everything which is produced by
nature, come about either always or usually in the same way,
30 whereas this is not so with anything coming about by luck or chance.
For it does not seem to be due to luck or coincidence that it frequently
rains in the winter, but in the summer, nor heat in the summer, but
in the winter. Now if these things seem either due to chance or for the
sake of something, but they are not due to chance or coincidence, they
35 must be for the sake of something. But all such things exist by
nature, as is acknowledged by those who say these things. Therefore,
there is 'that for the sake of which' among things which come about
and exist by nature.

Æ Further, among things in which there is some end, what is prior
40 and what follows that are for the sake of that end. As it happens, so it
is naturally [designed to occur], and as it is naturally [designed to
occur], so it happens, if nothing prevents it. But it happens for the
sake of something, and therefore it is naturally [designed to be] for
the sake of this. For example, if a house were among the things which
45 come about by nature, it would come about by nature in the same way
as it now comes about by art: and if things which come about by
nature not only came about by nature but also by art, they would
come about in the same way as they come about by nature. The one,
then, is for the sake of the other. And, in general, art partly completes
50 what nature cannot complete, and partly imitates nature. If, then,
artificial things are for the sake of something, so also are natural

things. For the latter [stages] are related to the former in the same
way in both natural and artificial things.

This is even more clear in the other animals, which make things
55 neither by art nor by inquiry or deliberation. And so some wonder
whether spiders, and ants, and animals of this sort, work by intellect
or by something else. But to the one who proceeds gradually in this
way it is apparent that even in plants certain things come about for
the sake of the end, for example, leaves are for the sake of protecting
60 the fruit. And so, if the swallow makes her nest, and the spider her
web, both by nature and for the sake of something, and if plants make
leaves for the sake of the fruit, and if roots grow, not up, but down, for
the sake of nourishment, it is clear that there is a cause of this sort
among things which come about and exist by nature. And since
65 nature is twofold, matter and form, and [form] is the end, and the
others are for the sake of the end, this [the form] will be the cause,
and 'that for the sake of which'.

Now mistakes occur even among artificial things (for a
grammarian has not written correctly and a doctor has not
70 administered the medicine correctly), so that this may clearly also
happen among natural things. If, then, there are some artificial
things which, rightly made, are for the sake of something, but which,
mistakenly made, were produced for the sake of something, which
was not attained, the same will also occur among natural things, and
75 monstrosities would be mistakes with respect to that for the sake of
which [it was done]. In the original combinations of things, then, the
'offspring of oxen', if they were unable to attain a certain limit, or end,
must have come about from the corruption of some principle, as
[such] things now come about from the corruption of seed.

80   Further, the seed must have come about first, and not the
animals all at once: and the expression "first the whole-natured"
referred to the seed.

Again, we also find 'that for the sake of which' among plants,
though it is less distinct. Would there have come about in plants,
85 then, 'olive-headed offspring of vines', much as the 'man-faced
offspring of oxen'? But this is ridiculous, yet it must have, since it also
occurred among the animals.

Again, things must have come about by chance among the seeds
of things. But he who asserts this completely destroys both natural

90   things and nature itself: for those things are natural which are continuously moved by reason of a certain principle within themselves, and so arrive at a specific end. Yet the same thing does not come about by reason of each principle, nor does any chance thing, but the same [principle] always arrives at the same end, unless
95   it is impeded.

     But 'that for the sake of which' [the end], and what is for the sake of *this* [the means], may also come about by chance, for example, we say that a stranger came by chance, paid the ransom, and left, when he did so *as if* he came for the sake of this, yet did not actually come
100   for this reason. And this is accidental (for chance is found among accidental causes, as we said earlier), but when this comes about either always or usually in this way, then it is neither accidental, nor by chance: and among natural things it always comes about in this way, unless something prevents it.

105   It is also absurd to think that things do not come about for the sake of something unless the agent is seen to deliberate. For neither does art deliberate: and if the ship-building art were in the wood, it would make [the same thing] by nature. So that if there is 'that for the sake of which' in art, this will also be found in nature. And this is
110   especially clear when someone heals himself: for nature is like this.

     That nature is a cause, then, and that it acts for the sake of something, is clear.

Questions To Consider

1   In the two remaining chapters of this book, Aristotle addresses the question whether there is some purpose in nature, whether things happen the way they do for some reason, or whether, rather, all things happen as they do because of necessity. Which of these alternatives did the philosophers prior to Aristotle choose: purpose, or necessity?

2   Aristotle begins with an argument given by those who say that everything happens by necessity. How might one explain the relation between rain falling and wheat growing in terms of necessity? How might the same be explained in terms of purpose? Does the fact that some rain, in falling, actually destroys wheat rather than helping it to grow, lend some probability to explanations in terms of necessity?

3   How might one explain the structure of teeth in terms of necessity? How might one explain the same thing in terms of purpose?

4   Aristotle next puts forth a position which has gained popular support in our time. What is the modern counterpart of the position he summarizes here?

5   Aristotle next gives the first of several direct arguments for the position that nature, rather than acting by necessity and chance, acts for the sake of an end, has purpose. What is characteristic of natural occurrences: do they occur mostly in the same way or seldom in the same way? Do things which occur by luck or chance occur mostly in the same way or seldom in the same way? Given these facts, how does Aristotle arrive at the conclusion that nature does not act by chance, but for the sake of an end?

6   In the second argument, Aristotle compares natural occurrences to those things which are brought about by art. How does this comparison lead him to conclude that nature must act for the sake of an end?

7   The third argument also concerns the relation between nature and art, and is quite similar to the second argument. Summarize this argument in your own words.

8   The fourth argument begins with those things which have natural functions which most closely resemble human activities which require thought and deliberation. How does this comparison enable Aristotle to conclude that nature has purpose?

9   Next, Aristotle gives the first of several indirect arguments, showing that those who held that nature does not act for the sake of an end reasoned incorrectly. One reason why someone might think that natural occurrences come about by chance is that certain things happen outside the normal course of things (such as birth defects, for example.) How does Aristotle use this very fact to prove that, given these errors in nature, nature must act for the sake of an end?

10 What does determinacy in nature show with respect to the question whether nature acts for the sake of an end? To what does Aristotle contrast nature in giving this argument?

11 Finally, Aristotle turns to the argument of those who think that nature does not act for a purpose because natural things do not

deliberate, or think, about what they are doing. How does Aristotle show that something can have purpose, and act for a purpose, even if it is not itself thinking about attaining that purpose?

Chapter 9

Does what occurs of necessity happen hypothetically, or simply? For they currently think that necessity is found in generation, as if someone were to think that a wall came about necessarily, because heavy things are naturally carried down and light things up, so that
5 the stones and foundation are lower, with the earth above them, since it is lighter, and wood at the very top, because it is the lightest. And yet, though the wall is not made without these things, nevertheless it is not a result of these, except as matter, rather, it comes about for the sake of sheltering and preserving things.
10 And so it is among all other things which come about for the sake of something, that they do not [come about] without things which have a necessary nature, and yet they do not come about as a result of such things, except as matter, rather, they are for the sake of something, for example: why is the saw the kind of thing it is? In
15 order that this may come about, or for the sake of this. Now this end [that for the sake of which] could not come about unless the saw were made of iron. It is necessary, then, that it be made of iron, *if* it is to be a saw and [do] its work. This necessity, then, is hypothetical, and not as an end: for necessity is in matter, but 'that for the sake of which' is
20 in the definition.

Necessity is found in mathematics in a way similar to what is found among things which come about by nature: for since a straight [line] is this sort of thing, it is necessary that a triangle should have its angles equal to two right angles: but it is not the case that since it
25 has its angles equal to two right angles it is a triangle: although if the angles were not equal to two right angles, neither would a straight line be this sort of thing. But the opposite happens among things which come about for the sake of something: for if the end will be, or is, that also which precedes [the end] will be, or is, otherwise, just as
30 the premise is not true when the conclusion is not true, so also the end, or 'that for the sake of which'. For it is also a principle, though of reasoning, not of action (in the other case [mathematics] it is the

principle of reasoning: for they are not actions). So that if a house is
to be made, it is necessary that certain things be made, or already be
35   there, or exist, or, in general, the matter which is for the sake of
something, bricks and stones if it is a house. And the end is not a
result of these things, except as matter, nor does it come to be
through them. Yet, in general, unless these exist, neither will the
house, come about unless there are stones, nor will the saw come
40   about unless there is iron, just as before the premises are not true
unless a triangle has its angles equal to two right angles.

Clearly, then, the necessity found in physical things is what we
call 'matter', as well as its motions. And both causes are to be stated
by the natural philosopher, but especially 'that for the sake of which'
45   [the end]: for this is the cause of the matter, whereas the matter is
not the cause of the end. And the end *is* 'that for the sake of which',
and the principle from the definition [is derived], as with artificial
things: since a house is of such a sort, certain things must necessarily
be made or already be there, and since health is such-and-such, other
50   things must necessarily come about or already be there—so too, if
man is such-and-such, certain things [must be], and if these, then
those.

Perhaps necessity is also found in definitions. For if the activity of
sawing were defined as a kind of division, this cannot be, unless it
55   has a certain sort of teeth, and they will not be [of the right sort]
unless they are [made of] iron. For in a definition there are also some
parts which are its matter, as it were.

Questions To Consider

1   Having shown how purpose is found in nature, Aristotle turns to
the second question, what sort of necessity is found in natural
things. What two sorts of necessity does Aristotle delineate in
this section? How would the wall of a house be explained in
terms of simple necessity?
2   Is it true to say that a metal saw must have weight? Is it true to
say that, if one is to make a saw, he must use a material which is
harder than what he intends to cut with it? Is the necessity of
each of these the same?
3   How does the type of necessity found in mathematics compare to
that found in the philosophy of nature?

4   Of matter and the final cause, which is of more importance in the philosophy of nature? Does this mean that matter will not be included in the definitions of natural things?

Physics III

Chapter 1

Now since nature is a principle of motion and of change, and since our inquiry is about nature, we must also ask what motion is: for if this remains unknown, nature also must remain unknown.

After we have defined motion, we must also try to treat of those
5 things which follow upon it in the same way. Now motion seems to be found among continuous things, and *the infinite* first appears in that which is continuous: so it often happens that those who define the continuous use the definition of the infinite, that which is divisible to infinity being continuous. In addition, it is impossible for motion to be
10 without *place*, and *void*, and *time*. Clearly, then, both for these reasons and because such things are common to all things, and universal, we should first consider each of them: (for a consideration of specifics should follow that of things which are general). But as we said, we must first take up *motion*.

15 Now there are certain things which exist only in act, and there are other things which exist both in potency and in act, such as 'this thing' [substance] or 'so much' [quantity] or 'of such a sort' quality] and so on with the other categories of being.

Further, of relative terms, one is said according to excess and
20 defect, another according to active and passive, or, generally, what can move and what can be moved: for the mover moves what is moved [by it], and what is moved is moved by the mover.

Motion, however, does not exist apart from things: for what is changed is always changed either in substance, or in quantity, or in
25 quality, or in place. But there is nothing common to these, as we said, which is neither 'this thing' [substance], nor quantity, nor quality, nor any of the other categories, so that there can be no motion or change of anything except the things mentioned, for there *is* nothing apart from these things.

30 But each of these is found in all things in a twofold way: for 'this thing' [substance], one is form and the other is privation, for quality, one is white and the other black, and for quantity, one is complete

and the other is incomplete. Similarly for locomotion, one is above
and another is below, or one is light and another is heavy. So that the
35 species of motion and change are as many as those of being.

Having distinguished between act and potency in each genus,
then, motion is *the actuality of that which is potential, as such,* for
example, the actuality of what can be altered, insofar as it can be
altered, is alteration, the actuality of what can be increased or of
40 what can be decreased is increase or decrease (there is no name
common to both), the actuality of what can be generated or corrupted
is generation or corruption, and the actuality of that which can be
moved in place is locomotion. And that this is what motion is is clear
in this way. For when the buildable, insofar as we call it that, is
45 actual, it is being built, and this is [the activity of] building; and so it
is with respect to learning, healing, rolling, leaping, and aging.

Now, since some things are both in potency and in act, though not
at the same time or in the same respect, for example, hot in potency
but cold in act, many things both act upon and are acted upon by each
50 other: for each of these will be able to act and able to be acted upon at
the same time. So that what causes motion in a physical way is also
moveable, for every such thing causes motion and is itself moved.
Some even think that everything which causes motion is also moved,
but whether this is so will be clear later on (for there *is* something
55 which causes motion, yet which is itself immovable).

So far, then, motion is the actuality of what is potential when it is
an actuality of that, not insofar as it is what it is, but insofar as it is
movable. And I say 'insofar as'. For bronze is potentially a statue, yet
motion is not the actuality of the bronze *as* bronze, for 'to be bronze' is
60 not the same as 'to be able to be moved', since if this were so simply,
and by definition, the actuality of bronze as bronze would *be* motion:
but they are not the same, as we have said. (And this is clear with
contraries: for what is potentially healthy and what is potentially sick
are different—otherwise being sick would be the same as being
65 healthy—but the subject, what is healthy and what is sick, whether it
be humor or blood, *is* one and the same.

But since they are not the same, as neither is color the same as
what is visible, clearly, motion is the actuality of what is potential
insofar as it is potential.

70   This [motion] *is* this, then, and that something happens to be
moved just when this actuality exists, and neither before nor after, is
clear, for everything is able at one time to be in act and at another
time not, for example, the buildable. And the actuality of the
buildable, as buildable, is [the process of] building (for [the process of]
75 building [something] is either the actuality of the buildable, or it is
the house: but when the house exists, it is no longer buildable: rather,
it is the buildable which is being built, and so [the process of] building
must be the actuality [and not the house]). And building is a type of
motion, and the same reasoning will also apply to other motions.

Aristotle

Metaphysics

Book IV, Chapter 8

In view of these distinctions it is obvious that the one-sided theories which some people express about all things cannot be valid—on the one hand the theory that nothing is true (for, say they, there is nothing to prevent every statement from being like the statement 'the diagonal of a square is commensurate with the side'), on the other hand the theory that everything is true. These views are practically the same as that of Heraclitus; for he who says that all things are true and all are false also makes each of these statements separately, so that since they are impossible, the double statement must be impossible too.

Again, there are obviously contradictories which cannot be at the same time true—nor on the other hand can all statements be false; yet this would seem more possible in the light of what has been said.—But against all such views we must postulate, as we said above,' not that something is or is not, but that something has a meaning, so that we must argue from a definition, viz. by assuming what falsity or truth means. If that which it is true to affirm is nothing other than that which it is false to deny, it is impossible that all statements should be false; for one side of the contradiction must be true. Again, if it is necessary with regard to everything either to assert or to deny it, it is impossible that both should be false; for it is one side of the contradiction that is false.—Therefore all such views are also exposed to the often expressed objection, that they destroy themselves. For he who says that everything is true makes even the statement contrary to his own true, and therefore his own not true (for the contrary statement denies that it is true), while he who says everything is false makes himself also false.—And if the former person excepts the contrary statement, saying it alone is not true,

while the latter excepts his own as being not false, none the less they
30 are driven to postulate the truth or falsity of an infinite number of
statements; for that which says the true statement is true is true, and
this process will go on to infinity.

Evidently, again, those who say all things are at rest are not
right, nor are those who say all things are in movement. For if all
35 things are at rest, the same statements will always be true and the
same always false,—but this obviously changes; for he who makes a
statement, himself at one time was not and again will not be. And if
all things are in motion, nothing will be true; everything therefore
will be false. But it has been shown that this is impossible. Again, it
40 must be that which is that changes; for change is from something to
something. But again it is not the case that all things are at rest or in
motion sometimes, and nothing for ever; for there is something which
always moves the things that are in motion, and the first mover is
itself unmoved.

Questions To Consider

1   What *are* the two 'one-sided theories' Aristotle is talking about
    here?
2   Two different 'one-sided theories' are addressed. What are they,
    and how does each refute itself?
3   Which of the Pre-Socratics holds the position that all things are at
    rest? That all things are in movement? How does Aristotle argue
    against each of these positions. What is the only remaining
    possibility, then? What sort of thing is Aristotle talking about
    when he says 'the first mover is itself unmoved'?

Thomas Aquinas

Thomas Aquinas was born in thirteenth-century Italy. He entered the Dominican Order, studying philosophy and theology at Paris and, under St. Albert the Great, in Cologne. He eventually taught at the University of Paris, then spent nine years traveling to various monasteries near Rome, returning at last to the University of Paris to teach. In 1274, he was called to Lyons to attend the Council there, though he died while on the way. He was canonized by Pope John XXII and declared the Angelic Doctor of the Church by Pope Pius V. He holds a pre-eminent place among the Fathers and Doctors of the Church. Popes from John XXII to the present Pope have acknowledged the value of his works, both philosophical and theological. Pope John Paul II had this to say about his philosophical works:

> The philosophy of St. Thomas deserves to be attentively studied and accepted with conviction by the youth of our day by reason of its spirit of openness and of universalism, characteristics which are hard to find in many trends of contemporary thought.

Thomas Aquinas was largely responsible for reconciling the philosophy of Aristotle with the Catholic faith. A considerable portion of his writings deal with various works of Aristotle, including the *Physics.* He also wrote two large summaries of the Catholic Faith, the *Summa Contra Gentiles* and the better-known *Summa Theologiae.* We have assembled here small sections of Aquinas' works dealing with the nature of things. The first, *On the Principles of Nature,* expresses in a succinct way the basic distinctions made by Aristotle in the first two Books of the *Physics. On the Mixture of Elements* presents a problem in explaining certain parts of nature, and Aquinas' solution to that problem. In the latter parts of our reading, we have taken segments from Aquinas' works dealing with human nature and the First Cause of all things from his *Summa Contra Gentiles* and *Summa Theologiae.*

Thomas Aquinas

On the Principles of Nature

Chapters 1-5

Chapter One: What are matter and form?

Since some things are able to be, even though they are not yet, and some things already are, that which is able both to be and not to be is said to be in potency, while that which already is, is said to be in
5 act. Being, however, is twofold: namely, essential being (or the substantial being of some thing, for example, that a man exists, and this is being simply) and accidental being (for example, that a man is white, and this is being in a qualified way.)

Now something is in potency with respect to each of these [types
10 of being.] For something is in potency to a man, (as the sperm and the egg,) and another thing is in potency to being white, for example, a man. And both that which is in potency to substantial being and that which is in potency to accidental being can be called matter, as the sperm is the matter of man and man is the matter of whiteness. But
15 these [types of matter] differ, since that which is in potency to substantial being is called the matter from which, while that which is in potency to accidental being is called the matter in which.

Likewise, properly speaking, that which is in potency to substantial being is called prime matter, while what is in potency to
20 accidental being is called a subject: for the subject gives being to the accident, namely, to the one already existing, since the accident has no being except through its subject, whence it is said that the accidental form is in a subject, while it is not said that the substantial form is in a subject. And [prime] matter differs from a subject in this
25 way, for the subject is what does not have being because something comes to it, rather, it exists through itself, and has complete being, just as a man does not have being [simply] through being white. But that is called [prime] matter which has being because something

comes to it, since, of itself, it is incomplete; rather, it has no being, as
30 Averroes says in the second book of his Commentary on the *De
Anima*. Hence, simply speaking, form gives being to matter, but an
accident does not give being to its subject, rather, the subject [gives
being] to the accident, although sometimes 'matter' is used for
'subject,' and vice-versa.

35   Now, just as everything which is in potency is able to be called
matter, thus everything from which something has being (whether it
be substantial being or accidental being) can be called form; just as a
man, when he is white in potency, becomes white in act through
whiteness, and the sperm, when it is potentially a man, becomes
40 actually a man through the soul. And because the form produces
being in act, form is called act. Nevertheless, what makes substantial
being in act is called substantial form, while what makes accidental
being in act is called accidental form.

        Since generation is a motion to form, to the two sorts of form
45 there correspond two sorts of generation: to the substantial form
there corresponds simple generation, to the accidental form there
corresponds generation in a qualified way. For when a substantial
form is introduced, it is said that something has come to be simply,
for example: a man has come to be, or: a man has been generated. But
50 when an accidental form has been introduced, it is not said that
something has come to be simply, but that it has come to be this
[such;] as when a man becomes white, we do not say that a man has
come to be or that a man has been generated simply, but that he has
come to be white [of such a color.]

55   And to this two-fold generation there is opposed a two-fold
corruption, namely, [corruption] simply, and [corruption] in a
qualified way. Simple generation and corruption are found in the
genus of substance; but qualified generation and corruption are found
in all other genera. And since generation is a certain change from
60 non-being to being, while corruption, on the contrary, is from being to
non-being, nevertheless generation does not come about from just any
non-being, but from that non-being which is a being in potency; just
as a statue [comes about] from bronze, which is a statue in potency
and not in act.

65   In order that there be generation, then, three things are required:
namely, being in potency, which is matter; and non-being in act,

which is privation; and that through which something comes to be in act, which is form. Just as when a statue is made out of bronze, the bronze, which is in potency to the form of the statue, is the matter;
70 that which is unshaped or indisposed is the privation; and the shape, by reason of which it is called a statue, is the form. Yet it is not a substantial form, since the bronze, before the coming of the shape, already has being in act, and its being does not depend upon that shape, rather, it is an accidental form. (For all artificial forms are
75 accidental forms.) For art only works upon what is already formed in a being perfected by nature.

Questions To Consider

1 How does Aquinas define 'being in potency', 'being in act', 'essential being', and 'accidental being'?
2 How do the two different types of matter differ? What are the two types of form?
3 What is generation, and what are the two types of generation? What is corruption, and what are the two types of corruption?
4 What sort of non-being is involved in a change? What, finally, are Aquinas' three principles of change?

Chapter Two: How are matter, form, and privation related?

There are, then, three principles of nature: namely, matter, form, and privation, of which one, the form, is that for the sake of which there is a generation; while the other two [matter and privation] are
5 on the part of that from which there is a generation. Hence, matter and privation are the same in subject but differ in definition. For bronze and 'the unshaped' are the same before the coming of the form: yet it is called bronze for one reason and unshaped for another. Hence, privation is not said to be a principle per se, but per accidens,
10 since it coincides with the matter; just as we say that it is accidental that the doctor builds: for it is not because he is a doctor, but because he is a builder, which coincides with the doctor in the same subject.

Yet there are two kinds of accident: namely, necessary, which is not separated from the thing, (as the risible from man,) and non-
15 necessary, which is separated, as white from a man. Hence, although privation is a principle accidentally, nevertheless it does not follow

that it is not necessary for generation, since matter is never completely without privation: for insofar as it has one form, it has the privation of another, and vice-versa, as in fire there is the privation of
20 air, and in air there is the privation of fire.

It must also be noted that, though generation is from non-being, we do not say that negation is the principle, but privation, since negation does not determine a subject to itself. For not to see is able to be said even of non-beings, as 'the chimera does not see' and also of
25 beings which do not naturally have sight, as of stones. But a privation is said only of a certain subject, in which it is natural for the positive state to come to be, just as blindness is only said of things which can see by nature. And since generation is not from non-being simply but from a non-being which is in some subject, and not in just any
30 subject, but in a certain one (since fire does not come to be from just any non-fire, but from a certain non-fire in which the form of fire naturally comes to be,) therefore it is said that privation is the principle and not negation.

But privation differs from the matter and form insofar as they are
35 principles both in being and in coming to be. For in order for a statue to come to be, it is necessary that there be bronze and that finally there be the shape of the statue; and also, when the statue already exists, these two must be there. But privation is a principle in coming to be and not in being: for while the statue is coming to be it is
40 necessary that there be no statue (yet). For if it already were, it could not come to be, since whatever comes to be does not (yet) exist (except in successive things, as in motion and time.) But since the statue already exists, the privation of statue is not there, since affirmation and negation are not found together, nor are privation and its positive
45 state. Further, privation is a per accidens principle, as was explained above, while the others are per se principles.

From what has been said, therefore, it is clear that matter differs from form and from privation according to its notion [definition]. For matter is that in which form and privation are understood: as in the
50 bronze is understood the shaped and the 'unshaped'. Nevertheless, sometimes matter is named with privation, at other times [it is named] without privation: just as bronze, when it is the matter of a statue, does not [of itself] imply a privation, since from this [alone], that I say 'bronze', the indisposed or 'unshaped' is not understood; but

55 flour, since it is the matter with respect to bread, implies in itself a privation of the form of bread, since from this, that I say 'flour', there is signified an indisposition or lack of order opposed to the form of bread. And since the matter or the subject remains in generation, but not privation, nor the composite of matter and privation, therefore

60 the matter which does not imply privation is the one which remains: while [the matter] which does [imply privation] passes away.

It should also be noted that some matter has [itself] a composition of form: for example, bronze, although it is matter with respect to a statue, is nevertheless itself composed of matter and form; and

65 therefore bronze is not called prime matter, since it has a form. But that matter which is understood without any form or privation whatsoever, but is subject to form and privation, is called prime matter, since there is not another matter before it.

Now since every definition and all understanding is through a

70 form, therefore prime matter can be neither defined nor known, except through a comparison to form; for example, it might be said that prime matter is that which is related to all forms and privations as bronze to the statue and to 'the shapeless'. And this matter is called prime simply.

75 It must also be noted that prime matter and form are neither generated nor corrupted, since every generation is from some thing to some thing. Now that from which there is a generation is matter, while that to which there is a generation is form. Therefore, if matter and form themselves were generated, there would be matter of

80 matter and form of form, and so on ad infinitum. Hence, properly speaking, there is generation only of the composite [of matter and form].

Note also that, though prime matter has no form or privation in its definition, (as in the definition of bronze itself there is neither

85 'shaped' nor 'shapeless',) nevertheless matter never exists without form and privation, for it is sometimes under one form and sometimes under another. Furthermore, it is never able to exist through itself, because it is not able to be in act (since it has no form in its definition, and since to be in act is only through a form,) rather, it is only in

90 potency. And thus whatever is in act cannot be called prime matter.

Questions To Consider

1   Which of the principles of nature are *that from which* a change takes place?
2   Is privation absolutely necessary for a change to occur? Why can *negation* (as opposed to *privation*) not be a principle of change?
3   Which of the principles make a thing the *kind* of thing that it is?
4   Which type of matter is itself made up of matter and form? Which is not?
5   If neither prime matter nor form can come into being or be destroyed, then what can?

Chapter Three: What are the four types of cause?

From what has been said it is clear that there are three principles of nature: namely, matter, form, and privation. But these [principles] are not sufficient for generation. For whatever is in potency cannot
5   reduce itself to act: for example, that bronze which is in potency to a statue does not make itself into a statue, but requires some worker, so that the form of the statue might be brought forth from potency into act. Nor is the form able to bring itself forth from potency into act (and I speak of the form of what is generated, which we say is the
10 term of generation); for the form only exists in the thing made: but what acts is in coming to be while the thing comes about. Therefore it is necessary that there be some principle, in addition to matter and form, which acts, and this is called the efficient cause, or the mover, or the agent, or that from which there is a beginning of motion.
15 And since, as Aristotle says in the second book of the Metaphysics, everything which acts only acts by intending something, it is necessary that there be a fourth [principle], namely, that which is intended by what acts: and this is called the end. It must also be noted that, although every agent, both natural and voluntary, intends
20 an end, nevertheless it does not follow that every agent knows the end, or deliberates about the end. Knowing the end is necessary among those [agents] whose actions are not determinate, but are related to opposite things, as with voluntary agents; and thus it is necessary that these [agents] know the end through which they might
25 determine their actions. But with natural agents the actions are

determinate: whence it is not necessary [that they] choose the means to the end. And Avicenna gives an example about the lute-player: it is not necessary that he deliberate about each and every striking of chords, since those strikings are determined with him; otherwise
30 there would be a delay in the strikings, which would be dissonant. But it seems [to pertain] more to the voluntary agent, that he deliberate, than to the natural agent. And so it is clear, by [an argument] *a maiori*, that if a voluntary agent, to which it seems [to pertain] more [to deliberate] does not deliberate sometimes, therefore
35 neither does a natural agent. Therefore it is possible for a natural agent to intend an end without deliberation: and this 'intention' is nothing other than to have a natural inclination to that [end]. From what has been said, it is clear that there are four causes: namely, the material cause, the efficient [or agent] cause, the formal cause, and
40 the final cause.

Now, although principle and cause are [sometimes] interchangeable, as is said in the fourth book of the Metaphysics, nevertheless, Aristotle gives four causes and three principles in the Physics. For he takes causes both for extrinsic and intrinsic
45 principles. But matter and form are said to be intrinsic to a thing, because they are parts which make something up; while the efficient and final causes are said to be extrinsic, since they are outside the thing. But he takes principles only for intrinsic causes. (Privation is not named among the causes, since it is an accidental principle, as
50 was said. And when we say there are four causes, we understand this to be about those which are per se causes, to which all per accidens causes, however, are reduced, since everything which is per accidens is reduced to that which is per se.)

Questions To Consider

1   Can change be explained in terms of the three principles alone?
2   What type of cause is there besides the material, formal, and agent causes?
3   We know that some agent causes do not deliberate about the purpose of their actions. Does it follow that they do not *intend* those purposes to come about?

4   What do matter and form have in common as causes? What do
    the agent and the end have in common as causes?
5   What sort of cause are elements?

Chapter Four: On the coincidence and priority of the causes.

Having seen that there are four kinds of cause, we must also
know that it is not impossible for the same thing to have many
causes: for example, a statue, the cause of which is bronze and an
5 artist: the artist as the efficient cause and bronze as the matter. Nor
is it impossible for the same thing to be a cause of contrary things: for
example, the pilot is the cause of the safety of the ship as well as of its
sinking: of its sinking through his absence and of its safety through
his presence, as the Philosopher [Aristotle] says in the second book of
10 the Physics.
It must also be noted that it is not impossible for the same thing
to be both the cause and what is caused [the effect] with respect to
the same thing: but in different ways: just as walking is sometimes
the cause of health as an efficient cause, but health is a cause of
15 walking as a final cause: for walking is sometimes the [agent] cause
of health, as well as for the sake of health. Also, the body is the
matter of the soul, and the soul is the form of the body.
Now the efficient cause is called a cause with respect to the end
[final cause], since the end is actual only through the activity of the
20 agent: but the end [final cause] is called the cause of the efficient
cause, since the efficient cause only acts through intending the end.
Whence the efficient cause is the cause of that which is the end: for
example, walking, that there may be health; nevertheless, it does not
make the end to be an end, and therefore it is not a cause of the
25 causality of the end, that is, it does not make the end a final cause:
for example, the doctor causes health to be in act, but he does not
make health an end.
And the end is not a cause of that which is the efficient cause, but
makes that which is the efficient cause to be an efficient cause: for
30 health does not make a doctor a doctor (and I speak of the health
which comes about by the activity of the doctor,) but makes the doctor
an efficient cause. Whence the end [final cause] is a cause of the
causality of the efficient cause, since it makes the efficient cause an
efficient cause: and in the same way, it makes the matter, matter and

35 the form, form, since matter only receives a form for the sake of some
end, and form perfects matter only through an end. Hence it is said
that the end is the cause of causes, since it is the cause of the
causality in all the causes. Matter is also said to be a cause of form,
insofar as form can only exist in matter; and similarly form is a cause
40 of matter, insofar as matter only has being in act through form. For
matter and form are said relatively to each other, as is said in the
second book of the *Physics*.

Questions To Consider

1   How can the same thing have more than one cause? How can the
same thing be both cause *and* effect?
2   Which of the causes is the cause of all the others?

Chapter Five: On the modes of the causes.

Having seen that there are four causes, namely, efficient, formal,
material, and final, we must note that each of these causes is said in
many ways. For one cause is called prior, while another is called
5 posterior, for example, art and a doctor are causes of health: but art is
a prior cause, and the doctor is a posterior cause; and it is similar
with the formal cause and the other causes. And it must be noted that
we ought always to ask the question about the first cause, for
example, if we were to ask: 'why is he healthy?' the answer might be:
10 'because the doctor healed him;' and further: 'why did the doctor heal
him?': 'in virtue of the art of healing which he possesses.'
    It should also be noted that what is called a proximate cause is
the same thing as a posterior cause, and what is called a remote
cause is [the same thing as] a prior cause. Whence these two divisions
15 of cause: some prior, others posterior, and again, some proximate,
others remote, mean the same thing. Yet this ought to be observed,
that what is more universal is called the remote cause, while what is
more specific is called the proximate cause: for example, we say that
the proximate form of man is his definition, namely, 'rational animal,'
20 but 'animal' is more remote, and 'substance' is even more remote. For
all the higher are forms of the lower. Similarly, the proximate matter
of the statue is the bronze, while the remote [matter] is 'metal,' and
matter which is even more remote is 'body.'

Next, some causes are per se causes, others are per accidens
25 causes. That which is a cause of some thing insofar as it is a thing of
that sort is said to be a per se cause, for example, the builder is a
cause of a house, and wood is a cause of a bench. That which happens
to belong to a per se cause is said to be a per accidens cause, for
example, that a grammarian builds. For a grammarian is said to be a
30 building cause only per accidens, for it is not insofar as he is a
grammarian [that he builds,] but insofar as it happens to belong to a
builder that he is [also] a grammarian. It is similar with the other
causes.

Next, certain causes are simple, while others are composite. A
35 cause is said to be a simple cause when it alone is that which is a per
se cause, or [when] it alone is that which is a per accidens [cause]: for
example, a builder is a [simple] cause of a house, and likewise a
doctor is a [simple] cause of a house. There is a composite cause when
it is said that both are the cause, for example, the doctor-builder is a
40 cause of the house.

Next, certain causes are actual, while others are potential. An
actual cause is that which is actually causing something, as the
builder while he builds, or bronze when a statue has been made from
it. A potential cause is that which, although it is not actually causing
45 something, is nevertheless able to cause it: for example, a builder, not
insofar as he is building [something], but insofar as he is able to build
[something], and the bronze while it is not a statue. And we must
note that, in speaking of actual causes, it is necessary that the cause
and the effect be simultaneous, in this way, that if one is present,
50 then the other is present also. For if there were a builder actually
[building something], there would have to be the activity of building,
and if there were actually the activity of building, there would have to
be a builder actually [building something]. But this is not necessary
with those causes which are merely potential. And we must
55 understand that a universal cause must be compared to a universal
effect, and a singular cause must be compared to a singular effect: for
example, a builder is the cause of a house and this builder is the
cause of this house.

Questions To Consider

1   How does a prior cause differ from a posterior cause?
2   How does a *per se* cause differ from a *per accidens* cause?
3   How does an actual cause differ from a potential cause?

Thomas Aquinas

On the Mixture of Elements

Many have difficulty with how elements are in a mixture.[1] It seemed to some that, with the active and passive qualities of the elements drawn together to a mean in some way through alteration, the substantial forms of the elements must remain: for if they did not
5 remain, it would seem to be a corruption of the elements, and not a mixture.

Further, if the substantial form of a mixed body [mixture] is the act of a matter which does not already have the forms of the simple bodies, then the simple bodies would lose the notion of elements. For
10 an element is that out of which a thing is first made, and which is in that thing, and which is indivisible in species; for with the substantial forms removed, a mixed body would not be made up of simple bodies such that they would remain in it.

But it is impossible that it be so; for it is impossible for matter to
15 receive the diverse forms of the elements in the same way. Therefore, if the substantial forms of the elements were to be preserved in a mixed body, it would be necessary that they be in different parts of the matter. But matter can have different parts only if quantity is already understood to be present; for with quantity removed,
20 substance remains indivisible, as is clear in the first book of the Physics. But a physical body is made up of matter, existing with a certain quantity, and the substantial form which comes [to it]. Therefore the different parts of the matter subsisting under the forms of the elements take on the notion of many bodies. But it is impossible
25 for many bodies to be in a single place. Therefore, the elements will not be in every part of the mixed body; and thus it will not be a true

---

[1] The problem here is whether elements are actually present in a compound, or not. For example: is salt simply a combination of sodium and chlorine in an equal ratio, or something different from both?

mixture, but [only] according to the senses, as happens in a collection of invisible or insensible bodies, on account of their smallness.

Further, every substantial form requires a proper disposition in matter, without which it cannot exist: whence, alteration is the way to generation and corruption. But it is impossible for the proper disposition which is required for the form of fire and that which is required for the form of water to come together in the same thing, since fire and water are contraries in virtue of such dispositions. And it is impossible for contraries to be together in the same thing equally. Therefore, it is impossible for the substantial forms of fire and water to be in the same part of the mixed body. If, therefore, a mixed body comes to be, with the substantial forms of the simple bodies remaining, it follows that it is not a true mixture, but only according to the senses, with the insensible parts placed next to each other, as it were, on account of their smallness.

Now others, wishing to avoid both these arguments, fell into an even greater difficulty. For, in order that the mixtures of the elements might be distinguished from their corruption, they said that the substantial forms of the elements do remain in the mixed body in some way; but lest they be compelled to say that the mixture is [merely] according to the senses and not according to the truth, they put it forth that the forms of the elements do not remain in the mixed body in their completeness, but are reduced to a certain mean; for they said that the forms of the elements admit of more and less and are contrary to one another.

Now because this is clearly against common opinion and the words of the Philosopher who says, in the Categories, that nothing is contrary to substance and that it does not admit of more and less, they continued, and said that the forms of the elements are the most imperfect, as they are closer to prime matter: whence they are means between substantial forms and accidental forms; and thus, insofar as they approach to the nature of an accidental form, they are able to admit of more and less, given that they may be contrary to one another.

But this position is improbable in many ways. First, because it is altogether impossible that there be a mean between substance and accidents: for there would [then also] be a mean between affirmation and negation. For it is proper to an accident to exist in a subject, but

65 [it is proper] to a substance not to be in a subject. Substantial forms are in matter, indeed, but not in a subject: for a subject is some individual thing; but the substantial form is what makes the subject some individual thing, it does not presuppose it.

Likewise it is ridiculous to say that there is a mean between those
70 things which are not of one kind; since it is necessary that the mean and the extremes be of one kind, as is proved in the tenth book of the Metaphysics. Therefore, nothing can be a mean between substance and accident.

Therefore it is necessary to find another way, in which the truth
75 of the mixture will be preserved and in which the elements will not be wholly corrupted, but may remain in the mixed body in some way. Therefore, we must consider that the active and passive qualities of the elements are contrary to each other, and admit of more and less. But from contrary qualities admitting of more and less a mean
80 quality can be constituted, which has the 'taste' of the nature of each extreme, as gray between white and black and warm between hot and cold. Therefore, with the extremes of the qualities of the elements removed, there is constituted from them a certain mean quality, which is the proper quality of a mixed body, differing, nevertheless, in
85 different ways according to the diverse proportion of the mixture: and this quality is, indeed, the proper disposition to the form of a mixed body, just as a simple quality is to the form of a simple body. Therefore, just as the extremes are found in the mean, which participates in the nature of each, so the qualities of the simple bodies
90 are found in the proper quality of a mixed body. But the quality of a simple body is, indeed, other than its substantial form, however, it acts in virtue of the substantial form; otherwise heat alone would heat, yet the substantial form would not become actual through its [the quality's] power; since nothing acts outside its own species.

95 In this way, therefore, the powers of the substantial forms of the simple bodies are preserved in mixed bodies. Thus the forms of the elements are in mixed bodies, not actually, but virtually: and this is what the Philosopher says in the first book of *On Generation and Corruption*: "therefore the elements do not remain in the mixed body
100 in act, as body and white, nor is one or both either corrupted or altered; for their power is preserved."

Questions To Consider

1   In Aquinas' terms, the problem addressed here becomes: do the
    substantial forms of the elements remain in a true mixture.
    What evidence does Aquinas offer to show that they *must* remain?

2   Yet there are arguments for the opposite view: that the
    substantial forms *do not* remain in the compound. Let us suppose
    that we shall produce salt from sodium and chlorine. Can the
    matter (which will receive the forms of sodium and chlorine) have
    the forms of both simultaneously? How might it?

3   If, then, the sodium and chlorine were in different parts of the
    matter, would the whole thing be what Aquinas calls a *true
    mixture*?

4   At the end of this treatise, Aquinas offers his own solution to the
    problem. Rather than reducing the substantial forms of the
    elements to a mean, he constructs a mean from the proper
    qualities of these same elements. So, just as fire requires a hot
    body in order to come about, and a liquid requires a (relatively)
    cooler one, their combination (if possible,) which would be a true
    mixture, would require a warm body: the mean between hot and
    cold. (Of course, this example is an oversimplification, but it is
    correct in principle.)

David Hume

David Hume was a Scottish philosopher of the Enlightenment period. He is perhaps best known for his withering attacks upon the whole notion of cause and effect, as well as for his biting criticisms of religion and his overall skeptical view of the mind's ability to know. In Hume we see continuing support for the ancient materialism found originally in the Pre-Socratic philosophers and later developed in the Hellenistic philosophy of Epicurus and the Roman Lucretius. In this selection, taken from his *Dialogues On Natural Religion*, Hume provides a defense of the Lucretian swerve.

Dialogue Concerning Natural Religion

Part 8

What you ascribe to the fertility of my invention, replied PHILO, is entirely owing to the nature of the subject. In subjects adapted to the narrow compass of human reason, there is commonly but one
5 determination, which carries probability or conviction with it; and to a man of sound judgement, all other suppositions, but that one, appear entirely absurd and chimerical. But in such questions as the present, a hundred contradictory views may preserve a kind of imperfect analogy; and invention has here full scope to exert itself.
10 Without any great effort of thought, I believe that I could, in an instant, propose other systems of cosmogony, which would have some faint appearance of truth, though it is a thousand, a million to one, if either yours or any one of mine be the true system.

For instance, what if I should revive the old EPICUREAN
15 hypothesis? This is commonly, and I believe justly, esteemed the most absurd system that has yet been proposed; yet I know not whether, with a few alterations, it might not be brought to bear a faint appearance of probability. Instead of supposing matter infinite, as EPICURUS did, let us suppose it finite. A finite number of particles is
20 only susceptible of finite transpositions: and it must happen, in an

eternal duration, that every possible order or position must be tried an infinite number of times. This world, therefore, with all its events, even the most minute, has before been produced and destroyed, and will again be produced and destroyed, without any bounds and

25   limitations. No one, who has a conception of the powers of infinite, in comparison of finite, will ever scruple this determination.

But this supposes, said DEMEA, that matter can acquire motion, without any voluntary agent or first mover.

And where is the difficulty, replied PHILO, of that supposition?

30   Every event, before experience, is equally difficult and incomprehensible; and every event, after experience, is equally easy and intelligible. Motion, in many instances, from gravity, from elasticity, from electricity, begins in matter, without any known voluntary agent: and to suppose always, in these cases, an unknown

35   voluntary agent, is mere hypothesis; and hypothesis attended with no advantages. The beginning of motion in matter itself is as conceivable a priori as its communication from mind and intelligence.

Besides, why may not motion have been propagated by impulse through all eternity, and the same stock of it, or nearly the same, be

40   still upheld in the universe? As much is lost by the composition of motion, as much is gained by its resolution. And whatever the causes are, the fact is certain, that matter is, and always has been, in continual agitation, as far as human experience or tradition reaches. There is not probably, at present, in the whole universe, one particle

45   of matter at absolute rest.

And this very consideration too, continued PHILO, which we have stumbled on in the course of the argument, suggests a new hypothesis of cosmogony, that is not absolutely absurd and improbable. Is there a system, an order, an economy of things, by which matter can

50   preserve that perpetual agitation which seems essential to it, and yet maintain a constancy in the forms which it produces? There certainly is such an economy; for this is actually the case with the present world. The continual motion of matter, therefore, in less than infinite transpositions, must produce this economy or order; and by its very

55   nature, that order, when once established, supports itself, for many ages, if not to eternity. But wherever matter is so poised, arranged, and adjusted, as to continue in perpetual motion, and yet preserve a constancy in the forms, its situation must, of necessity, have all the

same appearance of art and contrivance which we observe at present.

60 All the parts of each form must have a relation to each other, and to the whole; and the whole itself must have a relation to the other parts of the universe; to the element in which the form subsists; to the materials with which it repairs its waste and decay; and to every other form which is hostile or friendly. A defect in any of these

65 particulars destroys the form; and the matter of which it is composed is again set loose, and is thrown into irregular motions and fermentations, till it unite itself to some other regular form. If no such form be prepared to receive it, and if there be a great quantity of this corrupted matter in the universe, the universe itself is entirely

70 disordered; whether it be the feeble embryo of a world in its first beginnings that is thus destroyed, or the rotten carcass of one languishing in old age and infirmity. In either case, a chaos ensues; till finite, though innumerable revolutions produce at last some forms, whose parts and organs are so adjusted as to support the forms

75 amidst a continued succession of matter.

Suppose (for we shall endeavor to vary the expression), that matter were thrown into any position, by a blind, unguided force; it is evident that this first position must, in all probability, be the most confused and most disorderly imaginable, without any resemblance to

80 those works of human contrivance, which, along with a symmetry of parts, discover an adjustment of means to ends, and a tendency to self-preservation. If the actuating force cease after this operation, matter must remain for ever in disorder, and continue an immense chaos, without any proportion or activity. But suppose that the

85 actuating force, whatever it be, still continues in matter, this first position will immediately give place to a second, which will likewise in all probability be as disorderly as the first, and so on through many successions of changes and revolutions. No particular order or position ever continues a moment unaltered. The original force, still

90 remaining in activity, gives a perpetual restlessness to matter. Every possible situation is produced, and instantly destroyed. If a glimpse or dawn of order appears for a moment, it is instantly hurried away, and confounded, by that never-ceasing force which actuates every part of matter.

95 Thus the universe goes on for many ages in a continued succession of chaos and disorder. But is it not possible that it may

settle at last, so as not to lose its motion and active force (for that we
have supposed inherent in it), yet so as to preserve an uniformity of
appearance, amidst the continual motion and fluctuation of its parts?
100 This we find to be the case with the universe at present. Every
individual is perpetually changing, and every part of every individual;
and yet the whole remains, in appearance, the same. May we not
hope for such a position, or rather be assured of it, from the eternal
revolutions of unguided matter; and may not this account for all the
105 appearing wisdom and contrivance which is in the universe? Let us
contemplate the subject a little, and we shall find, that this
adjustment, if attained by matter of a seeming stability in the forms,
with a real and perpetual revolution or motion of parts, affords a
plausible, if not a true solution of the difficulty.
110   It is in vain, therefore, to insist upon the uses of the parts in
animals or vegetables, and their curious adjustment to each other. I
would fain know, how an animal could subsist, unless its parts were
so adjusted? Do we not find, that it immediately perishes whenever
this adjustment ceases, and that its matter corrupting tries some new
115 form? It happens indeed, that the parts of the world are so well
adjusted, that some regular form immediately lays claim to this
corrupted matter: and if it were not so, could the world subsist? Must
it not dissolve as well as the animal, and pass through new positions
and situations, till in great, but finite succession, it falls at last into
120 the present or some such order?
      It is well, replied CLEANTHES, you told us, that this hypothesis
was suggested on a sudden, in the course of the argument. Had you
had leisure to examine it, you would soon have perceived the
insuperable objections to which it is exposed. No form, you say, can
125 subsist, unless it possess those powers and organs requisite for its
subsistence: some new order or economy must be tried, and so on,
without intermission; till at last some order, which can support and
maintain itself, is fallen upon. But according to this hypothesis,
whence arise the many conveniences and advantages which men and
130 all animals possess? Two eyes, two ears, are not absolutely necessary
for the subsistence of the species. Human race might have been
propagated and preserved, without horses, dogs, cows, sheep, and
those innumerable fruits and products which serve to our satisfaction
and enjoyment. If no camels had been created for the use of man in

135 the sandy deserts of AFRICA and ARABIA, would the world have been dissolved? If no lodestone had been framed to give that wonderful and useful direction to the needle, would human society and the human kind have been immediately extinguished? Though the maxims of Nature be in general very frugal, yet instances of this
140 kind are far from being rare; and any one of them is a sufficient proof of design, and of a benevolent design, which gave rise to the order and arrangement of the universe.

At least, you may safely infer, said PHILO, that the foregoing hypothesis is so far incomplete and imperfect, which I shall not
145 scruple to allow. But can we ever reasonably expect greater success in any attempts of this nature? Or can we ever hope to erect a system of cosmogony, that will be liable to no exceptions, and will contain no circumstance repugnant to our limited and imperfect experience of the analogy of Nature? Your theory itself cannot surely pretend to
150 any such advantage, even though you have run into Anthropomorphism, the better to preserve a conformity to common experience. Let us once more put it to trial. In all instances which we have ever seen, ideas are copied from real objects, and are ectypal, not archetypal, to express myself in learned terms: You reverse this
155 order, and give thought the precedence. In all instances which we have ever seen, thought has no influence upon matter, except where that matter is so conjoined with it as to have an equal reciprocal influence upon it. No animal can move immediately any thing but the members of its own body; and indeed, the equality of action and
160 reaction seems to be an universal law of nature: But your theory implies a contradiction to this experience. These instances, with many more, which it were easy to collect, (particularly the supposition of a mind or system of thought that is eternal, or, in other words, an animal ingenerable and immortal); these instances, I say,
165 may teach all of us sobriety in condemning each other, and let us see, that as no system of this kind ought ever to be received from a slight analogy, so neither ought any to be rejected on account of a small incongruity. For that is an inconvenience from which we can justly pronounce no one to be exempted.

170 All religious systems, it is confessed, are subject to great and insuperable difficulties. Each disputant triumphs in his turn; while he carries on an offensive war, and exposes the absurdities,

barbarities, and pernicious tenets of his antagonist. But all of them,
on the whole, prepare a complete triumph for the Skeptic; who tells
175   them, that no system ought ever to be embraced with regard to such
subjects: For this plain reason, that no absurdity ought ever to be
assented to with regard to any subject. A total suspense of judgement
is here our only reasonable resource. And if every attack, as is
commonly observed, and no defense, among Theologians, is
180   successful; how complete must be his victory, who remains always,
with all mankind, on the offensive, and has himself no fixed station or
abiding city, which he is ever, on any occasion, obliged to defend?

Questions To Consider

1   Demea offers an objection to Philo: how can matter ever acquire
motion without a first mover? Does Epicurus himself address this
objection? Does Lucretius?

2   In the remaining selections, Philo (Hume himself, it is likely)
offers an explanation for an ordered universe arising from
disorder, apart from any first mover (God). How like
contemporary explanations is this?

3   What is Philo's ultimate philosophical position on the question of
the origins of the universe, then? Is he an atheist? Is he an
agnostic?

Jean-Henri Fabre

Jean-Henri Fabre was a nineteenth-century entomologist whose studies were recorded in a collection of works called *Souvenirs Entomologiques*. Fabre was a contemporary of Charles Darwin, who called him "an incomparable observer". He is probably best-known popularly for his probing questions concerning animal behavior and instinct, an account of which is provided in these selections.

The Hunting Wasps

Chapter 8

The Languedocian Sphex

When the chemist has fully prepared his plan of research, he mixes his reagent at the most convenient moment and lights a flame
5 under his retort. He is the master of time, place and circumstances. He chooses his hour, shuts himself up in his laboratory, where nothing can come to disturb the business in hand; he produces at will this or that condition which reflection suggests to him: he is in quest of the secrets of inorganic matter, whose chemical activities science
10 can awaken whenever it thinks fit.

The secrets of living matter—not those of anatomical structure, but really, those of life in action, especially of instinct—present much more difficult and delicate conditions to the observer. Far from being able to choose his own time, he is the slave of the season, of the day,
15 of the hour, of the very moment. When the opportunity offers, he must seize it as it comes, without hesitation, for it may be long before it presents itself again. And, as it usually arrives at the moment when he is least expecting it, nothing is in readiness for making the most of it. He must then and there improvise his little stock of
20 experimenting-material, contrive his plans, evolve his tactics, devise

133

his tricks; and he can think himself lucky if inspiration comes fast enough to allow him to profit by the chance offered. This chance, moreover, hardly ever comes except to those who look for it. You must watch for it patiently for days and days, now on sandy slopes exposed
25   to the full glare of the sun, now on some path walled in by high banks, where the heat is like that of an oven, or again on some sandstone ledge which is none too steady. If it is in your power to set up your observatory under a meager olive tree that pretends to protect you from the rays of a pitiless sun, you may bless the fate that
30   treats you as a sybarite: your lot is an Eden. Above all, keep your eyes open. The spot is a good one; and—who knows?—the opportunity may come at any moment.

It came, late, it is true; but still it came. Ah, if you could now observe at your ease, in the quiet of your study, with nothing to
35   distract your mind from your subject, far from the profane wayfarer who, seeing you so busily occupied at a spot where he sees nothing, will stop, overwhelm you with queries, take you for some water-diviner, or—a graver suspicion this—regard you as some questionable character searching for buried treasure and discovering by means of
40   incantations where the old pots full of coin lie hidden! Should you still wear a Christian aspect in his eyes, he will approach you, look to see what you are looking at and smile in a manner that leaves no doubt as to his poor opinion of people who spend their time in watching Flies. You will be lucky indeed if the troublesome visitor, with his
45   tongue in his cheek, walks off at last without disturbing things and without repeating in his innocence the disaster brought about by my two conscripts' boots.

Should your inexplicable doings not puzzle the passerby, they will be sure to puzzle the village keeper, that uncompromising representative of the law in the ploughed acres. He has long had his
50   eye on you. He has so often seen you wandering about, like a lost soul, for no appreciable reason; he has so often caught you rooting in the ground, or with infinite precautions, knocking down some strip of wall in a sunken road, that in the end he has come to look upon you
55   with dark suspicion. You are nothing to him but a gypsy, a tramp, a poultry-thief, a shady person or, at the best, a madman. Should you be carrying your botanizing-case, it will represent to him the poacher's ferret-cage; and you would never get it out of his head that,

regardless of the game-laws and the rights of landlords, you are
60 clearing all the neighboring warrens of their rabbits. Take care.
However thirsty you may be, do not lay a finger on the nearest bunch
of grapes: the man with the municipal badge will be there, delighted
to have a case at last and so to receive an explanation of your highly
perplexing behavior.

65   I have never, I can safely say, committed any such misdemeanor;
and yet, one day, lying on the sand, absorbed in the details of a
Bembex' household, I suddenly heard beside me: "In the name of the
law, I arrest you! You come along with me!"

It was the keeper of Les Angles, who, after vainly waiting for an
70 opportunity to catch me at fault and being daily more anxious for an
answer to the riddle that was worrying him, at last resolved upon the
brutal expedient of a summons. I had to explain things. The poor man
seemed anything but convinced: "Pooh!" he said. "Pooh! You will
never make me believe that you come here and roast in the sun just
75 to watch Flies. I shall keep an eye on you, mark you! And, the first
time I...! However, that'll do for the present."

And he went off. I have always believed that my red ribbon had a
good deal to do with his departure. And I also put down to that red
ribbon certain other little services by which I benefited during my
80 entomological and botanical excursions. It seemed to me—or was I
dreaming?—it seemed to me that, on my botanizing-expeditions up
Mont Ventoux, the guide was more tractable and the donkey less
obstinate.

The aforesaid bit of scarlet ribbon did not always spare me the
85 tribulations which the entomologist must expect when experimenting
on the public way. Here is a characteristic example. Ever since
daybreak I have been ambushed, sitting on a stone, at the bottom of a
ravine. The subject of my matutinal visit is the Languedocian Sphex.
Three women, vine-pickers, pass in a group, on the way to their work.
90 They give a glance at the man seated, apparently absorbed in
reflection. At sunset, the same pickers pass again, carrying their full
baskets on their heads. The man is still there, sitting on the same
stone, with his eyes fixed on the same place. My motionless attitude,
my long persistency in remaining at that deserted spot, must have
95 impressed them deeply. As they passed by me, I saw one of them tap
her forehead and heard her whisper to the others:

Un paouré inoucènt, pécaïre!

And all three made the sign of the Cross.

An innocent, she had said, *un inoucènt*, an idiot, a poor creature,
100 quite harmless, but half-witted; and they had all made the sign of the
Cross, an idiot being to them one with God's seal stamped upon him.

"How now!" thought I. "What a cruel mockery of fate! You, who
are so laboriously seeking to discover what is instinct in the animal
and what is reason, you yourself do not even possess your reason in
105 these good women's eyes! What a humiliating reflection!"

No matter: *pécaïre*, that expression of supreme compassion, in the
Provencal dialect, *pécaïre*, coming from the bottom of the heart, soon
made me forget *inoucènt*.

It is in this ravine with its three grape-gathering women that I
110 would meet the reader, if he be not discouraged by the petty
annoyances of which I have given him a foretaste. The Languedocian
Sphex frequents these points, not in tribes congregating at the same
spot when nest-building work begins, but as solitary individuals,
sparsely distributed, settling wherever the chances of their
115 vagabondage lead them. Even as her kinswoman, the Yellow-winged
Sphex, seeks the society of her kind and the animation of a yard full
of workers, the Languedocian Sphex prefers isolation, quiet and
solitude. Graver of gait, more formal in her manners, of a larger size
and also more somberly clad, she always lives apart, not caring what
120 others do, disdaining company, a genuine misanthrope among the
Sphegidae. The one is sociable, the other is not: a profound difference
which in itself is enough to characterize them.

This amounts to saying that, with the Languedocian Sphex, the
difficulties of observation increase. No long-meditated experiment is
125 possible in her case; nor, when the first attempts have failed, can one
hope to try them again, on the same occasion, with a second or a third
subject and so on. If you prepare the materials for your observation in
advance, if, for instance, you have in reserve a piece of game which
you propose to substitute for that of the Sphex, it is to be feared, nay,
130 it is almost certain that the huntress will not appear; and, when she
does come at last, your materials are no longer fit for use and
everything has to be improvised in a hurry, that very moment, under
conditions that are not always satisfactory.

Let us take heart. The site is a first-rate one. Many a time
135   already I have surprised the Sphex here, sunning herself on a vine-
leaf. The insect, spread out flat, is basking voluptuously in the heat
and light. From time to time it has a sort of frenzied outburst of
pleasure: it quivers with content; it rapidly taps its feet on its couch,
producing a tattoo not unlike that of rain falling heavily on the leaf.
140   The joyous thrum can be heard several feet away. Then immobility
begins again, soon followed by a fresh nervous commotion and by the
whirling of the tarsi, a symbol of supreme felicity. I have known some
of these passionate sun-lovers suddenly to leave the work yard, when
the larva's cave has been half-dug, and go to the nearest vine to take
145   a bath of heat and light, after which they would come back to the
burrow, as though reluctantly, just to give a perfunctory sweep and
soon end by knocking off work, unable to resist the exquisite
temptation of luxuriating on the vine-leaves.

It may be that the voluptuous couch is also an observatory,
150   whence the Wasp surveys the surrounding country in order to
discover and select her prey. Her exclusive game is the Ephippiger of
the Vine, scattered here and there on the branches or on any
brambles hard by. The joint is a substantial one, especially as the
Sphex favors solely the females, whose bellies are swollen with a
155   mighty cluster of eggs.

Let us take no notice of the repeated trips, the fruitless searches,
the tedium of frequent long waiting, but rather present the Sphex
suddenly to the reader as she herself appears to the observer. Here
she is, at the bottom of a sunken road with high, sandy banks. She
160   comes on foot, but gets help from her wings in dragging her heavy
prize. The Ephippiger's antennae, long and slender as threads, are
the harnessing-ropes. Holding her head high, she grasps one of them
in her mandibles. The antenna gripped passes between her legs; and
the game follows, turned over on its back. Should the soil be too
165   uneven and so offer resistance to this method of carting, the Wasp
clasps her unwieldy burden and carries it with very short flights,
interspersed, as often as possible, with journeys on foot. We never see
her undertake a sustained flight, for long distances, holding the game
in her legs, as is the practice of those expert aviators, the Bembeces
170   and Cerceres, for instance, who bear through the air for more than
half a mile their respective Flies or Weevils, a very light booty

compared with the huge Ephippiger. The overpowering weight of her capture compels the Languedocian Sphex, to make the whole or nearly the whole journey on foot, her method of transport being
175 consequently slow and laborious.

The same reason, the bulk and weight of the prey, have entirely reversed the usual order which the Burrowing Wasps follow in their operations. This order we know: it consists in first digging a burrow and then stocking it with provisions. As the victim is not out of
180 proportion to the strength of the spoiler, it is quite simple to carry it flying, which means that the Wasp can choose any site that she likes for her dwelling. She does not mind how far afield she goes for her prey: once she has captured her quarry, she comes flying home at a speed which makes questions of distance quite immaterial. Hence she
185 prefers as the site for her burrow the place where she herself was born, the place where her forbears lived; she here inherits deep galleries, the accumulated work of earlier generations; and, by repairing them a little, she makes them serve as approaches to new chambers, which are in this way better protected than they would be
190 if they depended upon the labors of a single Wasp, who had to start boring from the surface each year. This happens, for instance, in the case of the Great Cerceris and the Bee-eating Philanthus. And, should the ancestral abode not be strong enough to withstand the rough weather from one year to the next and to be handed down to
195 the offspring, should the burrower have each time to start her tunneling afresh, at least the Wasp finds greater safety in places consecrated by the experience of her forerunners. Consequently she goes there to dig her galleries, each of which serves as a corridor to a group of cells, thus effecting an economy in the aggregate labor
200 expended upon the whole business of the laying.

In this way are formed not real societies, for there are no concerted efforts towards a common object, but at least assemblies where the sight of her kinswomen and her neighbors doubtless puts heart into the labor of the individual. We can observe, in fact,
205 between these little tribes, springing from the same stock, and the burrowers who do their work alone, a difference in activity which reminds us of the emulation prevailing in a crowded yard and the indifference of laborers who have to work in solitude. Action is contagious in animals as in men; it is fired by its own example.

210   To sum up: when of a moderate weight for its captor, the prey can
be conveyed flying, to a great distance. The Wasp can then choose any
site that she pleases for her burrow. She adopts by preference the
spot where she was born and uses each passage as a common corridor
giving access to several cells. The result of this meeting at a common
215 birthplace is the formation of groups, like turning to like, which is a
source of friendly rivalry. This first step towards social life comes
from facilities for traveling. Do not things happen in the same way
with man, if I may be permitted the comparison?

When he has nothing but trackless paths, man builds a solitary
220 hut; when supplied with good roads, he and his fellows collect in
populous cities; when served by railways which, so to speak,
annihilate distance, they assemble in those immense human hives
called London or Paris.

The situation of the Languedocian Sphex is just the reverse. Her
225 prey is a heavy Ephippiger, a single dish representing by itself the
sum total of provisions which the other freebooters amass on
numerous journeys, insect by insect. What the Cerceres and the other
plunderers strong on the wing accomplish by dividing the labor she
does in a single journey. The weight of the prey makes any distant
230 flight impossible; it has to be brought home slowly and laboriously,
for it is a troublesome business to cart things along the ground. This
alone makes the site of the burrow dependent on the accidents of the
chase: the prey comes first and the dwelling next. So there is no
assembling at a common meeting-place, no association of kindred
235 spirits, no tribes stimulating one another in their work by mutual
example, but isolation in the particular spot where the chances of the
day have taken the Sphex, solitary labor, carried on without
animation though with unfailing diligence. First of all, the prey is
sought for, attacked, reduced to helplessness. Not until after that
240 does the digger trouble about the burrow. A favorable place is chosen,
as near as possible to the spot where the victim lies, so as to cut short
the tedious work of transport; and the chamber of the future larva is
rapidly hollowed out and at once receives the egg and the victuals.
There you have an example of the inverted method of the
245 Languedocian Sphex, a method, as all my observations go to prove,
diametrically opposite to that of the other Hymenoptera. I will give
some of the more striking of these observations.

When caught digging, the Languedocian Sphex is always alone, sometimes at the bottom of a dusty recess left by a stone that has 250 dropped out of an old wall, sometimes ensconced in the shelter formed by a flat, projecting bit of sandstone, a shelter much sought after by the fierce Eyed Lizard to serve as an entrance-hall to his lair. The sun beats full upon it; it is an oven. The soil, consisting of old dust that has fallen little by little from the roof, is very easy to dig. The cell is 255 soon scooped out with the mandibles, those pincers which are also used for digging, and the tarsi, which serve as rubbish-rakes. Then the miner flies off, but with a slow flight and no sudden display of wing-power, a manifest sign that the insect is not contemplating a distant expedition. We can easily follow it with our eyes and perceive 260 the spot where it alights, usually ten or twelve yards away. At other times, it decides to walk. It goes off and makes hurriedly for a spot where we will have the indiscretion to follow it, for our presence does not trouble it at all. On reaching its destination, either on foot or on the wing, it looks round for some time, as we gather from its 265 undecided attitude and its journeys hither and thither. It looks round; at last it finds or rather retrieves something. The object recovered is an Ephippiger, half-paralyzed, but still moving her tarsi, antennae and ovipositor. She is a victim which the Sphex certainly stabbed not long ago with a few stings. After the operation, the Wasp 270 left her prey, an embarrassing burden amid the suspense of house-hunting; she abandoned it perhaps on the very spot where she captured it, contenting herself with making it more or less conspicuous by placing it on some grass-tuft, in order to find it more easily later; and, trusting to her good memory to return presently to 275 the spot where the booty lies, she set out to explore the neighborhood with the object of finding a suitable site and there digging a burrow. Once the home was ready, she came back to her prize, which she found again without much hesitation, and she now prepares to lug it home. She bestrides the victim, seizes one or both of the antenna and 280 off she goes, tugging and dragging with all the strength of her loins and jaws.

Sometimes, she has only to make one journey; at other times and more often, the carter suddenly plumps down her load and quickly runs home. Perhaps it occurs to her that the entrance-door is not 285 wide enough to admit so substantial a morsel; perhaps she

remembers some lack of finish that might hamper the storing. And, in point of fact, the worker does touch up her work: she enlarges the doorway, smooths the threshold, strengthens the ceiling. It is all done with a few strokes of the tarsi. Then she returns to the Ephippiger,
290 lying yonder, on her back, a few steps away. The hauling begins again. On the road, the Sphex seems struck with a new idea, which flashes through her quick brain. She has inspected the door, but has not looked inside. Who knows if all is well in there? She hastens to see, dropping the Ephippiger before she goes. The interior is
295 inspected; and apparently a few pats of the trowel are administered with the tarsi, giving a last polish to the walls. Without lingering too long over these delicate after touches, the Wasp goes back to her booty and harnesses herself to its antennae. Forward! Will the journey be completed this time? I would not answer for it. I have
300 known a Sphex, more suspicious than the others, perhaps, or more neglectful of the minor architectural details, to repair her omissions, to dispel her doubts, by abandoning her prize on the way five or six times running, in order to hurry to the burrow, which each time was touched up a little or merely inspected within. It is true that others
305 make straight for their destination, without even stopping to rest. I must also add that, when the Wasp goes home to improve the dwelling, she does not fail to give a glance from a distance every now and then at the Ephippiger over there, to make sure that nothing has happened to her. This solicitude recalls that of the Sacred Beetle
310 when he leaves the hall which he is excavating in order to come and feel his beloved pellet and bring it a little nearer to him.

The inference to be drawn from the details which I have related is manifest. The fact that every Languedocian Sphex surprised in her mining-operations, even though it be at the very beginning of the
315 digging, at the first stroke of the tarsus in the dust, afterwards, when the home is prepared, makes a short excursion, now on foot, anon flying, and invariably finds herself in possession of a victim already stabbed, already paralyzed, compels us to conclude, in all certainty, that this Wasp does her work as a huntress first and as a burrower
320 after, so that the place of the capture decides the place of the home.

This reversal of procedure, which causes the food to be prepared before the larder, whereas hitherto we have seen the larder come before the food, I attribute to the weight of the Sphex' prey, a prey

which it is not possible to carry far through the air. It is not that the
325 Languedocian Sphex is ill-built for flight: on the contrary, she can
soar magnificently; but the prey which she hunts would weigh her
down if she had no other support than her wings. She needs the
support of the ground for her hauling-work, in which she displays
wonderful strength. When laden with her prey, she always goes afoot,
330 or takes but very short flights, even under conditions when flight
would save her time and trouble. I will quote an instance taken from
my latest observations on this curious Wasp.

A Sphex appears unexpectedly, coming I know not whence. She is
on foot, dragging her Ephippiger, a capture which apparently she has
335 made that moment in the neighborhood. In the circumstances, it
behooves her to dig herself a burrow. The site is as bad as bad can be.
It is a well-beaten path, hard as stone. The Sphex, who has no time to
make laborious excavations, because the already captured prize must
be stored as quickly as possible, the Sphex wants soft ground,
340 wherein the larva's chamber can be contrived in one short spell of
work. I have described her favorite soil, namely, the dust of years
which has accumulated at the bottom of some hole in a wall or of
some little shelter under the rocks. Well, the Sphex whom I am now
observing stops at the foot of a house with a newly-whitewashed front
345 some twenty to twenty-five feet high. Her instinct tells her that up
there, under the red tiles of the roof, she will find nooks rich in old
dust. She leaves her prey at the foot of the house and flies up to the
roof. For some time, I see her looking here, there and everywhere.
After finding a proper site, she begins to work under the curve of a
350 pantile. In ten minutes or fifteen at most, the home is ready. The
insect now flies down again. The Ephippiger is promptly found. She
has to be taken up. Will this be done on the wing, as circumstances
seem to demand? Not at all. The Sphex adopts the toilsome method of
scaling a perpendicular wall, with a surface smoothed by the mason's
355 trowel and measuring twenty to twenty-five feet in height. Seeing her
take this road, dragging the game between her legs, I at first think
the feat impossible; but I am soon reassured as to the outcome of the
bold attempt. Getting a foothold on the little roughnesses in the
mortar, the plucky insect, despite the hindrance of her heavy load,
360 walks up this vertical plane with the same assured gait and the same
speed as on level ground. The top is reached without the least

accident; and the prey is laid temporarily on the edge of the roof, upon the rounded back of a tile. While the digger gives a finishing touch to the burrow, the badly-balanced prey slips and drops to the
365 foot of the wall. The thing must be done all over again and once more by laboriously climbing the height. The same mistake is repeated. Again the prey is incautiously left on the curved tile, again it slips and again it falls to the ground. With a composure which accidents such as these cannot disturb, the Sphex for the third time hoists up
370 the Ephippiger by scaling the wall and, better advised, drags her forthwith right into the home.

As even under these conditions no attempt has been made to carry the prey on the wing, it is clear that the Wasp is incapable of long flight with so heavy a load. To this incapacity we owe the few
375 characteristics that form the subject of this chapter. A quarry that is not too big to permit the effort of flying makes of the Yellow-winged Sphex a semi-social species, that is to say, one seeking the company of her fellows; a quarry too heavy to carry through the air makes of the Languedocian Sphex a species vowed to solitary labor, a sort of
380 savage disdainful of the pleasures that come from the proximity of one's kind. The lighter or heavier weight of the game selected here determines the fundamental character of the huntress.

Questions To Consider

1   What distinction does Fabre make between a study of anatomy and what he is doing in his study of insects? What does he hope to learn from his study?
2   Is Fabre concerned more with the question *whether* the Languedocian Sphex can (or does) transport its prey by flying or *why* it does so? Support your answer.
3   What reason does Fabre discover in answer to the above question? What evidence does he give to support it?

Chapter 9

The Wisdom of Instinct

To paralyze her prey, the Languedocian Sphex, I have no doubt,
pursues the method of the Cricket-huntress and drives her lancet
5   repeatedly into the Ephippiger's breast in order to strike the ganglia
of the thorax. The process of wounding the nerve centers must be
familiar to her; and I am convinced beforehand of her consummate
skill in that scientific operation. This is an art thoroughly known to
all the Hunting Wasps, who carry a poisoned dart that has not been
10 given them in vain. At the same time, I must confess that I have
never yet succeeded in witnessing the deadly performance. This
omission is due to the solitary life led by the Languedocian Sphex.
When a number of burrows are dug on a common site and then
provisioned, one has but to wait on the spot to see how one huntress
15 and now another arrive with the game which they have caught. It is
easy in these circumstances to try upon the new arrivals the
substitution of a live prey for the doomed victim and to repeat the
experiment as often as we wish. Besides, the certainty that we shall
not lack subjects of observation, as and when wanted, enables us to
20 arrange everything in advance. With the Languedocian Sphex, these
conditions of success do not exist. To set out expressly to look for her,
with one's material prepared, is almost useless, as the solitary insect
is scattered one by one over vast expanses of ground. Moreover, if you
do come upon her, it will most often be in an idle hour and you will
25 get nothing out of her. As I said before, it is nearly always
unexpectedly, when your thoughts are elsewhere engaged, that the
Sphex appears, dragging her Ephippiger after her.
This is the moment, the only propitious moment to attempt a
substitution of prey and invite the huntress to let you witness her
30 lancet-thrusts. Quick, let us procure an alternative morsel, a live
Ephippiger! Hurry, time presses: in a few minutes, the burrow will
have received the victuals and the glorious occasion will be lost! Must
I speak of my mortification at these moments of good fortune, the
mocking bait held out by chance?
35 Here, before my eyes, is matter for interesting observations; and I
cannot profit by it! I cannot surprise the Sphex' secret for the lack of
something to offer her in the place of her prize! Try it for yourself, try

setting out in quest of an alternative piece with only a few minutes at
your disposal, when it took me three days of wild running about
40 before I found Weevils for my Cerceres! And yet I made the desperate
experiment twice over. Ah, if the keeper had caught me this time,
tearing like mad through the vineyards, what a good opportunity it
would have been for crediting me with robbery and having me up
before the magistrate! Vine-branches and clusters of grapes: not a
45 thing did I respect in my mad rush, hampered by the trailing shoots. I
must have an Ephippiger at all costs, I must have him that moment.
And once I did get my Ephippiger during one of these frenzied
expeditions. I was radiant with joy, never suspecting the bitter
disappointment in store for me.

50   If only I arrive in time, if only the Sphex be still engaged in
transport work! Thank heaven, everything is in my favor! The Wasp
is still some distance away from her burrow and still dragging her
prize along. With my forceps I pull gently at it from behind. The
huntress resists, stubbornly clutches the antenna! of her victim and
55 refuses to let go. I pull harder, even drawing the carter back as well;
it makes no difference: the Sphex does not loose her hold. I have with
me a pair of sharp scissors, belonging to my little entomological case.
I use them and promptly cut the harness-ropes, the Ephippiger's long
antennae. The Sphex continues to move ahead, but soon stops,
60 astonished at the sudden decrease in the weight of the burden which
she is trailing, for this burden is now reduced merely to the two
antennae, snipped off by my mischievous wiles. The real load, the
heavy, pot-bellied insect, remains behind and is instantly replaced by
my live specimen. The Wasp turns round, lets go the ropes that now
65 draw nothing after them and retraces her steps. She come face to face
with the prey substituted for her own. She examines it, walks round
it gingerly, then stops, moistens her foot with saliva and begins to
wash her eyes. In this attitude of meditation, can some such thought
as the following pass through her mind:
70   "Come now I Am I awake or am I asleep ? Do I know what I am
about or do I not? That thing's not mine. Who or what is trying to
humbug me?"

    At any rate, the Sphex shows no great hurry to attack my prey
with her mandibles. She keeps away from it and shows not the
75 smallest wish to seize it. To excite her, I offer the insect to her in my

fingers, I almost thrust the antennae under her teeth. I know that
she does not suffer from shyness; I know that she will come and take
from your fingers, without hesitation, the prey which you have
snatched from her and afterwards present to her. But what is this?
80 Scorning my offers, the Sphex retreats instead of snapping up what I
place within her reach. I put down the Ephippiger, who, obeying a
thoughtless impulse, unconscious of danger, goes straight to his
assassin. Now we shall see! Alas, no: the Sphex continues to recoil,
like a regular coward, and ends by flying away. I never saw her
85 again. Thus ended, to my confusion, an experiment that had filled me
with such enthusiasm.

Later and by degrees, as I inspected an increasing number of
burrows, I came to understand my failure and the obstinate refusal of
the Sphex. I always found the provisions to consist, without a single
90 exception, of a female Ephippiger, harboring in her belly a copious
and succulent cluster of eggs. This appears to be the favorite food of
the grubs. Well, in my hurried rush through the vines, I had laid my
hands on an Ephippiger of the other sex. I was offering the Sphex a
male. More far-seeing than I in this important question of provender,
95 the Wasp would have nothing to say to my game:

"A male, indeed! Is that a dinner for my larvae? What do you take
them for?"

What nice discrimination they have, these dainty epicures, who
are able to differentiate between the tender flesh of the female and
100 the comparatively dry flesh of the males! What an unerring glance,
which can distinguish at once between the two sexes, so much alike in
shape and color! The female carries a sword at the tip of her
abdomen, the ovipositor wherewith the eggs are buried in the ground;
and that is about the only external difference between her and the
105 male. This distinguishing feature never escapes the perspicacious
Sphex; and that is why, in my experiment, the Wasp rubbed her eyes,
hugely puzzled at beholding swordless a prey which she well knew
carried a sword when she caught it. What must not have passed
through her little Sphex brain at the sight of this transformation?

110 Let us now watch the Wasp when, having prepared the burrow,
she goes back for her victim, which, after its capture and the
operation that paralyzed it, she has left at no great distance. The
Ephippiger is in a condition similar to that of the Cricket sacrificed by

the Yellow-winged Sphex, a condition proving for certain that stings
115 have been driven into her thoracic ganglia. Nevertheless, a good
many movements still continue; but they are disconnected, though
endowed with a certain vigor. Incapable of standing on its legs, the
insect lies on its side or on its back. It flutters its long antenna and
also its palpi; it opens and closes its mandibles and bites as hard as in
120 the normal state. The abdomen heaves rapidly and deeply. The
ovipositor is brought back sharply under the belly, against which it
almost lies flat. The legs stir, but languidly and irregularly; the
middle legs seem more torpid than the others. If pricked with a
needle, the whole body shudders convulsively; efforts are made to get
125 up and walk, but without success. In short, the insect would be full of
life, but for its inability to move about or even to stand upon its legs.

We have here therefore a wholly local paralysis, a paralysis of the
legs, or rather a partial abolition and ataxy of their movements. Can
this very incomplete inertia be caused by some special arrangement
130 of the victim's nervous system, or does it come from this, that the
Wasp perhaps administers only a single prick, instead of stinging
each ganglion of the thorax, as the Cricket-huntress does? I cannot
tell.

Still, for all its shivering, its convulsions, its disconnected
135 movements, the victim is none the less incapable of hurting the larva
that is meant to devour it. I have taken from the burrow of the Sphex
Ephippigers struggling just as lustily as when they were first half-
paralyzed; and nevertheless the feeble grub, hatched but a few hours
since, was digging its teeth into the gigantic victim in all security; the
140 dwarf was biting into the colossus without danger to itself. This
striking result is due to the spot selected by the mother for laying her
egg. I have already said how the Yellow-winged Sphex glues her egg
to the Cricket's breast, a little to one side, between the first and
second pair of legs. Exactly the same place is chosen by the White-
145 edged Sphex; and a similar place, a little farther back, towards the
root of one of the large hind-thighs, is adopted by the Languedocian
Sphex, all three thus giving proof, by this uniformity, of wonderful
discernment in picking out the spot where the egg is bound to be safe.

Consider the Ephippiger pent in the burrow. She lies stretched
150 upon her back, absolutely incapable of turning. In vain, she struggles,
in vain she writhes: the disordered movements of her legs are lost in

space, the room being too wide to afford them the support of its walls. The grub cares nothing for the victim's convulsions: it is at a spot where naught can reach it, not tarsi, nor mandibles, nor ovipositor,
155   nor antennae; a spot absolutely stationary, devoid of so much as a surface tremor. It is in perfect safety, on the sole condition that the Ephippiger cannot shift her position, turn over, get upon her feet; and this one condition is admirably fulfilled.

But, with several heads of game, all in the same stage of
160   paralysis, the larva's danger would be great. Though it would have nothing to fear from the insect first attacked, because of its position out of the reach of its victim, it would have every occasion to dread the proximity of the others, which, stretching their legs at random, might strike it and rip it open with their spurs. This is perhaps the
165   reason why the Yellow-winged Sphex, who heaps up three or four Crickets in the same cell, practically annihilates all movement in its victims, whereas the Languedocian Sphex, victualling each burrow with a single piece of game, leaves her Ephippigers the best part of their power of motion and contents herself with making it impossible
170   for them to change their position or stand upon their legs. She may thus, though I cannot say so positively, economize her dagger-thrusts.

While the only half-paralyzed Ephippiger cannot imperil the larva, fixed on a part of the body where resistance is impossible, the case is different with the Sphex, who has to cart her prize home.
175   First, having still, to a great extent, preserved the use of its tarsi, the victim clutches with these at any blade of grass encountered on the road along which it is being dragged; and this produces an obstacle to the hauling-process which is difficult to overcome. The Sphex, already heavily burdened by the weight of her load, is liable to exhaust
180   herself with her efforts to make the other insect relax its desperate grip in grassy places. But this is the least serious drawback. The Ephippiger preserves the complete use of her mandibles, which snap and bite with their customary vigor. Now what these terrible nippers have in front of them is just the slender body of the enemy, at a time
185   when she is in her hauling-attitude. The antennae, in fact, are grasped not far from their roots, so that the mouth of the victim dragged along on its back faces either the thorax or the abdomen of the Sphex, who, standing high on her long legs, takes good care, I am convinced, not to be caught in the mandibles yawning underneath

190 her. At all events, a moment of forgetfulness, a slip, the merest trifle
can bring her within the reach of two powerful nippers, which would
not neglect the opportunity of taking a pitiless vengeance. In the
more difficult cases at any rate, if not always, the action of those
formidable pincers must be done away with; and the fish-hooks of the
195 legs must be rendered incapable of increasing their resistance to the
process of transport.

How will the Sphex go to work to obtain this result? Here man,
even the man of science, would hesitate, would waste his time in
barren efforts and would perhaps abandon all hope of success. He can
200 come and take one lesson from the Sphex. She, without ever being
taught it, without ever seeing it practiced by others, understands her
surgery through and through. She knows the most delicate mysteries
of the physiology of the nerves, or rather she behaves as if she did.
She knows that under her victim's skull there is a circlet of nervous
205 nuclei, something similar to the brain of the higher animals. She
knows that this main center of innervation controls the action of the
mouth-parts and moreover is the seat of the will, without whose
orders not a single muscle acts; lastly, she knows that, by injuring
this sort of brain, she will cause all resistance to cease, the insect no
210 longer possessing any will to resist. As for the mode of operating, this
is the easiest matter in the world to her; and, when we have been
taught in her school, we are free to try her process in our turn. The
instrument employed is no longer the sting: the insect, in its wisdom,
has deemed compression preferable to a poisoned thrust. Let us
215 accept its decision, for we shall see presently how prudent it is to be
convinced of our own ignorance in the presence of the animal's
knowledge. Lest by editing my account I should fail to give a true
impression of the sublime talent of this masterly operator, I here copy
out my note as I penciled it on the spot, immediately after the stirring
220 spectacle.

The Sphex finds that her victim is offering too much resistance,
hooking itself here and there to blades of grass. She then stops to
perform upon it the following curious operation, a sort of *coup de
grâce*. The Wasp, still astride her prey, forces open the articulation of
225 the neck, high up, at the nape. Then she seizes the neck with her
mandibles and, without making any external wound, probes as far
forward as possible under the skull, so as to seize and chew up the

ganglia of the head. When this operation is done, the victim is utterly
motionless, incapable of the least resistance, whereas previously the
230   legs, though deprived of the power of connected movement needed for
walking, vigorously opposed the process of traction.

There is the fact in all its eloquence. With the points of its
mandibles, the insect, while leaving uninjured the thin and supple
membrane of the neck, goes rummaging into the skull and munching
235   the brain. There is no effusion of blood, no wound but simply an
external pressure. Of course, I kept for my own purposes the
Ephippiger paralyzed before my eyes, in order to ascertain the effects
of the operation at my leisure; also of course, I hastened to repeat in
my turn, upon live Ephippigers, what the Sphex had just taught me. I
240   will here compare my results with the Wasp's.

Two Ephippigers whose cervical ganglia I squeeze and compress
with a forceps fall rapidly into a state resembling that of the victims
of the Sphex. Only, they grate their cymbals if I tease them with a
needle; and the legs still retain a few disordered and languid
245   movements. The difference no doubt is due to the fact that my
patients were not previously injured in their thoracic ganglia, as were
those of the Sphex, who were first stung on the breast. Allowing for
this important condition, we see that I was none too bad a pupil and
that I imitated pretty closely my teacher of physiology, the Sphex. I
250   confess, it was not without a certain satisfaction that I succeeded in
doing almost as well as the insect.

As well? What am I talking about? Wait a bit and you shall see
that I still have much to learn from the Sphex. For what happens is
that my two patients very soon die: I mean, they really die; and, in
255   four or five days, I have nothing but putrid corpses before my eyes.
And the Wasp's Ephippiger? I need hardly say that the Wasp's
Ephippiger, even ten days after the operation, is perfectly fresh, just
as she will be required by the larva for which she has been destined.
Nay, more: only a few hours after the operation under the skull, there
260   reappeared, as though nothing had occurred, the disorderly
movements of the legs, antennae, palpi, ovipositor and mandibles; in
a word, the insect returned to the condition wherein it was before the
Sphex bit its brain. And these movements were kept up after, though
they became feebler every day. The Sphex had merely reduced her
265   victim to a passing state of torpor, lasting amply long enough to

enable her to bring it home without resistance; and I, who thought myself her rival, was but a clumsy and barbarous butcher: I killed my prize. She, with her inimitable dexterity, shrewdly compressed the brain to produce a lethargy of a few hours; I, brutal through 270 ignorance, perhaps crushed under my forceps that delicate organ, the main seat of life. If anything could prevent me from blushing at my defeat, it would be the conviction that very few, if any, could vie with these clever ones in cleverness.

Ah, I now understand why the Sphex does not use her sting to 275 injure the cervical ganglia! A drop of poison injected here, at the center of vital force, would destroy the whole nervous system; and death would follow soon after. But it is not death that the huntress wishes to obtain; the larva have not the least use for dead game, for a corpse, in short, smelling of corruption; and all that she wants to 280 bring about is a lethargy, a passing torpor, which will put a stop to the victim's resistance during the carting process, this resistance being difficult to overcome and moreover dangerous for the Sphex. The torpor is obtained by a method known in laboratories of experimental physiology: compression of the brain. The Sphex acts 285 like a Flourens, who, laying bare an animal's brain and bearing upon the cerebral mass, forthwith suppresses intelligence, will, sensibility and movement. The pressure is removed; and everything reappears. Even so do the remains of the Ephippiger's life reappear, as the lethargic effects of a skillfully-directed pressure pass off. The ganglia 290 of the skull, squeezed between the mandibles but without fatal contusions, gradually recover their activity and put an end to the general torpor. Admit that it is all alarmingly scientific.

Fortune has her entomological whims: you run after her and catch no glimpse of her; you forget about her and behold, she comes 295 tapping at your door! How vainly I watched and waited, how many useless journeys I made to see the Languedocian Sphex sacrifice her Ephipiggers! Twenty years pass; these pages are in the printer's hands; and, one day early this month, on the 8th of August 1878, my son Émile comes rushing into my study:

300 "Quick!" he shouts. "Come quick: there's a Sphex dragging her prey under the plane-trees, outside the door of the yard!"

Émile knew all about the business, from what I had told him, to amuse him when we used to sit up late, and better still from similar

incidents which he had witnessed in our life out of doors. He is right.
305 I run out and see a magnificent Languedocian Sphex dragging a
paralyzed Ephippiger by the antennae. She is making for the hen-
house close by and seems anxious to scale the wall, with the object of
fixing her burrow under some tile on the roof; for, a few years ago, in
the same place, I saw a Sphex of the same species accomplish the
310 ascent with her game and make her home under the arch of a badly-
joined tile. Perhaps the present Wasp is descended from the one who
performed that arduous climb.

A like feat seems about to be repeated; and this time before
numerous witnesses, for all the family, working under the shade of
315 the plane-trees, come and form a circle around the Sphex. They
wonder at the unceremonious boldness of the insect, which is not
diverted from its work by a gallery of onlookers; all are struck by its
proud and lusty bearing, as, with raised head and the victim's
antennae firmly gripped in its mandibles, it drags the enormous
320 burden after it. I, alone among the spectators, feel a twinge of regret
at the sight:

"Ah, if only I had some live Ephippigers!" I cannot help saying,
with not the least hope of seeing my wish realized,

"Live Ephippigers?" replies Émile. "Why, I have some perfectly
325 fresh ones, caught this morning!"

He dashes upstairs, four steps at a time, and runs to his little
den, where a fence of dictionaries encloses a park for the rearing of
some fine caterpillars of the Spurge Hawkmoth. He brings me three
Ephippigers, the best that I could wish for, two females and a male.

330 How did these insects come to be at hand, at the moment when
they were wanted, for an experiment tried in vain twenty years ago?
That is another story. A Lesser Gray Shrike had nested in one of the
tall plane-trees of the avenue. Now a few days earlier, the mistral,
the brutal north-west wind of our parts, blew with such violence as to
335 bend the branches as well as the reeds; and the nest, turned upside
down by the swaying of its support, had dropped its contents, four
small birds. Next morning, I found the brood upon the ground; three
were killed by the fall, the fourth was still alive. The survivor was
entrusted to the cares of Émile, who went Cricket-hunting twice a
340 day on the neighboring grass-plots for the benefit of his young charge.
But Crickets are small and the nursling's appetite called for many of

them. Another dish was preferred, the Ephippiger, of whom a stock
was collected from time to time among the stalks and prickly leaves of
the eryngo. The three insects which Émile brought me came from the
Shrike's larder. My pity for the fallen nestling had procured me this
unhoped-for success.

After making the circle of spectators stand back so as to leave the
field clear for the Sphex, I take away her prey with a pair of pincers
and at once give her in exchange one of my Ephippigers, carrying a
sword at the end of her belly, like the game which I have abstracted.
The dispossessed Wasp stamps her feet two or three times; and that
is the only sign of impatience which she gives. She goes for her new
prey, which is too stout, too obese even to try to avoid pursuit, grips it
with her mandibles by the saddle-shaped corselet, gets astride and,
curving her abdomen, slips the end of it under the Ephippiger's
thorax. Here, no doubt, some stings are administered, though I am
unable to state the number exactly, because of the difficulty of
observation. The Ephippiger, a peaceable victim, suffers herself to be
operated on without resistance; she is like the silly Sheep of our
slaughter-houses. The Sphex takes her time and wields her lancet
with a deliberation which favors accuracy of aim. So far, the observer
has nothing to complain of; but the prey touches the ground with its
breast and belly and exactly what happens underneath escapes his
eye. As for interfering and lifting the Ephippiger a little, so as to see
better, that must not be thought of: the murderess would resheath
her weapon and retire. The act that follows is easy to observe. After
stabbing the thorax, the tip of the abdomen appears under the
victim's neck, which the operator forces open by pressing the nape. At
this point, the sting probes with marked persistency, as if the prick
administered here were more effective than elsewhere. One would be
inclined to think that the nerve center attacked is the lower part of
the esophageal chain; but the continuance of movement in the mouth-
parts—the mandibles, jaws and palpi—controlled by this seat of
innervation shows that such is not the case. Through the neck, the
Sphex reaches simply the ganglia of the thorax, or at any rate the
first of them, which is more easily accessible through the thin skin of
the neck than through the integuments of the chest.

And in a moment it is all over. Without the least shiver denoting
pain, the Ephippiger becomes henceforth an inert mass. I remove the

380 Sphex' patient for the second time and replace it by the other female
at my disposal. The same proceedings are repeated, followed by the
same result. The Sphex has performed her skillful surgery thrice
over, almost in immediate succession, first with her own prey and
then with my substitutes. Will she do so a fourth time with the male
385 Ephippiger whom I still have left? I have my doubts, not because the
Wasp is tired, but because the game does not suit her. I have never
seen her with any prey but females, who, crammed with eggs, are the
food which the larvae appreciate above all others. My suspicion is
well-founded; deprived of her capture, the Sphex stubbornly refuses
390 the male whom I offer to her. She runs hither and thither, with
hurried steps, in search of the vanished game; three or four times, she
goes up to the Ephippiger, walks round him, casts a scornful glance at
him; and at last she flies away. He is not what her larvae want;
experiment demonstrates this once again after an interval of twenty
395 years.

The three females stabbed, two of them before my eyes, remain in
my possession. In each case, all the legs are completely paralyzed.
Whether lying naturally, on its belly or on its back or side, the insect
retains indefinitely whatever position we give it. A continued
400 fluttering of the antennae, a few intermittent pulsations of the belly
and the play of the mouth-parts are the only signs of life. Movement
is destroyed but not susceptibility; for, at the least prick administered
to a thin-skinned spot, the whole body gives a slight shudder.
Perhaps, some day, physiology will find in such victims the material
405 for valuable work on the functions of the nervous system. The Wasp's
sting, so incomparably skillful at striking a particular point and
administering a wound which affects that point alone, will
supplement, with immense advantage, the experimenter's brutal
scalpel, which rips open where it ought to give merely a light touch.
410 Meanwhile, here are the results which I have obtained from the three
victims, but in another direction.

As only the movement of the legs has been destroyed, without any
wound save that of the nerve centers, which are the seat of that
movement, the insect must die of inanition and not of its injuries. The
415 experiment was conducted as follows: two sound and healthy
Ephipiggers, just as I picked them up in the fields, were imprisoned
without food, one in the dark, the other in the light. The second died

in four days, the first in five. This difference of a day is easily
explained. In the light, the insect made greater exertions to recover
420 its liberty; and, as every movement of the animal machine is
accompanied by a corresponding expenditure of energy, a greater sum
total of activity has involved a more rapid consumption of the reserve
force of the organism. In the light, there is more restlessness and a
shorter life; in the dark, less restlessness and a longer life, while no
425 food at all was taken in either case.

One of my three stabbed Ephipiggers was kept in the dark,
fasting. In her case, there were not only the conditions of complete
abstinence and darkness, but also the serious wounds inflicted by the
Sphex; and nevertheless for seventeen days I saw her continually
430 waving her antennae. As long as this sort of pendulum keeps on
swinging, the clock of life does not stop. On the eighteenth day, the
creature ceased its antennary movements and died. The badly-
wounded insect therefore lived, under the same conditions, four times
as long as the insect that was untouched. What seemed as though it
435 should be a cause of death was really a cause of life.

However paradoxical it may seem at first sight, this result is
exceedingly simple. When untouched, the insect exerts itself and
consequently uses up its reserves. When paralyzed, it has merely the
feeble, internal movements which are inseparable from any organism;
440 and its substance is economized in proportion to the weakness of the
action displayed. In the first case, the animal machine is at work and
wears itself out; in the second, it is at rest and saves itself. There
being no nourishment now to repair the waste, the moving insect
spends its nutritive reserves in four days and dies; the motionless
445 insect does not spend them and lives for eighteen days. Life is a
continual dissolution, the physiologists tell us; and the Sphex' victims
give us the neatest possible demonstration of the fact.

One remark more. Fresh food is absolutely necessary for the
Wasp's larvae. If the prey were warehoused in the burrow intact, in
450 four or five days it would be a corpse abandoned to corruption; and
the scarce-hatched grub would find nothing to live upon but a putrid
mass. Pricked with the sting, however, it can keep alive for two or
three weeks, a period more than long enough to allow the egg to hatch
and the larva to grow. The paralyzing of the victim therefore has a
455 twofold result: first, the living dish remains motionless and the safety

of the delicate grub is not endangered; secondly, the meat keeps good a long time and thus ensures wholesome food for the larva. Man's logic, enlightened by science, could discover nothing better.

My two other Ephippigers stung by the Sphex were kept in the
460 dark with food. To feed inert insects, hardly differing from corpses except by the perpetual waving of their long antenna, seems at first an impossibility; still, the play of the mouth-parts gave me some hope and I tried. My success exceeded my anticipations. There was no question here, of course, of giving them a lettuce-leaf or any other
465 piece of green stuff on which they might have browsed in their normal state; they were feeble valetudinarians, who needed spoon-feeding, so to speak, and supporting with liquid nourishment. I used sugar-and-water.

Laying the insect on its back, I place a drop of the sugary fluid on
470 its mouth with a straw. The palpi at once begin to stir; the mandibles and jaws move. The drop is swallowed with evident satisfaction, especially after a somewhat prolonged fast. I repeat the dose until it is refused. The meal takes place once a day, sometimes twice, at irregular intervals, lest I should become too much of a slave to my
475 patients. Well, one of the Ephippigers lived for twenty-one days on this meager fare. It was not much, compared with the eighteen days of the one whom I had left to die of starvation. True, the insect had twice had a bad fall, having dropped from the experimenting-table to the floor owing to some piece of awkwardness on my part. The bruises
480 which it received must have hastened its end. The other, which suffered no accidents, lived for forty days. As the nourishment employed, sugar-and-water, could not indefinitely take the place of the natural green food, it is very likely that the insect would have lived longer still if the usual diet had been possible. And so the point
485 which I had in view is proved: the victims stung by the Digger-wasps die of starvation and not of their wounds.

Questions To Consider

1   The title of the chapter is *The Wisdom of Instinct*. What evidence
    does Fabre give that instinct is intelligent in what it does:
    remarkably so, in fact?
2   What significance do Fabre's own attempts at reduplicating the
    Sphex's activities have for his overall study?

Chapter 10

The Ignorance of Instinct

        The Sphex has shown us how infallibly and with what
   transcendental art she acts when guided by the unconscious
 5 inspiration of her instinct; she is now going to show us how poor she
   is in resource, how limited in intelligence, how illogical even, in
   circumstances outside of her regular routine. By a strange
   inconsistency, characteristic of the instinctive faculties, profound
   wisdom is accompanied by an ignorance no less profound. To instinct
10 nothing is impossible, however great the difficulty may be. In
   building her hexagonal cells, with their floors consisting of three
   lozenges, the Bee solves with absolute precision the arduous problem
   of how to achieve the maximum result at a minimum cost, a problem
   whose solution by man would demand a powerful mathematical mind.
15 The Wasps whose larvae live on prey display in their murderous art
   methods hardly rivaled by those of a man versed in the intricacies of
   anatomy and physiology. Nothing is difficult to instinct, so long as the
   act is not outside the unvarying cycle of animal existence; on the
   other hand, nothing is easy to instinct, if the act is at all removed
20 from the course usually pursued. The insect which astounds us,
   which terrifies us with its extraordinary intelligence surprises us, the
   next moment, with its stupidity, when confronted with some simple
   fact that happens to lie outside its ordinary practice. The Sphex will
   supply us with a few instances.
25   Let us follow her dragging her Ephippiger home. If fortune smile
   upon us, we may witness some such little scene as that which I will
   now describe. When entering her shelter under the rock, where she
   has made her burrow, the Sphex finds, perched on a blade of grass, a
   Praying Mantis, a carnivorous insect which hides cannibal habits

30 under a pious appearance. The danger threatened by this robber
    ambushed on her path must be known to the Sphex, for she lets go
    her game and pluckily rushes upon the Mantis, to inflict some heavy
    blows and dislodge her, or at all events to frighten her and inspire her
    with respect. The robber does not move, but closes her lethal
35 machinery, the two terrible saws of the arm and fore-arm. The Sphex
    goes back to her capture, harnesses herself to the antennae and
    boldly passes under the blade of grass whereon the other sits perched.
    By the direction of her head we can see that she is on her guard and
    that she holds the enemy rooted, motionless, under the menace of her
40 eyes. Her courage meets with the reward which it deserves: the prey
    is stored away without further mishap.

    A word more on the Praying Mantis, or, as they say in Provence,
    lou Prégo Diéou, the Pray-to-God. Her long, pale-green wings, like
    spreading veils, her head raised heavenwards, her folded arms,
45 crossed upon her breast, are in fact a sort of travesty of a nun in
    ecstasy. And yet she is a ferocious creature, loving carnage. Though
    not her favorite spots, the work-yards of the various Digger-wasps
    receive her visits pretty frequently. Posted near the burrows, on some
    bramble or other, she waits for chance to bring within her reach some
50 of the arrivals, forming a double capture for her, as she seizes both
    the huntress and her prey. Her patience is long put to the test: the
    Wasp suspects something and is on her guard; still, from time to
    time, a rash one gets caught. With a sudden rustle of wings half-
    unfurled as by the violent release of a clutch, the Mantis terrifies the
55 newcomer, who hesitates for a moment, in her fright. Then, with the
    sharpness of a spring, the toothed fore-arm folds back on the toothed
    upper arm; and the insect is caught between the blades of the double
    saw. It is as though the jaws of a Wolf-trap were closing on the
    animal that had nibbled at its bait. Thereupon, without unloosing the
60 cruel machine, the Mantis gnaws her victim by small mouthfuls. Such
    are the ecstasies, the prayers, the mystic meditations of the *Prégo
    Diéou.*

    Of the scenes of carnage which the Praying Mantis has left in my
    memory, let me relate one. The thing happens in front of a-work-yard
65 of Bee-eating Philanthi. These diggers feed their larvae on Hive-bees,
    whom they catch on the flowers while gathering pollen and honey. If
    the Philanthus who has made a capture feels that her Bee is swollen

with honey, she never fails, before storing her, to squeeze her crop, either on the way or at the entrance of the dwelling, so as to make her
70 disgorge the delicious syrup, which she drinks by licking the tongue which her unfortunate victim, in her death-agony, sticks out of her mouth at full length. This profanation of a dying creature, whose enemy squeezes its belly to empty it and feast on the contents, has something so hideous about it that I should denounce the Philanthus
75 as a brutal murderess, if animals were capable of wrongdoing. At the moment of some such horrible banquet, I have seen the Wasp, with her prey, seized by the Mantis: the bandit was rifled by another bandit. And here is an awful detail: while the Mantis held her transfixed under the points of the double saw and was already
80 munching her belly, the Wasp continued to lick the honey of her Bee, unable to relinquish the delicious food even amid the terrors of death. Let us hasten to cast a veil over these horrors.

We will return to the Sphex, with whose burrow we must make ourselves acquainted before we go further. This burrow is a hole
85 made in fine sand, or rather in a sort of dust at the bottom of a natural shelter. Its entrance-passage is very short, merely an inch or two, without a bend, and leads to a single, roomy, oval chamber. The whole thing is a rough den, hastily dug out, rather than a leisurely and artistically excavated dwelling. I have explained that the reason
90 for this simplicity is that the game is captured first and set down for a moment on the hunting-field while the Wasp hurriedly makes a burrow in the vicinity, a method of procedure which allows of but one chamber or cell to each retreat. For who can tell whither the chances of the day will lead the huntress for her second capture? The prisoner
95 is heavy and the burrow must therefore be near; so today's home, which is too far away for the next Ephippiger to be conveyed to it, cannot be utilized tomorrow. Thus, as each prey is caught, there is a fresh excavation, a fresh burrow, with its single chamber, now here, now there. Having said this, we will try a few experiments to see how
100 the insect behaves when we create circumstances new to it.

Experiment I

A Sphex, dragging her prey along, is a few inches from the burrow. Without disturbing her, I cut with a pair of scissors the Ephippiger's antenna, which the Wasp, as we know, uses for harness-

105 ropes. On recovering from the surprise caused by the sudden
lightening of her load, the Sphex goes back to her victim and, without
hesitation, now seizes the root of the antenna, the short stump left by
the scissors. It is very short indeed, hardly a millimeter; no matter: it
is enough for the Sphex, who grips this fag-end of a rope and resumes
110 her hauling. With the greatest precaution, so as not to injure the
Wasp, I now cut the two antennary stumps level with the skull.
Finding nothing left to catch hold of at the familiar points, the insect
seizes, close by, one of the victim's long palpi and continues its
hauling-work, without appearing at all perturbed by this change in
115 the harness. I leave it alone. The prey is brought home and placed so
that its head faces the entrance to the burrow; and the Wasp goes in
by herself, to make a brief inspection of the inside of the cell before
proceeding to warehouse the provisions. Her behavior reminds us of
that of the Yellow-winged Sphex in similar circumstances. I take
120 advantage of this short moment to seize the abandoned prey, remove
all its palpi and place it a little farther off, about half a yard from the
burrow. The Sphex reappears and goes straight to her captive, whom
she has seen from her threshold. She looks at the top of the head, she
looks underneath, on either side and finds nothing to take hold of. A
125 desperate attempt is made: the Wasp, opening wide her mandibles,
tries to grab the Ephippiger by the head; but the pincers have not a
sufficient compass to take in so large a bulk and they slip off the
round, polished skull. She makes several fresh endeavors, each time
without result. She is at length convinced of the uselessness of her
130 efforts. She draws back a little to one side and appears to be
renouncing further attempts. One would say that she was
discouraged; at least, she smooths her wings with her hind legs, while
with her front tarsi, which she first puts into her mouth, she washes
her eyes. This, so it has always seemed to me, is a sign in
135 Hymenoptera of giving up a job.

Nevertheless there is no lack of parts by which the Ephippiger
might be seized and dragged along as easily as by the antennae and
the palpi. There are the six legs, there is the ovipositor: all organs
slender enough to be gripped boldly and to serve as hauling ropes. I
140 agree that the easiest way to effect the storing is to introduce the
prey head first, drawn down by the antennae; but it would enter
almost as readily if drawn by a leg, especially one of the front legs, for

the orifice is wide and the passage short or sometimes even non-existent. Then how is it that the Sphex did not once try to seize one of
145 the six tarsi or the tip of the ovipositor, whereas she attempted the impossible, the absurd, in striving to grip, with her much too short mandibles, the huge skull of her prey? Can it be that the idea did not occur to her? Then we will try to suggest it.

I offer her, right under her mandibles, first a leg, next the end of
150 the abdominal rapier. The insect obstinately refuses to bite; my repeated blandishments lead to nothing. A singular huntress, to be embarrassed by her game, not knowing how to seize it by a leg when she is not able to take it by the horns! Perhaps my prolonged presence and the unusual events that have just occurred have disturbed her
155 faculties. Then let us leave the Sphex to herself, between her Ephippiger and her burrow; let us give her time to collect herself and, in the calm of solitude, to think out some way of managing her business. I leave her therefore and continue my walk; and, two hours later, I return to the same place. The Sphex is gone, the burrow is
160 still open and the Ephippiger is lying just where I placed her. Conclusion: the Wasp has tried nothing; she went away, abandoning everything, her home and her game, when, to utilize them both, all that she had to do was to take her prey by one leg. And so this rival of Flourens, who but now was startling us with her cleverness as she
165 dexterously squeezed her victim's brain to produce lethargy, becomes incredibly helpless in the simplest case outside her usual habits. She, who so well knows how to attack a victim's thoracic ganglia with her sting and its cervical ganglia with her mandibles; she, who makes such a judicious difference between a poisoned prick annihilating the
170 vital influence of the nerves for ever and a pressure causing only momentary torpor, cannot grip her prey by this part when it is made impossible for her to grip it by any other. To understand that she can take a leg instead of an antenna is utterly beyond her powers. She must have the antenna, or some other string attached to the head,
175 such as one of the palpi. If these cords did not exist her race would perish, for lack of the capacity to solve this trivial problem.

Experiment II

The Wasp is engaged in closing her burrow where the prey has been stored and the egg laid upon it. With her front tarsi, she brushes

180 her doorstep, working backwards and sweeping into the entrance a
stream of dust which passes under her belly and spurts behind in a
parabolic spray as continuous as a liquid spray, so nimble is the
sweeper in her actions. From time to time, the Sphex picks out with
her mandibles a few grains of sand, so many solid blocks which she
185 inserts one by one into the mass of dust, causing it all to cake
together by beating and compressing it with her forehead and
mandibles. Walled up by this masonry, the entrance-door soon
disappears from sight.

I intervene in the middle of the work. Pushing the Sphex aside, I
190 carefully clear the short gallery with the blade of a knife, take away
the materials that close it and restore full communication between
the cell and the outside. Then, with my forceps, without damaging the
edifice, I take the Ephippiger from the cell, where she lies with her
head at the back and her ovipositor towards the entrance. The Wasp's
195 egg is on the victim's breast, at the usual place, the root of one of the
hinder thighs: a proof that the Sphex was giving the finishing touch
to the burrow, with the intention of never returning.

Having done this and put the stolen prey safely away in a box, I
yield my place to the Sphex, who has been on the watch beside me
200 while I was rifling her home. Finding the door open, she goes in and
stays for a few moments. Then she comes out and resumes her work
where I interrupted it, that is to say, she starts conscientiously
stopping the entrance to the cell by sweeping dust backwards and
carrying grains of sand, which she continues to heap up with
205 scrupulous care, as though she were doing useful work. When the
door is once again thoroughly walled up, the insect brushes itself,
seems to give a glance of satisfaction at the task accomplished and
finally flies away.

The Sphex must have known that the burrow contained nothing,
210 because she went inside and even stayed there for some time; and yet,
after this inspection of the pillaged abode, she once more proceeds to
close up the cell with the same care as though nothing out of the way
had happened. Can she be proposing to use this burrow later, to
return to it with a fresh victim and lay a new egg there? If so, her
215 work of closing would be intended to prevent the access of intruders
to the dwelling during her absence; it would be a measure of prudence
against the attempts of other diggers who might covet the ready-

made chamber; it might also be a wise precaution against internal dilapidations. And, as a matter of fact, some Hunting Wasps do take
220 care to protect the entrance to the burrow by closing it temporarily, when the work has to be suspended for a time. Thus I have seen certain Ammophilae, whose burrow is a perpendicular shaft, block the entrance to the home with a small flat stone when the insect goes off hunting or ceases its mining operations at sunset, the hour for
225 striking work. But this is a slight affair, a mere slab laid over the mouth of the shaft. When the insect comes, it only takes a moment to remove the little flat stone; and the entrance is free.

On the other hand, the obstruction which we have just seen built by the Sphex is a solid barrier, a stout piece of masonry, where dust
230 and gravel form alternate layers all the way down the passage. It is a definite performance and not a provisional defense, as is proved by the care with which it is constructed. Besides, as I think I have shown pretty clearly, it is very doubtful, considering the way in which she acts, whether the Sphex will ever return to make use of the home
235 which she has prepared. The next Ephippiger will be caught elsewhere; and the warehouse destined to receive her will be dug elsewhere too. But these, after all, are only arguments: let us rather have recourse to experiment, which is more conclusive here than logic.

240   I allowed nearly a week to elapse, in order to give the Sphex time to return to the burrow which she had so methodically closed and to make use of it for her next laying if such were her intention. Events corresponded with the logical inferences: the burrow was in the condition wherein I left it, still firmly dosed, but without provisions,
245 egg or larva. The proof was decisive: the Wasp had not been back.

So the plundered Sphex enters her house, makes a leisurely inspection of the empty chamber and, a moment afterwards, behaves as though she had not perceived the disappearance of the bulky prey which but now filled the cell. Did she, in fact, fail to notice the
250 absence of the provisions and the egg? Is she, who is so clear-sighted in her murderous proceedings, dense enough not to realize that the cell is empty? I dare not accuse her of such stupidity. She is aware of it. But then why that other piece of stupidity which makes her close—and very conscientiously close—an empty burrow, one which
255 she does not purpose to victual later? Here the work of closing is

useless, is supremely absurd; no matter: the insect performs it with
the same ardor as though the larva's future depended on it. The
insect's various instinctive actions are then fatally linked together.
Because one thing has been done, a second thing must inevitably be
260 done to complete the first or to prepare the way for its completion;
and the two acts depend so closely upon each other that the
performing of the first entails that of the second, even when, owing to
casual circumstances, the second has become not only inopportune
but sometimes actually opposed to the insect's interests. What object
265 can the Sphex have in blocking up a burrow which has become
useless, now that it no longer contains the victim and the egg, and
which will always remain useless, since the insect will not return to
it? The only way to explain this inconsequent action is to look upon it
as the inevitable complement of the actions that went before. In the
270 normal order of things, the Sphex hunts down her prey, lays an egg
and closes her burrow. The hunting has been done; the game, it is
true, has been withdrawn by me from the cell; never mind: the
hunting has been done, the egg has been laid; and now comes the
business of closing up the home. This is what the insect does, without
275 another thought, without in the least suspecting the futility of her
present labors.

Experiment III

To know everything and to know nothing, according as it acts
under normal or exceptional conditions: that is the strange antithesis
280 presented by the insect race. Other examples, also drawn from the
Sphex tribe, will confirm this conclusion. The White-edged Sphex *(S.
albisecta)* attacks medium-sized Locusts, whereof the different
species to be found in the neighborhood of the burrow all furnish her
with their tribute of victims. Because of the abundance of these
285 Acridians, there is no need to go hunting far afield. When the burrow,
which takes the form of a perpendicular shaft, is ready, the Sphex
merely explores the purlieus of her lair, within a small radius, and is
not long in finding some Locust browsing in the sunshine. To pounce
upon her and sting her, despite her kicking, is to the Sphex the
290 matter of a moment. After some fluttering of its wings, which unfurl
their carmine or azure fan, after some drowsy stretching of its legs,
the victim ceases to move. It has now to be brought home, on foot. For

this laborious operation, the Sphex employs the same method as her
kinswomen, that is to say, she drags her prize along between her legs,
295 holding one of its antennae in her mandibles. If she encounters some
grassy jungle, she goes hopping and flitting from blade to blade,
without ever letting slip her prey. When at last she comes within a
few feet of her dwelling, she performs a maneuver which is also
practiced by the Languedocian Sphex; but she does not attach as
300 much importance to it, for she frequently neglects it. Leaving her
captive on the road, the Wasp hurries home, though no apparent
danger threatens her abode, and puts her head through the entrance
several times, even going part of the way down the burrow. She next
returns to the Locust and, after bringing her nearer the goal, leaves
305 her a second time to revisit the burrow. This performance is repeated
over and over again always with the same anxious haste.

These visits are sometimes followed by grievous accidents. The
victim, rashly abandoned on hilly ground, rolls to the bottom of the
slope; and the Sphex on her return, no longer finding it where she left
310 it, is obliged to seek for it, sometimes fruitlessly. If she find it, she
must renew a toilsome climb, which does not prevent her from once
more abandoning her booty on the same unlucky declivity. Of these
repeated visits to the mouth of the shaft, the first can be very
logically explained. The Wasp, before arriving with her heavy burden,
315 inquires whether the entrance to the home be really clear, whether
nothing will hinder her from bringing in her game. But, once this first
reconnaissance is made, what can be the use of the rest, following one
after the other, at close intervals? Is the Sphex so volatile in her ideas
that she forgets the visit which she has just paid and runs afresh to
320 the burrow a moment later, only to forget this new inspection also
and to start doing the same thing over and over again? That would be
a memory with very fleeting recollections, whence the impression
vanished almost as soon as it was produced. Let us not linger too long
on this obscure point.

325   At last the game is brought to the brink of the shaft, with its
antennae hanging down the hole. We now again see, faithfully
imitated, the method employed in the like case by the Yellow-winged
Sphex and also, but under less striking conditions, by the
Languedocian Sphex. The Wasp enters alone, inspects the interior,
330 reappears at the entrance, lays hold of the antennae and drags the

Locust down. While the Locust-huntress was making her examination of the home, I have pushed her prize a little farther back; and I obtained results similar in all respects to those which the Cricket-huntress gave me. Each Sphex displays the same obstinacy in diving
335 down her burrow before dragging in the prey. Let us recall here that the Yellow-winged Sphex does not always allow herself to be caught by this trick of pulling away her Cricket. There are picked tribes, strong-minded families which, after a few disappointments, see through the experimenter's wiles and know how to baffle them. But
340 these revolutionaries, fit subjects for progress, are the minority; the remainder, mulish conservatives clinging to the old manners and customs, are the majority, the crowd. I am unable to say whether the Locust-huntress also varies in ingenuity according to the district which she hails from.
345   But here is something more remarkable; and it is this with which I wanted to conclude the present experiment. After repeatedly withdrawing the White-edged Sphex' prize from the mouth of the pit and compelling her to come and fetch it again, I take advantage of her descent to the bottom of the shaft to seize the prey and put it in a
350 place of safety where she cannot find it. The Sphex comes up, looks about for a long time and, when she is convinced that the prey is really lost, goes down into her home again. A few moments after, she reappears. Is it with the intention of resuming the chase? Not the least in the world: the Sphex begins to stop up the burrow. And what
355 we see is not a temporary closing, effected with a small flat stone, a slab covering the mouth of the well; it is a final closing, carefully done with dust and gravel swept into the passage until it is filled up. The White-edged Sphex makes only one cell at the bottom of her shaft and puts one head of game into this cell. That single Locust has been
360 caught and dragged to the edge of the hole. If she was not stored away, it was not the huntress' fault, but mine. The Wasp performed her task according to the inflexible rule; and, also according to the inflexible rule, she completes her work by stopping up the dwelling, empty though it be. We have here an exact repetition of the useless
365 exertions made by the Languedocian Sphex whose home has just been plundered.

Experiment IV

It is almost impossible to make certain whether the Yellow-winged Sphex, who constructs several cells at the end of the same
370 passage and stacks several Crickets in each, is equally illogical when accidentally disturbed in her proceedings. A cell can be closed though empty or imperfectly victualled and the Wasp will none the less continue to come to the same burrow in order to work at the others. Nevertheless, I have reason to believe that this Sphex is subject to
375 the same aberrations as her two kinswomen. My conviction is based on the following facts: the number of Crickets found in the cells, when all the work is done, is usually four to each cell, although it is not uncommon to find only three, or even two. Four appears to me to be the normal number, first, because it is the most frequent and,
380 secondly, because, when rearing young larvae dug up while they were still engaged on their first joint, I found that all of them, those actually provided with only two or three pieces of game as well as those which had four, easily managed the various Crickets wherewith I served them one by one, up to and including the fourth, but that
385 after this they refused all nourishment, or barely touched the fifth ration. If four Crickets are necessary to the larva to acquire the full development called for by its organization, why are sometimes only three, sometimes only two provided for it? Why this enormous difference in the quantity of the victuals, some larvae having twice as
390 much as the others? It cannot be because of any difference in the size of the dishes provided to satisfy the grub's appetite, for all have very much the same dimensions; and it can therefore be due only to the wastage of game on the way. We find, in fact, at the foot of the banks whose upper stages are occupied by the Sphex-wasps, Crickets that
395 have been paralyzed but lost, owing to the slope of the ground, down which they have slipped when the huntresses have momentarily left them, for some reason or other. These Crickets fall a prey to the Ants and Flies; and the Sphex-wasps who come across them take good care not to pick them up, for, if they did, they would themselves be
400 admitting enemies into the house.

These facts seem to me to prove that, while the Yellow-winged Sphex' arithmetical powers enable her to calculate exactly how many victims to capture, she cannot achieve a census of those which have

safely reached their destination. It is as though the insect had no
405 mathematical guide beyond an irresistible impulse that prompts her
to hunt for game a definite number of times. When the Sphex has
made the requisite number of journeys, when she has done her
utmost to store the captures that result from these, her work is
ended; and she closes the cell whether completely or incompletely
410 provisioned. Nature has endowed her with only those faculties called
for in ordinary circumstances by the interests of her larvae; and, as
these blind faculties, which cannot be modified by experience, are
sufficient for the preservation of the race, the insect is unable to go
beyond them.
415   I conclude therefore as I began: instinct knows everything, in the
undeviating paths marked out for it; it knows nothing, outside those
paths. The sublime inspirations of science and the astounding
inconsistencies of stupidity are both its portion, according as the
insect acts under normal or accidental conditions.

Questions To Consider

1 The title of the chapter is *The Ignorance of Instinct.* What
   evidence does Fabre give that instinct is also quite stupid in what
   it does?
2 Summarize, in your own words, each of Fabre's four experiments.
   What do they collectively show?
3 Explain, in your own words, Fabre's conclusions at the end of this
   reading.

II. THE SOUL

We now move on to some of the implications of various views of natural things, beginning with ourselves: for human beings are also part of the natural world. If a view of nature is consistent and true, it should apply to human nature as well as to other natural things. We have chosen the immortality of the human soul as a sort of focal point, in terms of which we can see the implications of materialism, Platonic formalism, and the Aristotelian and Thomistic account of nature.

Here, Epicurus and Lucretius represent the Pre-Socratic and materialist position. Lucretius in particular has a well-developed account of human nature in his work *On the Nature of Things*. (Recall that Lucretius, like Democritus, explained nature in terms of atoms and the void.) He also specifically addresses the question of the immortality of the human soul. The question we must ask ourselves is: Do the Pre-Socratic view of nature and materialism imply the conclusion Lucretius draws about the soul? (We also look at some later materialist accounts of the immortality of the human soul.)

One finds Plato's formalist account of the immortality of the human soul in *the Phaedo*. Famous among Plato's dialogues, *the Phaedo* recounts Socrates' last hours, spent in discourse with friends about his own upcoming death and the possibility, or even necessity, of life after death.

We have selected a few chapters from Aquinas' *Summa Contra Gentiles* which deal with this specific question about the immortality of the human soul, and which illustrate particular difficulties hylomorphism confronts when dealing with this question. Aquinas is careful to present both sides of the issue, and he ends by resolving those arguments which go contrary to his own conclusion.

Lucretius

On the Nature of Things

Selections from Book III

Again if all motion is ever linked together and a new motion ever springs from another in a fixed order and first-beginnings do not by swerving make some commencement of motion to break through the decrees of fate, that cause follow not cause from everlasting, whence
5 have all living creatures here on earth, whence, I ask, has been wrested from the fates the power by which we go forward whither the will leads each, by which likewise we change the direction of our motions neither at a fixed time nor fixed place; but when and where the mind itself has prompted? For beyond a doubt in these things his
10 own will makes for each a beginning and from this beginning motions are welled through the limbs. See you not too, when the barriers are thrown open at a given moment, that yet the eager powers of the horses cannot start forward so instantaneously as the mind itself desires? The whole store of matter through the whole body must be
15 sought out, in order that stirred up through all the frame it may follow with undivided effort the bent of the mind; so that you see the beginning of motion is born from the heart, and the action first commences in the will of the mind and next is transmitted through the whole body and frame. Quite different is the case when we move
20 on propelled by a stroke inflicted by the strong might and strong compulsion of another; for then it is quite clear that all the matter of the whole body moves and is hurried on against our inclination, until the will has reined it in throughout the limbs. Do you see then in this case that, though an outward force often pushes men on and compels
25 them frequently to advance against their will and to be hurried headlong on, there yet is something in our breast sufficient to struggle against and resist it? And when too this something chooses the store of matter is compelled sometimes to change its course through the limbs and frame, and after it has been forced forward, is
30 reined in and settles back into its place. Wherefore in seeds too you

must admit the same, admit that besides blows and weights there is another cause of motions, from which this power of free action has been begotten in us, since we see that nothing can come from nothing. For weight forbids that all things be done by blows through as it were
35 an outward force; but that the mind itself does not feel an internal necessity in all its actions and is not as it were overmastered and compelled to bear and put up with this, is caused by a minute swerving of first-beginnings at no fixed part of space and no fixed time.

40   Since I have shown what the beginnings of all things are like and how diverse with varied shapes as they fly spontaneously, driven on in everlasting motion, and how all things can be severally produced out of these, next after these questions the nature of the mind and soul should, I think, be cleared up by my verses, and that dread of
45 Acheron be driven headlong forth, troubling as it does the life of man from its inmost depths and overspreading all things with the blackness of death, allowing no pleasure to be pure and unalloyed. For as to what men often give out that diseases and a life of shame are more to be feared than Tartarus, place of death, and that they
50 know the soul to be of blood or it may be of wind, if perhaps their choice so direct, and that they have no need at all of our philosophy, you may perceive for the following reasons that all these boasts are thrown out more for glory's sake than because the thing is really believed. These very men, exiles from their country and banished far
55 from the sight of men, live degraded by foul charge of guilt, sunk in a word in every kind of misery, and wherever the poor wretches go, they yet do offer sacrifices to the dead and slaughter black sheep and make libations to the gods Manes and in times of distress turn their thoughts to religion much more earnestly. Wherefore you can better
60 test the man in doubts and dangers and mid adversity learn who he is; for then and not till then the words of truth are forced out from the bottom of his heart: the mask is torn off, the reality is left. Avarice again and blind lust of honors which constrain unhappy men to overstep the bounds of right and sometimes as partners and agents of
65 crimes to strive night and day with surpassing effort to struggle up to the summit of power,—these sores of life are in no small measure fostered by the dread of death. For foul scorn and pinching want in every case are seen to be far removed from a life of pleasure and

security and to be a loitering so to say before the gates of death. And
70 while men, driven on by an unreal dread, wish to escape far away
from these and keep them far from them, they amass wealth by civil
bloodshed and greedily double their riches piling up murder on
murder; cruelly triumph in the sad death of a brother and hate and
fear the tables of kinsfolk. Often likewise from the same fear envy
75 causes them to pine: they make moan that before their very eyes he is
powerful, he attracts attention, who walks arrayed in gorgeous
dignity, while they are wallowing in darkness and dirt. Some wear
themselves to death for the sake of statues and a name. And often to
such a degree through dread of death does hate of life and of the sight
80 of daylight seize upon mortals, that they commit self-murder with a
sorrowing heart, quite forgetting that this fear is the source of their
cares, this fear which urges men to every sin, prompts this one to put
all shame to rout, another to burst asunder the bonds of friendship,
and in fine to overturn duty from its very base; since often before now
85 men have betrayed country and dear parents in seeking to shun the
Acherusian quarters. For even as children are flurried and dead all
things in the thick darkness, thus we in the daylight fear at times
things not a whit more to be dreaded than what children shudder at
in the dark and fancy sure to be. This terror therefore and darkness
90 of mind must be dispelled not by the rays of the sun and glittering
shafts of day, but by the aspect and law of nature.

   First then I say that the mind, which we often call the
understanding, in which dwells the directing and governing principle
of life, is no less part of the man, than hand and foot and eyes are
95 parts of the whole living creature. Some, however, affirm that the
sense of the mind does not dwell in a distinct part, but is a certain
vital state of the body, which the Greeks call *harmonia*, because by it,
they say, we live with sense, though the understanding is in no one
part; just as when good health is said to belong to the body, though
100 yet it is not any one part of the man in health. In this way they do not
assign a distinct part to the sense of the mind; in all which they
appear to me to be grievously at fault in more ways than one.
Oftentimes the body which is visible to sight, is sick, while yet we
have pleasure in another hidden part; and oftentimes the case is the
105 very reverse, the man who is unhappy in mind feeling pleasure in his
whole body; just as if, while a sick man's foot is pained, the head

meanwhile should be in no pain at all. Moreover, when the limbs are
consigned to soft sleep and the burdened body lies diffused without
sense, there is yet something else in us which during that time is
110 moved in many ways and admits into it all the motions of joy and
unreal cares of the heart. Now that you may know that the soul as
well is in the limbs and that the body does not have sense by any
harmony, this is a main proof: when much of the body has been taken
away, still life often stays in the limbs; and yet the same life, when a
115 few bodies of heat have been dispersed abroad and some air has been
forced out through the mouth, abandons at once the veins and quits
the bones: by this you may perceive that all bodies have not functions
of like importance nor alike uphold existence, but rather that those
seeds which constitute wind and heat, cause life to stay in the limbs.
120 Therefore vital heat and wind are within the body and abandon our
frame at death. Since, then, the nature of the mind and that of the
soul have been proved to be a part, as it were, of the man, surrender
the name of harmony, whether brought down to musicians from high
Helicon, or whether, rather, they have themselves taken it from
125 something else and transferred it to that thing which then was in
need of a distinctive name; whatever it be, let them keep it: do you
take in the rest of my precepts.

Now I assert that the mind and the soul are kept together in close
union and make up a single nature, but that the directing principle
130 which we call mind and understanding, is the head so to speak and
reigns paramount in the whole body. It has a fixed seat in the middle
region of the breast: here throb fear and apprehension, about these
spots dwell soothing joys; therefore here is the understanding or
mind. All the rest of the soul disseminated through the whole body
135 obeys and moves at the will and inclination of the mind. It by itself
alone knows for itself, rejoices for itself, at times when the impression
does not move either soul or body together with it. And as when some
part of us, the head or the eye, suffers from an attack of pain, we do
not feel the anguish at the same time over the whole body, thus the
140 mind sometimes suffers pain by itself or is inspirited with joy, when
all the rest of the soul throughout the limbs and frame is stirred by
no novel sensation. But when the mind is excited by some more
vehement apprehension, we see the whole soul feel in unison through
all the limbs, sweats and paleness spread over the whole body, the

145 tongue falter, the voice die away, a mist cover the eyes, the ears ring, the limbs sink under one; in short we often see men drop down from terror of mind; so that anybody may easily perceive from this that the soul is closely united with the mind, and, when it has been smitten by the influence of the mind, forthwith pushes and strikes the body.

150 This same principle teaches that the nature of the mind and soul is bodily; for when it is seen to push the limbs, rouse the body from sleep, and alter the countenance and guide and turn about the whole man, and when we see that none of these effects can take place without touch nor touch without body, must we not admit that the

155 mind and the soul are of a bodily nature? Again you perceive that our mind in our body suffers together with the body and feels in unison with it. When a weapon with a shudder-causing force has been driven in and has laid bare bones and sinews within the body, if it does not take life, yet there ensues a faintness and a lazy sinking to the

160 ground and on the ground the turmoil of mind which arises, and sometimes a kind of undecided inclination to get up. Therefore the nature of the mind must be bodily, since it suffers from bodily weapons and blows.

I will now go on to explain in my verses of what kind of body the

165 mind consists and out of what it is formed. First of all I say that it is extremely fine and formed of exceedingly minute bodies. That this is so you may, if you please to attend, clearly perceive from what follows: nothing that is seen takes place with a velocity equal to that of the mind when it starts some suggestion and actually sets it going;

170 the mind therefore is stirred with greater rapidity than any of the things whose nature stands out visible to sight. But that which is so passing nimble, must consist of seeds exceedingly round and exceedingly minute, in order to be stirred and set in motion by a small moving power. Thus water is moved and heaves by ever so

175 small a force, formed as it is of small particles apt to roll. But on the other hand the nature of honey is more sticky, its liquid more sluggish and its movement more dilatory; for the whole mass of matter coheres more closely, because sure enough it is made of bodies not so smooth, fine, and round. A breeze however gentle and light can

180 force, as you may see, a high heap of poppy seed to be blown away from the top downwards; but on the other hand Eurus itself cannot move a heap of stones. Therefore bodies possess a power of moving in

proportion to their smallness and smoothness; and on the other hand
the greater weight and roughness bodies prove to have, the more
185 stable they are. Since then the nature of the mind has been found to
be eminently easy to move, it must consist of bodies exceedingly
small, smooth, and round. The knowledge of which fact, my good
friend, will on many accounts prove useful and be serviceable to you.
The following fact too likewise demonstrates how fine the texture is of
190 which its nature is composed, and how small the room is in which it
can be contained, could it only be collected into one mass: soon as the
untroubled sleep of death has gotten hold of a man and the nature of
the mind and soul has withdrawn, you can perceive then no
diminution of the entire body either in appearance or weight: death
195 makes all good save the vital sense and heat. Therefore the whole
soul must consist of very small seeds and be inwoven through veins
and flesh and sinews; inasmuch as, after it has all withdrawn from
the whole body, the exterior contour of the limbs preserves itself
entire and not a bit of the weight is lost. Just in the same way when
200 the flavor of wine is gone or when the delicious aroma of a perfume
has been dispersed into the air or when the savor has left some body,
yet the thing itself does not therefore look smaller to the eye, nor does
anything seem to have been taken from the weight, because many
minute seeds make up the savors and the odor in the whole body of
205 the several things. Therefore, again and again I say, you are to know
that the nature of the mind and the soul has been formed of
exceedingly minute seeds, since at its departure it takes away none of
the weight.

Now mark me: that you may know that the minds and light souls
210 of living creatures have birth and are mortal, I will go on to set forth
verses worthy of your attention, got together by long study and
invented with welcome effort. Do you mind to link to one name both
of them alike, and when for instance I shall choose to speak of the
soul, showing it to be mortal, believe that I speak of the mind as well,
215 inasmuch as both make up one thing and are one united substance.

First of all then since I have shown the soul to be fine and to be
formed of minute bodies and made up of much smaller first-
beginnings than is the liquid of water or mist or smoke:—for it far
surpasses these in nimbleness and is moved when struck by a far
220 more slender cause; inasmuch as it is moved by images of smoke and

mist; as when for instance sunk in sleep we see altars steam forth their heat and send up their smoke on high; for beyond a doubt images are begotten for us from these things:—well then, since you see on the vessels being shattered the water flow away on all sides, and since mist and smoke pass away into air, believe that the soul too is shed abroad and perishes much more quickly and dissolves sooner into its first bodies, when once it has been taken out of the limbs of a man and has withdrawn. For, when the body that serves for its vessel cannot hold it, if shattered from any cause and rarefied by the withdrawal of blood from the veins, how can you believe that this soul can be held by any air? How can that air which is rarer than our body hold it in?

Again we perceive that the mind is begotten along with the body and grows up together with it and becomes old along with it. For even as children go about with a tottering and weakly body, so slender sagacity of mind follows along with it; then when their life has reached the maturity of confirmed strength, the judgement too is greater and the power of the mind more developed. Afterwards when the body has been shattered by the mastering might of time and the frame has drooped with its forces dulled, then the intellect halts, the tongue dotes, the mind gives way, all faculties fail and are found wanting at the same time. It naturally follows, then, that the whole nature of the soul is dissolved, like smoke, into the high air; since we see it is begotten along with the body and grows up along with it and, as I have shown, breaks down at the same time worn out with age.

Moreover, we see that even as the body is liable to violent diseases and severe pain, so is the mind to sharp cares and grief and fear; it naturally follows therefore that it is its partner in death as well.

Again in diseases of the body the mind often wanders and goes astray; for it loses its reason and drivels in its speech and often in a profound lethargy is carried into deep and never-ending sleep with drooping eyes and head; out of which it neither bears the voices nor can recognize the faces of those who stand around calling it back to life and bedewing with tears, face and cheeks. Therefore you must admit that the mind too dissolves, since the infection of disease reaches to it; for pain and disease are both forgers of death: a truth we have fully learned ere now by the death of many.

Again, when the pungent strength of wine has entered into a man
260 and its spirit has been infused into and transmitted through his
veins, why is it that a heaviness of the limbs follows along with this,
his legs are hampered as he reels about, his tongue falters, his mind
is besotted, his eyes swim, shouting, hiccuping, wranglings are rife,
together with all the other usual concomitants, why is all this, if not
265 because the overpowering violence of the wine disorders the soul
within the body? But whenever things can be disordered and
hampered, they give token that if a somewhat more potent cause
gained an entrance, they would perish and be robbed of all further
existence.

270   Moreover, it often happens that some one constrained by the
violence of disease suddenly drops down before our eyes, as by a
stroke of lightning, and foams at the mouth, moans and shivers
through his frame, loses his reason, stiffens his muscles, is racked,
gasps for breath fitfully, and wearies his limbs with tossing. Sure
275 enough, because the violence of the disease spreads itself through his
frame and disorders him, he foams as he tries to eject his soul, just as
in the salt sea the waters boil with the mastering might of the winds.
A moan too is forced out, because the limbs are seized with pain, and
mainly because seeds of voice are driven forth and are carried in a
280 close mass out by the mouth, the road which they are accustomed to
take and where they have a well-paved way. Loss of reason follows,
because the powers of the mind and soul are disordered and, as I have
shown, are riven and forced asunder, torn to pieces by the same
baneful malady. Then, after the cause of the disease has bent its
285 course back, and the acrid humors of the distempered body return to
their biding-places, then he first gets up like one reeling, and by little
and little comes back into full possession of his senses and regains his
soul. Since therefore even within the body mind and soul are
harassed by such violent distempers and so miserably racked by
290 sufferings, why believe that they without the body in the open air can
continue existence battling with fierce winds?

And since we perceive that the mind is healed like the sick body,
and we see that it can be altered by medicine, this too gives warning
that the mind has a mortal existence. For it is natural that whoever
295 attempts to change the mind or seeks to alter any other nature you
like, should add new parts or change the arrangement of the present,

or withdraw in short some little bit from the sum. But that which is immortal wills not to have its parts transposed nor any addition to be made nor one bit to ebb away; for whenever a thing changes and quits

300 its proper limits, this change is at once the death of that which was before. Therefore the mind, whether it is sick or whether it is altered by medicine, alike, as I have shown, gives forth mortal symptoms. So invariably is truth found to make head against false reason and to cut off all retreat from the assailant and by a two-fold refutation to put

305 falsehood to rout.

Again the quickened powers of body and mind by their joint partnership enjoy health and life; for the nature of the mind cannot by itself alone without the body give forth vital motions nor can the body again bereft of the soul continue to exist and make use of its

310 senses: just, you are to know, as the eye itself torn away from its roots cannot see anything when apart from the whole body, thus the soul and mind cannot it is plain do anything by themselves. Sure enough, because mixed up through veins and flesh, sinews and bones, their first-beginnings are confined by all the body and are not free to bound

315 away leaving great spaces between, therefore thus shut in they make those sense-giving motions which they cannot make after death when forced out of the body into the air by reason that they are not then confined in a like manner; for the air will be a body and a living thing, if the soul shall be able to keep itself together and to enclose in

320 it those motions which it used before to perform in the sinews and within the body.

Moreover even while it yet moves within the confines of life, often the soul shaken from some cause or other is seen to wish to pass out and be loosed from the whole body, the features are seen to droop as

325 at the last hour and all the limbs to sink flaccid over the bloodless trunk: just as happens, when the phrase is used, the mind is in a bad way, or the soul is quite gone; when all is hurry and every one is anxious to keep from parting the last tie of life; for then the mind and the power of the soul are shaken throughout and both are quite

330 loosened together with the body, so that a cause somewhat more powerful can quite break them up. Why doubt I would ask that the soul when driven forth out of the body, when in the open air, feeble as it is, stripped of its covering, not only cannot continue through eternity, but is unable to hold together the smallest fraction of time?

335 Therefore, again and again I say, when the enveloping body has been
all broken up and the vital airs have been forced out, you must admit
that the senses of the mind and the soul are dissolved, since the cause
of destruction is one and inseparable for both body and soul.

Again a tree cannot exist in the ether, nor clouds in the deep sea
340 nor can fishes live in the fields nor blood exist in woods nor sap in
stones. Where each thing can grow and abide is fixed and ordained.
Thus the nature of the mind cannot come into being alone without the
body nor exist far away from the sinews and blood. But if (for this
would be much more likely to happen than that) the force itself of the
345 mind might be in the head or shoulders or heels or might be born in
any other part of the body, it would after all be wont to abide in one
and the same man or vessel. But since in our body even it is fixed and
seen to be ordained where the soul and the mind can severally be and
grow, it must still more strenuously be denied that it can abide and
350 be carried out of the body altogether. Therefore when the body has
died, we must admit that the soul has perished, wrenched away
throughout the body. To link a mortal thing with an everlasting thing
and suppose that they can have sense in common and can be
reciprocally acted upon, is sheer folly; for what can be conceived more
355 incongruous, more discordant and inconsistent with itself, than a
thing which is mortal, linked with an immortal and everlasting thing,
trying in such union to weather furious storms? But if perhaps the
soul is to be accounted immortal for this reason rather, because it is
kept sheltered from death-bringing things, either because things
360 hostile to its existence do not approach at all, or because those which
do approach, in some way or other retreat discomfited before we can
feel the harm they do, manifest experience proves that this cannot be
true. For besides that it sickens in sympathy with the maladies of the
body, it is often attacked by that which frets it on the score of the
365 future and keeps it on the rack of suspense and wears it out with
cares; and when ill deeds are in the past, remorse for sins yet gnaws:
then there is madness peculiar to the mind and forgetfulness of all
things; then too it often sinks into the black waters of lethargy.

Death therefore to us is nothing, concerns us not a bit, since the
370 nature of the mind is proved to be mortal; and as in time gone by we
felt no distress, when the Poeni from all sides came together to do
battle, and all things shaken by war's troublous uproar shuddered

and quaked beneath high heaven, and mortal men were in doubt
which of the two peoples it should be to whose empire all must fall by
375   sea and land alike, thus when we shall be no more, when there shall
have been a separation of body and soul, out of both of which we are
each formed into a single being, to us, you may be sure, who then
shall be no more, nothing whatever can happen to excite sensation,
not if earth shall be mingled with sea and sea with heaven. And even
380   supposing the nature of the mind and power of the soul do feel, after
they have been severed from our body, yet that is nothing to us who
by the binding tie of marriage between body and soul are formed each
into one single being. And if time should gather up our matter after
our death and put it once more into the position in which it now is,
385   and the light of life be given to us again, this result even would
concern us not at all, when the chain of our self-consciousness has
once been snapped asunder. So now we give ourselves no concern
about any self which we have been before, nor do we feel any distress
on the score of that self. For when you look back on the whole past
390   course of immeasurable time and think how manifold are the shapes
which the motions of matter take, you may easily credit this too, that
these very same seeds of which we now are formed, have often before
been placed in the same order in which they now are; and yet we
cannot recover this in memory: a break in our existence has been
395   interposed, and all the motions have wandered to and fro far astray
from the sensations they produced. For he whom evil is to befall,
must in his own person exist at the very time it comes, if the misery
and suffering are even to have any place at all; but since death
precludes this, and forbids him to be, upon whom the ills can be
400   brought, you may be sure that we have nothing to fear after death,
and that he who exists not, cannot become miserable, and that it
matters not a whit whether he has been born into life at any other
time, when immortal death has taken away his mortal life.

Therefore when you see a man bemoaning his hard case, that
405   after death he shall either rot with his body laid in the grave or be
devoured by flames or the jaws of wild beasts, you may be sure that
his ring betrays a flaw and that there lurks in his heart a secret goad,
though he himself declare that he does not believe that any sense will
remain to him after death. He does not, I think, really grant the
410   conclusion which he professes to grant nor the principle on which he

so professes, nor does he take and force himself root and branch out of
life, but all unconsciously imagines something of self to survive. For
when any one in life suggests to himself that birds and beasts will
rend his body after death, he makes moan for himself: he does not
415   separate himself from that self, nor withdraw himself fully from the
body so thrown out, and fancies himself that other self and stands by
and impregnates it with his own sense. Hence he makes much moan
that he has been born mortal, and sees not that after real death there
will be no other self to remain in life and lament to self that his own
420   self has met death, and there to stand and grieve that his own self
there lying is mangled or burnt. For if it is an evil after death to be
pulled about by the devouring jaws of wild beasts, I cannot see why it
should not be a cruel pain to be laid on fires and burn in hot flames,
or to be placed in honey and stifled, or to stiffen with cold, stretched
425   on the smooth surface of an icy slab of stone, or to be pressed down
and crushed by a load of earth above.

'Now no more shall thy house admit thee with glad welcome,
nor a most virtuous wife and sweet children run to be the first to
snatch kisses and touch thy heart with a silent joy. No more
430   mayst thou be prosperous in thy doings, a safeguard to thine own.
One disastrous day has taken from thee luckless man in luckless
wise all the many prizes of life.'

This do men say; but add not thereto:

'and now no longer does any craving for these things beset
435   thee withal.'

For if they could rightly perceive this in thought and follow up the
thought in words, they would release themselves from great distress
and apprehension of mind.

'Thou, even as now thou art, sunk in the sleep of death, shalt
440   continue so to be all time to come, freed from all distressful pains;
but we with a sorrow that would not be sated wept for thee, when
close by thou didst turn to an ashen hue on thy appalling funeral
pile, and no length of days shall pluck from our hearts our ever-
during grief.'

445   This question therefore should be asked of this speaker, what
there is in it so passing bitter, if it come in the end to sleep and rest,
that any one should pine in never-ending sorrow.

This too men often, when they have reclined at table cup in hand and shade their brows with crowns, love to say from the heart,

450   'short is this enjoyment for poor weak men; presently it will have been and never after may it be called back'.

As if after their death it is to be one of their principal afflictions that thirst and parching drought is to burn them up hapless wretches, or a craving for any thing else is to beset them. What folly!

455 no one feels the want of himself and life at the time when mind and body are together sunk in sleep; for all we care this sleep might be everlasting, no craving whatever for ourselves then moves us. And yet by no means do those first-beginnings throughout our frame wander at that time far away from their sense-producing motions, at the

460 moment when a man starts up from sleep and collects himself. Death therefore must be thought to concern us much less, if less there can be than what we see to be nothing; for a greater dispersion of the mass of matter follows after death, and no one wakes up, upon whom the chill cessation of life has once come.

465   Once more, what evil lust of life is this which constrains us with such force to be so mightily troubled in doubts and dangers? A sure term of life is fixed for mortals, and death cannot be shunned, but meet it we must. Moreover we are ever engaged, ever involved in the same pursuits, and no new pleasure is struck out by living on; but

470 while what we crave is wanting, it seems to transcend all the rest; then, when it has been gotten, we crave something else, and ever does the same thirst of life possess us, as we gape for it open-mouthed. Quite doubtful it is what fortune the future will carry with it or what chance will bring us or what end is at hand. Nor by prolonging life do

475 we take one bit from the time past in death nor can we fret anything away, whereby we may haply be a less long time in the condition of the dead. Therefore you may complete as many generations as you please during your life; none the less however will that everlasting death await you; and for no less long a time will he be no more in

480 being, who beginning with to-day has ended his life, than the man who has died many months and years ago.

Plato

The Phaedo

Selections

Were you yourself, Phaedo, in the prison with Socrates on the day when he drank the poison?

Yes, Echecrates, I was.

I should so like to hear about his death. What did he say in his
5 last hours? We were informed that he died by taking poison, but no one knew anything more; for no Phliasian ever goes to Athens now, and it is a long time since any stranger from Athens has found his way here; so that we had no clear account.

Did you not hear of the proceedings at the trial?
10 Yes: someone told us about the trial, and we could not understand why, having been condemned, he should have been put to death, not at the time, but long afterwards. What was the reason of this?

An accident, Echecrates: the stern of the ship which the Athenians send to Delos happened to have been crowned on the day
15 before he was tried.

What is this ship?

It is the ship in which, according to Athenian tradition, Theseus went to Crete when he took with him the fourteen youths, and was the savior of them and of himself. And they are said to have vowed to
20 Apollo at the time, that if they were saved they would send a yearly mission to Delos. Now this custom still continues, and the whole period of the voyage to and from Delos, beginning when the priest of Apollo crowns the stern of the ship, is a holy season, during which the city is not allowed to be polluted by public executions; and when the
25 vessel is detained by contrary winds, the time spent in going and returning is very considerable. As I was saying, the ship was crowned on the day before the trial, and this was the reason why Socrates lay in prison and was not put to death until long after he was condemned.

What was the manner of his death, Phaedo? What was said or
30 done? And which of his friends were with him? Or did the authorities

forbid them to be present—so that he had no friends near him when he died?

No; there were several of them with him.

If you have nothing to do, I wish that you would tell me what passed, as exactly as you can.

I have nothing at all to do, and will try to gratify your wish. To be reminded of Socrates is always the greatest delight to me, whether I speak myself or hear another speak of him.

You will have listeners who are of the same mind with you, and I hope that you will be as exact as you can.

I had a singular feeling at being in his company. For I could hardly believe that I was present at the death of a friend, and therefore I did not pity him, Echecrates; he died so fearlessly, and his words and bearing were so noble and gracious, that to me he appeared blessed. I thought that in going to the other world he could not be without a divine call, and that he would be happy, if any man ever was, when he arrived there; and therefore I did not pity him as might have seemed natural at such an hour. But I had not the pleasure which I usually feel in philosophical discourse (for philosophy was the theme of which we spoke). I was pleased, but in the pleasure there was also a strange admixture of pain; for I reflected that he was soon to die, and this double feeling was shared by us all; we were laughing and weeping by turns, especially the excitable Apollodorus—you know the sort of man?

Yes.

He was quite beside himself; I and all of us were greatly moved.

Who were present?

Of native Athenians there were, besides Apollodorus, Critobulus and his father Crito, Hermogenes, Epigenes, Aeschines... Plato, if I am not mistaken, was ill.

Were there any strangers?

Yes, there were; Simmias the Theban, and Cebes, and Phaedondes; Euclid and Terpsion, who came from Megara.

And was Aristippus there, and Cleombrotus?

No, they were said to be in Aegina.

Any one else?

I think that these were nearly all.

Well, and what did you talk about?

I

I will begin at the beginning, and endeavor to repeat the entire conversation. On the previous days we had been in the habit of assembling early in the morning at the court in which the trial took place, and which is not far from the prison. There we used to wait
5 talking with one another until the opening of the doors (for they were not opened very early); then we went in and generally passed the day with Socrates. On the last morning we assembled sooner than usual, having heard on the day before when we quitted the prison in the evening that the sacred ship bad come from Delos; and so we
10 arranged to meet very early at the accustomed place. On our arrival the jailer who, answered the door, instead of admitting us, came out and told us to stay until he called us. 'For the Eleven,' he said, 'are now with Socrates; they are taking off his chains, and giving orders that he is to die today.' He soon returned and said that we might
15 come in. On entering we found Socrates just released from chains, and Xanthippè, whom you know, sitting by him, and holding his child in her arms. When she saw us she uttered a cry and said, as women will: 'O Socrates, this is the last time that either you will converse with your friends, or they with you.' Socrates turned to Crito and
20 said: 'Crito, let some one take her home.' Some of Crito's people accordingly led her away, crying out and beating herself. And when she was gone, Socrates, sitting up on the couch, bent and rubbed his leg, saying, as he was rubbing: How singular is the thing called pleasure, and how curiously related to pain, which might be thought
25 to be the opposite of it; for they are never present to a man at the same instant, and yet he who pursues either is generally compelled to take the other; their bodies are two, but they are joined by a single head. And I cannot help thinking that if Aesop had remembered them, he would have made a fable about God trying to reconcile their
30 strife, and how, when he could not, he fastened their heads together; and this is the reason why when one comes the other follows: as I know by my own experience now, when after the pain in my leg which was caused by the chain pleasure appears to succeed.

Upon this Cebes said: I am glad, Socrates, that you have
35 mentioned the name of Aesop. For it reminds me of a question which has been asked by many, and was asked of me only the day before yesterday by Evenus the poet—he will be sure to ask it again, and

therefore if you would like me to have an answer ready for him, you
may as well tell me what I should say to him:—he wanted to know
40 why you, who never before wrote a line of poetry, now that you are in
prison are turning Aesop's fables into verse, and also composing that
hymn in honor of Apollo.

Tell this to Evenus, Cebes, and bid him be of good cheer; say that
I would have him come after me if he be a wise man, and not tarry;
45 and that today I am likely to be going, for the Athenians say that I
must.

Simmias said: What a message for such a man! having been a
frequent companion of his I should say that, as far as I know him, he
will never take your advice unless he is obliged.

50   Why, said Socrates—is not Evenus a philosopher?
I think that he is, said Simmias.

Then he, or any man who has the spirit of philosophy, will be
willing to die; but he will not take his own life, for that is held to be
unlawful.

55   Here he changed his position, and put his legs off the couch on to
the ground, and during the rest of the conversation he remained
sitting.

And now, my judges, (said Socrates), I desire to prove to you that
the real philosopher has reason to be of good cheer when he is about
60 to die, and that after death he may hope to obtain the greatest good in
the other world. And how this may be, Simmias and Cebes, I will
endeavor to explain. For I deem that the true votary of philosophy is
likely to be misunderstood by other men; they do not perceive that he
is always pursuing death and dying; and if this be so, and he has had
65 the desire of death all his life long, why when his time comes should
he repine at that which he has been always pursuing and desiring?

Simmias said laughingly: Though not in a laughing humor, you
have made me laugh, Socrates; for I cannot help thinking that the
many when they hear your words will say how truly you have
70 described philosophers, and our people at home will likewise say that
the life which philosophers desire is in reality death, and that they
have found them out to be deserving of the death which they desire.

And they are right, Simmias, in thinking so, with the exception of
the words *they have found them out*; for they have not found out
75 either what is the nature of that death which the true philosopher

deserves, or how he deserves or desires death. But enough of them:—let us discuss the matter among ourselves. Do we believe that there is such a thing as death?

To be sure, replied Simmias.

80 Is it not the separation of soul and body? And to be dead is the completion of this; when the soul exists in herself, and is released from the body and the body is released from the soul, what is this but death?

Just so, he replied.

85 There is another question, which will probably throw light on our present inquiry if you and I can agree about it:—Ought the philosopher to care about the pleasures—if they are to be called pleasures—of eating and drinking?

Certainly not, answered Simmias.

90 And what about the pleasures of love—should he care for them?

By no means.

And will he think much of the other ways of indulging the body, for example, the acquisition of costly raiment, or sandals, or other adornments of the body? Instead of caring about them, does he not 95 rather despise anything more than nature needs? What do you say?

I should say that the true philosopher would despise them.

Would you not say that he is entirely concerned with the soul and not with the body? He would like, as far as he can, to get away from the body and to turn to the soul.

100 Quite true.

In matters of this sort philosophers, above all other men, may be observed in every sort of way to dissever the soul from the communion of the body.

Very true.

105 Whereas, Simmias, the rest of the world are of opinion that to him who has no sense of pleasure and no part in bodily pleasure, life is not worth having; and that he who is indifferent about them is as good as dead.

That is also true.

110 What again shall we say of the actual acquirement of knowledge?—is the body, if invited to share in the inquiry, a hinderer or a helper? I mean to say, have sight and hearing any truth in them? Are they not, as the poets are always telling us, inaccurate witnesses?

and yet, if even they are inaccurate and indistinct, what is to be said
115 of the other senses?—for you will allow that they are the best of
them?

Certainly, he replied.

Then when does the soul attain truth?—for in attempting to
consider anything in company with the body she is obviously
120 deceived.

True.

Then must not true existence be revealed to her in thought, if at
all?

Yes.

125 And thought is best when the mind is gathered into herself and
none of these things trouble her—neither sounds nor sights nor pain
nor any pleasure,—when she takes leave of the body, and has as little
as possible to do with it, when she has no bodily sense or desire, but
is aspiring after true being?

130 Certainly.

And in this the philosopher dishonors the body; his soul runs
away from his body and desires to be alone and by herself?

That is true.

Well, but there is another thing, Simmias: Is there or is there not
135 an absolute justice?

Assuredly there is.

And an absolute beauty and absolute good?

Of course.

But did you ever behold any of them with your eyes?

140 Certainly not.

Or did you ever reach them with any other bodily sense?—and I
speak not of these alone, but of absolute greatness, and health, and
strength, and of the essence or true nature of everything. Has the
reality of them ever been perceived by you through the bodily organs?
145 or rather, is not the nearest approach to the knowledge of their
several natures made by him who so orders his intellectual vision as
to have the most exact conception of the essence of each thing which
he considers?

Certainly.

150 And he attains to the purest knowledge of them who goes to each
with the mind alone, not introducing or intruding in the act of

thought sight or any other sense together with reason, but with the very light of the mind in her own clearness searches into the very truth of each; he who has got rid, as far as he can, of eyes and ears
155 and, so to speak, of the whole body, these being in his opinion distracting elements which when they infect the soul hinder her from acquiring truth and knowledge—who, if not he, is likely to attain to the knowledge of true being?

What you say has a wonderful truth in it, Socrates, replied
160 Simmias.

And when real philosophers consider all these things, will they not be led to make a reflection which they will express in words something like the following? *Have we not found,* they will say, *a path of thought which seems to bring us and our argument to the*
165 *conclusion, that while we are in the body, and while the soul is infected with the evils of the body, our desire will not be satisfied? and our desire is of the truth. For the body is a source of endless trouble to us by reason of the mere requirement of food; and is liable also to diseases which overtake and impede us in the search after true being:*
170 *it fills us full of loves, and lusts, and fears, and fancies of all kinds, and endless foolery, and in fact, as men say, takes away from us the power of thinking at all. Whence come wars, and fightings, and factions? whence but from the body and the lusts of the body? Wars are occasioned by the love of money, and money has to be acquired for the*
175 *sake and in the service of the body; and by reason of all these impediments we have no time to give to philosophy; and, last and worst of all, even if we are at leisure and betake ourselves to some speculation, the body is always breaking in upon us, causing turmoil and confusion in our enquiries, and so amazing us that we are*
180 *prevented from seeing the truth. It has been proved to us by experience that if we would have pure knowledge of anything we must be quit of the body—the soul in herself must behold things in themselves: and then we shall attain the wisdom which we desire, and of which we say that we are lovers; not while we live, but after death; for if while in*
185 *company with the body, the soul cannot have pure knowledge, one of two things follows—either knowledge is not to be attained at all, or, if at all, after death. For then, and not till then, the soul will be parted from the body and exist in herself alone. In this present life, I reckon that we make the nearest approach to knowledge when we have the*

190 *least possible intercourse or communion with the body, and are not*
surfeited with the bodily nature, but keep ourselves pure until the hour
when God himself is pleased to release us. And thus having got rid of
the foolishness of the body we shall be pure and hold converse with the
pure, and know of ourselves the clear light everywhere, which is no
195 *other than the light of truth.* For the impure are not permitted to
approach the pure. These are the sort of words, Simmias, which the
true lovers of knowledge cannot help saying to one another, and
thinking. You would agree; would you not?

Undoubtedly, Socrates.

200   But, my friend, if this be true, there is great reason to hope that,
going whither I go, when I have come to the end of my journey, I shall
attain that which has been the pursuit of my life. And therefore I go
on my way rejoicing, and not I only, but every other man who believes
that his mind has been made ready and that he is in a manner
205 purified.

Certainly, replied Simmias.

And what is purification but the separation of the soul from the
body, as I was saying before; the habit of the soul gathering and
collecting herself into herself from all sides out of the body; the
210 dwelling in her own place alone, as in another life, so also in this, as
far as she can;—the release of the soul from the chains of the body?

Very true, he said.

And this separation and release of the soul from the body is
termed death?

215   To be sure, he said.

And the true philosophers, and they only, are ever seeking to
release the soul. Is not the separation and release of the soul from the
body their special study?

That is true.

220   And, as I was saying at first, there would be a ridiculous
contradiction in men studying to live as nearly as they can in a state
of death, and yet repining when it comes upon them.

Clearly.

And the true philosophers, Simmias, are always occupied in the
225 practice of dying, wherefore also to them least of all men is death
terrible. Look at the matter thus:—if they have been in every way the
enemies of the body, and are wanting to be alone with the soul, when

this desire of theirs is granted, how inconsistent would they be if they trembled and repined, instead of rejoicing at their departure to that
230 place where, when they arrive, they hope to gain that which in life they desired—and this was wisdom—and at the same time to be rid of the company of their enemy. Many a man has been willing to go to the world below animated by the hope of seeing there an earthly love, or wife, or son, and conversing with them. And will he who is a true
235 lover of wisdom[1] and is strongly persuaded in like manner that only in the world below he can worthily enjoy her, still repine at death? Will he not depart with joy? Surely he will, my friend, if he be a true philosopher. For he will have a firm conviction that there, and there only, he can find wisdom in her purity. And if this be true, he would
240 be very absurd, as I was saying, if he were afraid of death.

He would indeed, replied Simmias.

And when you see a man who is repining at the approach of death, is not his reluctance a sufficient proof that he is not a lover of wisdom, but a lover of the body, and probably at the same time a
245 lover of either money or power, or both?

Quite so, he replied.

And therefore I maintain that I am right, Simmias and Cebes, in not grieving or repining at parting from you and my masters in this world, for I believe that I shall equally find good masters and friends
250 in another world. But most men do not believe this saying; if then I succeed in convincing you by my defense better than I did the Athenian judges, it will be well.

Cebes answered: I agree, Socrates, in the greater part of what you say. But in what concerns the soul, men are apt to be incredulous;
255 they fear that when she has left the body her place may be nowhere, and that on the very day of death she may perish and come to an end—immediately on her release from the body, issuing forth dispersed like smoke or air and in her flight vanishing away into nothingness. If she could only be collected into herself after she has
260 obtained release from the evils of which you were speaking, there would be good reason to hope, Socrates, that what you say is true. But surely it requires a great deal of argument and many proofs to show

---

[1]   Lover of wisdom is a literal translation of the Greek word for philosopher, *philosophos.*

that when the man is dead his soul yet exists, and has any force or intelligence.

265   True, Cebes, said Socrates; and shall I suggest that we converse a little of the probabilities of these things?

I am sure, said Cebes, that I should greatly like to know your opinion about them.

I reckon, said Socrates, that no one who heard me now, not even if
270 he were one of my old enemies, the Comic poets, could accuse me of idle talking about matters in which I have no concern—If you please, then, we will proceed with the inquiry.

II

When I was young, Cebes, (said Socrates), I had a prodigious desire to know that department of philosophy which is called the investigation of nature; to know the causes of things, and why a thing is and is created or destroyed appeared to me to be a lofty profession;
5 and I was always agitating myself with the consideration of questions such as these:—Is the growth of animals the result of some decay which the hot and cold principle contracts, as some have said? Is the blood the element with which we think, or the air, or the fire? or perhaps nothing of the kind—but the brain may be the originating
10 power of the perceptions of hearing and sight and smell, and memory and opinion may come from them, and science may be based on memory and opinion when they have attained fixity. And then I went on to examine the corruption of them, and then to the things of heaven and earth, and at last I concluded myself to be utterly and
15 absolutely incapable of these inquiries, as I will satisfactorily prove to you. For I was fascinated by them to such a degree that my eyes grew blind to things which I had seemed to myself, and also to others, to know quite well; I forgot what I had before thought self-evident truths; e.g. such a fact as that the growth of man is the result of
20 eating and drinking; for when by the digestion of food flesh is added to flesh and bone to bone, and whenever there is an aggregation of congenial elements, the lesser bulk becomes larger and the small man great. Was not that a reasonable notion?

Yes, said Cebes, I think so.

25   Well; but let me tell you something more. There was a time when I thought that I understood the meaning of greater and less pretty

well; and when I saw a great man standing by a little one, I fancied
that one was taller than the other by a head; or one horse would
appear to be greater than another horse: and still more clearly did I
30 seem to perceive that ten is two more than eight, and that two cubits
are more than one, because two is the double of one.

And what is now your notion of such matters? said Cebes.

I should be far enough from imagining, he replied, that I knew
the cause of any of them, by heaven I should; for I cannot satisfy
35 myself that, when one is added to one, the one to which the addition
is made becomes two, or that the two units added together make two
by reason of the addition. I cannot understand how, when separated
from the other, each of them was one and not two, and now, when
they are brought together, the mere juxtaposition or meeting of them
40 should be the cause of their becoming two: neither can I understand
how the division of one is the way to make two; for then a different
cause would produce the same effect,—as in the former instance the
addition and juxtaposition of one to one was the cause of two, in this
the separation and subtraction of one from the other would be the
45 cause. Nor am I any longer satisfied that I understand the reason
why one or anything else is either generated or destroyed or is at all,
but I have in my mind some confused notion of a new method, and
can never admit the other.

Then I heard some one reading, as he said, from a book of
50 Anaxagoras, that mind was the disposer and cause of all, and I was
delighted at this notion, which appeared quite admirable, and I said
to myself: If mind is the disposer, mind will dispose all for the best,
and put each particular in the best place; and I argued that if any one
desired to find out the cause of the generation or destruction or
55 existence of anything, he must find out what state of being or doing or
suffering was best for that thing, and therefore a man had only to
consider the best for himself and others, and then he would also know
the worse, since the same science comprehended both. And I rejoiced
to think that I had found in Anaxagoras a teacher of the causes of
60 existence such as I desired, and I imagined that he would tell me first
whether the earth is flat or round; and whichever was true, he would
proceed to explain the cause and the necessity of this being so, and
then he would teach me the nature of the best and show that this was
best; and if he said that the earth was in the center, he would further

65 explain that this position was the best, and I should be satisfied with
the explanation given, and not want any other sort of cause. And I
thought that I would then go on and ask him about the sun and moon
and stars, and that he would explain to me their comparative
swiftness, and their returnings and various states, active and passive,
70 and how all of them were for the best. For I could not imagine that
when he spoke of mind as the disposer of them, he would give any
other account of their being as they are, except that this was best;
and I thought that when he had explained to me in detail the cause of
each and the cause of all, he would go on to explain to me what was
75 best for each and what was good for all. These hopes I would not have
sold for a large sum of money, and I seized the books and read them
as fast as I could in my eagerness to know the better and the worse.

What expectations I had formed, and how grievously was I
disappointed! As I proceeded, I found my philosopher altogether
80 forsaking mind or any other principle of order, but having recourse to
air, and ether, and water, and other eccentricities. I might compare
him to a person who began by maintaining generally that mind is the
cause of the actions of Socrates, but who, when he endeavored to
explain the causes of my several actions in detail, went on to show
85 that I sit here because my body is made up of bones and muscles—
and the bones, as he would say, are hard and have joints which divide
them, and the muscles are elastic, and they cover the bones, which
have also a covering or environment of flesh and skin which contains
them; and as the bones are lifted at their joints by the contraction or
90 relaxation of the muscles, I am able to bend my limbs, and this is why
I am sitting here in a curved posture—that is what he would say; and
he would have a similar explanation of my talking to you, which he
would attribute to sound, and air, and hearing, and he would assign
ten thousand other causes of the same sort, forgetting to mention the
95 true cause, which is, that the Athenians have thought fit to condemn
me, and accordingly I have thought it better and more right to remain
here and undergo my sentence; for I am inclined to think that these
muscles and bones of mine would have gone off long ago to Megara or
Boeotia—by the dog, they would, if they had been moved only by their
100 own idea of what was best, and if I had not chosen the better and
nobler part, instead of playing truant and running away, of enduring
any punishment which the state inflicts. There is surely a strange

confusion of causes and conditions in all this. It may be said, indeed, that without bones and muscles and the other parts of the body I
105 cannot execute my purposes. But to say that I do as I do because of them, and that this is the way in which mind acts, and not from the choice of the best, is a very careless and idle mode of speaking. I wonder that they cannot distinguish the cause from the condition, which the many, feeling about in the dark, are always mistaking and
110 misnaming. And thus one man makes a vortex all round and steadies the earth by the heaven; another gives the air as a support to the earth, which is a sort of broad trough. Any power which in arranging them as they are arranges them for the best never enters into their minds; and instead of finding any superior strength in it, they rather
115 expect to discover another Atlas of the world who is stronger and more everlasting and more containing than the good; of the obligatory and containing power of the good they think nothing; and yet this is the principle which I would fain learn if any one would teach me. But as I have failed either to discover myself, or to learn of any one else,
120 the nature of the best, I will exhibit to you, if you like, what I have found to be the second best mode of inquiring into the cause.

I should very much like to hear, he replied.

Socrates proceeded:—I thought that as I had failed in the contemplation of true existence, I ought to be careful that I did not
125 lose the eye of my soul; as people may injure their bodily eye by observing and gazing on the sun during an eclipse, unless they take the precaution of only looking at the image reflected in the water, or in some similar medium. So in my own case, I was afraid that my soul might be blinded altogether if I looked at things with my eyes or tried
130 to apprehend them by the help of the senses. And I thought that I had better have recourse to the world of mind and seek there the truth of existence. I dare say that the simile is not perfect—for I am very far from admitting that he who contemplates existences through the medium of thought, sees them only 'through a glass darkly,' any more
135 than he who considers them in action and operation. However, this was the method which I adopted: I first assumed some principle which I judged to be the strongest, and then I affirmed as true whatever seemed to agree with this, whether relating to the cause or to anything else; and that which disagreed I regarded as untrue. But

140 I should like to explain my meaning more clearly, as I do not think that you as yet understand me.

No indeed, replied Cebes, not very well.

There is nothing new, he said, in what I am about to tell you; but only what I have been always and everywhere repeating in the
145 previous discussion and on other occasions: I want to show you the nature of that cause which has occupied my thoughts. I shall have to go back to those familiar words which are in the mouth of every one, and first of all assume that there is an absolute beauty and goodness and greatness, and the like; grant me this, and I hope to be able to
150 show you the nature of the cause, and to prove the immortality of the soul.

Cebes said: You may proceed at once with the proof, for I grant you this.

Well, he said, then I should like to know whether you agree with
155 me in the next step; for I cannot help thinking, if there be anything beautiful other than absolute beauty should there be such, that it can be beautiful only in so far as it partakes of absolute beauty—and I should say the same of everything. Do you agree in this notion of the cause?

160 Yes, he said, I agree.

He proceeded: I know nothing and can understand nothing of any other of those wise causes which are alleged; and if a person says to me that the bloom of color, or form, or any such thing is a source of beauty, I leave all that, which is only confusing to me, and simply and
165 singly, and perhaps foolishly, hold and am assured in my own mind that nothing makes a thing beautiful but the presence and participation of beauty in whatever way or manner obtained; for as to the manner I am uncertain, but I stoutly contend that by beauty all beautiful things become beautiful. This appears to me to be the safest
170 answer which I can give, either to myself or to another, and to this I cling, in the persuasion that this principle will never be overthrown, and that to myself or to any one who asks the question, I may safely reply, That by beauty beautiful things become beautiful. Do you not agree with me?

175 I do.

And that by greatness only great things become great and greater greater, and by smallness the less become less?

True.

Then if a person were to remark that A is taller by a head than B, and B less by a head than A, you would refuse to admit his statement, and would stoutly contend that what you mean is only that the greater is greater by, and by reason of, greatness, and the less is less only by, and by reason of, smallness; and thus you would avoid the danger of saying that the greater is greater and the less less by the measure of the head, which is the same in both, and would also avoid the monstrous absurdity of supposing that the greater man is greater by reason of the head, which is small. You would be afraid to draw such an inference, would you not?

Indeed, I should, said Cebes, laughing.

In like manner you would be afraid to say that ten exceeded eight by, and by reason of, two; but would say by, and by reason of, number; or you would say that two cubits exceed one cubit not by a half, but by magnitude?—for there is the same liability to error in all these cases.

Very true, he said.

Again, would you not be cautious of affirming that the addition of one to one, or the division of one, is the cause of two? And you would loudly asseverate that you know of no way in which anything comes into existence except by participation in its own proper essence, and consequently, as far as you know, the only cause of two is the participation in duality—this is the way to make two, and the participation in one is the way to make one. You would say: I will let alone puzzles of division and addition—wiser heads than mine may answer them; inexperienced as I am, and ready to start, as the proverb says, at my own shadow, I cannot afford to give up the sure ground of a principle. And if any one assails you there, you would not mind him, or answer him until you had seen whether the consequences which follow agree with one another or not, and when you are further required to give an explanation of this principle, you would go on to assume a higher principle, and a higher, until you found a resting-place in the best of the higher; but you would not confuse the principle and the consequences in your reasoning, like the Eristics—at least if you wanted to discover real existence. Not that this confusion signifies to them, who never care or think about the matter at all, for they have the wit to be well pleased with themselves

215 however great may be the turmoil of their ideas. But you, if you are a
philosopher, will certainly do as I say.

What you say is most true, said Simmias and Cebes, both
speaking at once.

(Phaedo) After all this had been admitted, and they had agreed
220 *that ideas exist, and that other things participate in them and derive*
their names from them, Socrates, if I remember rightly, said:

This is your way of speaking; and yet when you say that Simmias
is greater than Socrates and less than Phaedo, do you not predicate of
Simmias both greatness and smallness?

225 Yes, I do.

But still you allow that Simmias does not really exceed Socrates,
as the words may seem to imply, because he is Simmias, but by
reason of the size which he has; just as Simmias does not exceed
Socrates because he is Simmias, any more than because Socrates is
230 Socrates, but because he has smallness when compared with the
greatness of Simmias?

True.

And if Phaedo exceeds him in size, this is not because Phaedo is
Phaedo, but because Phaedo has greatness relatively to Simmias, who
235 is comparatively smaller?

That is true.

And therefore Simmias is said to be great, and is also said to be
small, because he is in a mean between them, exceeding the
smallness of the one by his greatness, and allowing the greatness of
240 the other to exceed his smallness. He added, laughing, I am speaking
like a book, but I believe that what I am saying is true.

Simmias assented.

I speak as I do because I want you to agree with me in thinking,
not only that absolute greatness will never be great and also small,
245 but that greatness in us or in the concrete will never admit the small
or admit of being exceeded: instead of this, one of two things will
happen, either the greater will fly or retire before the opposite, which
is the less or at the approach of the less has already ceased to exist;
but will not, if allowing or admitting of smallness, be changed by that;
250 even as I, having received and admitted smallness when compared
with Simmias, remain just as I was, and am the same small person.
And as the idea of greatness cannot condescend ever to be or become

small, in like manner the smallness in us cannot be or become great;
nor can any other opposite which remains the same ever be or become
255 its own opposite, but either passes away or perishes in the change.

That, replied Cebes, is quite my notion.

Hereupon one of the company, though I do not exactly remember
which of them, said: In heaven's name, is not this the direct contrary
of what was admitted before—that out of the greater came the less
260 and out of the less the greater, and that opposites were simply
generated from opposites; but now this principle seems to be utterly
denied.

Socrates inclined his head to the speaker and listened. I like your
courage, he said, in reminding us of this. But you do not observe that
265 there is a difference in the two cases. For then we were speaking of
opposites in the concrete, and now of the essential opposite which, as
is affirmed, neither in us nor in nature can ever be at variance with
itself: then, my friend, we were speaking of things in which opposites
are inherent and which are called after them, but now about the
270 opposites which are inherent in them and which give their name to
them; and these essential opposites will never, as we maintain, admit
of generation into or out of one another. At the same time, turning to
Cebes, he said: Are you at all disconcerted, Cebes, at our friend's
objection?

275 No, I do not feel so, said Cebes; and yet I cannot deny that I am
often disturbed by objections.

Then we are agreed after all, said Socrates, that the opposite will
never in any case be opposed to itself?

To that we are quite agreed, he replied.

280 Yet once more let me ask you to consider the question from
another point of view, and see whether you agree with me:—There is
a thing which you term heat, and another thing which you term cold?

Certainly.

But are they the same as fire and snow?

285 Most assuredly not.

Heat is a thing different from fire, and cold is not the same as
snow?

Yes.

And yet you will surely admit, that when snow, as was before
290 said, is under the influence of heat, they will not remain snow and

heat; but at the advance of the heat, the snow will either retire or perish?

Very true, he replied.

And the fire too at the advance of the cold will either retire or
295   perish; and when the fire is under the influence of the cold, they will not remain as before, fire and cold.

That is true, he said.

And in some cases the name of the idea is not only attached to the idea in an eternal connection, but anything else which, not being the
300   idea, exists only in the form of the idea, may also lay claim to it. I will try to make this clearer by an example:—The odd number is always called by the name of odd?

Very true.

But is this the only thing which is called odd? Are there not other
305   things which have their own name, and yet are called odd, because, although not the same as oddness, they are never without oddness?—that is what I mean to ask—whether numbers such as the number three are not of the class of odd. And there are many other examples: would you not say, for example, that three may be called by
310   its proper name, and also be called odd, which is not the same as three? and this may be said not only of three but also of five, and of every alternate number—each of them without being oddness is odd; and in the same way two and four, and the other series of alternate numbers, has every number even, without being evenness. Do you
315   agree?

Of course.

Then now mark the point at which I am aiming:—not only do essential opposites exclude one another, but also concrete things, which, although not in themselves opposed, contain opposites; these, I
320   say, likewise reject the idea which is opposed to that which is contained in them, and when it approaches them they either perish or withdraw. For example; Will not the number three endure annihilation or anything sooner than be converted into an even number, while remaining three?
325   Very true, said Cebes.

And yet, he said, the number two is certainly not opposed to the number three?

It is not.

Then not only do opposite ideas repel the advance of one another, but also there are other natures which repel the approach of opposites.

True he said.

Suppose, he said, that we endeavor, if possible, to determine what these are.

By all means.

Are they not, Cebes, such as compel the things of which they have possession, not only to take their own form, but also the form of some opposite?

What do you mean?

I mean, as I was just now saying, and as I am sure that you know, that those things which are possessed by the number three must not only be three in number, but must also be odd.

Quite true.

And on this oddness, of which the number three has the impress, the opposite idea will never intrude?

No.

And this impress was given by the odd principle?

Yes.

And to the odd is opposed the even?

True.

Then the idea of the even number will never arrive at three?

No.

Then three has no part in the even?

None.

Then the triad or number three is uneven?

Very true.

To return then to my distinction of natures which are not opposed, and yet do not admit opposites—as, in the instance given, three, although not opposed to the even, does not any the more admit of the even, but always brings the opposite into play on the other side; or as two does not receive the odd, or fire the cold—from these examples (and there are many more of them) perhaps you may be able to arrive at the general conclusion, that not only opposites will not receive opposites, but also that nothing which brings the opposite will admit the opposite of that which it brings, in that to which it is brought. And here let me recapitulate—for there is no harm in

repetition. The number five will not admit the nature of the even, any more than ten, which is the double of five, will admit the nature of the odd. The double has another opposite, and is not strictly opposed
370 to the odd, but nevertheless rejects the odd altogether. Nor again will parts in the ratio 3 : 2, nor any fraction in which there is a half, nor again in which there is a third, admit the notion of the whole,. although they are not opposed to the whole: You will agree?

Yes, he said, I entirely agree and go along with you in that.

375   And now, he said, let us begin again; and do not you answer my question in the words in which I ask it: let me have not the old safe answer of which I spoke at first, but another equally safe, of which the truth will be inferred by you from what has been just said. I mean that if any one asks you 'what that is, of which the inherence makes
380 the body hot,' you will reply not heat (this is what I call the safe and stupid answer), but fire, a far superior answer, which we are now in a condition to give. Or if any one asks you 'why a body is diseased,' you will not say from disease, but from fever; and instead of saying that oddness is the cause of odd numbers, you will say that the monad is
385 the cause of them: and so of things in general, as I dare say that you will understand sufficiently without my adducing any further examples.

Yes, he said, I quite understand you.

Tell me, then, what is that of which the inherence will render the
390 body alive?

The soul, he replied.

And is this always the case?

Yes, he said, of course.

Then whatever the soul possesses, to that she comes bearing life?
395   Yes, certainly.

And is there any opposite to life?

There is, he said.

And what is that?

Death.

400   Then the soul, as has been acknowledged, will never receive the opposite of what she brings.

Impossible, replied Cebes.

And now, he said, what did we just now call that principle which repels the even?

405   The odd.

And that principle which repels the musical or the just?

The unmusical, he said, and the unjust.

And what do we call that principle which does not admit of death?

The immortal, he said.

410   And does the soul admit of death?

No.

Then the soul is immortal?

Yes, he said.

And may we say that this has been proven?

415   Yes abundantly proven, Socrates, he replied.

Supposing that the odd were imperishable, must not three be imperishable?

Of course.

And if that which is cold were imperishable, when the warm
420 principle came attacking the snow, must not the snow have retired whole and unmelted—for it could never have perished, nor could it have remained and admitted the heat?

True, he said.

Again, if the uncooling or warm principle were imperishable, then
425 fire when assailed by cold would not have perished or have been extinguished, but would have gone away unaffected?

Certainly, he said.

And the same may be said of the immortal: if the immortal is also imperishable, the soul when attacked by death cannot perish; for the
430 preceding argument shows that the soul will not admit of death, or ever be dead, any more than three or the odd number will admit of the even, or fire, or the heat in the fire, of the cold. Yet a person may say: 'But although the odd will not become even at the approach of the even, why may not the odd perish and the even take the place of
435 the odd?' Now to him who makes this objection, we cannot answer that the odd principle is imperishable; for this has not been acknowledged, but if this had been acknowledged, there would have been no difficulty in contending that at the approach of the even the odd principle and the number three took their departure; and the
440 same argument would have held good of fire and heat and any other thing.

Very true.

And the same may be said of the immortal: if the immortal is also imperishable, then the soul will be imperishable as well as immortal;
445 but if not, some other proof of her imperishableness will have to be given.

No other proof is needed, he said; for if the immortal, being eternal, is liable to perish, then nothing is imperishable.

Yes, replied Socrates, and yet all men will agree that God, and
450 the essential form of life, and the immortal in general, will never perish.

Yes, all men, he said—that is true; and what is more, gods, if I am not mistaken, as well as men.

Seeing then that the immortal is indestructible, must not the
455 soul, if she is immortal, be also imperishable?

Most certainly.

Then when death attacks a man, the mortal portion of him may be supposed to die, but the immortal retires at the approach of death and is preserved safe and sound?
460   True.

Then, Cebes, beyond question, the soul is immortal and imperishable, and our souls will truly exist in another world!

I am convinced, Socrates, said Cebes, and have nothing more to object; but if my friend Simmias, or any one else, has any further
465 objection to make, he had better speak out, and not keep silence, since I do not know to what other season he can defer the discussion, if there is anything which he wants to say or to have said.

But I have nothing more to say, replied Simmias; nor can I see any reason for doubt after what has been said. But I still feel and
470 cannot help feeling uncertain in my own mind, when I think of the greatness of the subject and the feebleness of man.

Yes, Simmias, replied Socrates, that is well said: and I may add that first principles, even if they appear certain, should be carefully considered; and when they are satisfactorily ascertained, then, with a
475 sort of hesitating confidence in human reason, you may, I think, follow the course of the argument; and if that be plain and clear, there will be no need for any further inquiry.

Very true.

But then, my friends, he said, if the soul is really immortal, what
480 care should be taken of her, not only in respect of the portion of time

which is called life, but of eternity! And the danger of neglecting her from this point of view does indeed appear to be awful. If death had only been the end of all, the wicked would have had a good bargain in dying, for they would have been happily quit not only of their body,
485 but of their own evil together with their souls. But now, inasmuch as the soul is manifestly immortal, there is no release or salvation from evil except the attainment of the highest virtue and wisdom. For the soul when on her progress to the world below takes nothing with her but nurture and education; and these are said greatly to benefit or
490 greatly to injure the departed, at the very beginning of his journey there.

III

You, Simmias and Cebes, and all other men, will depart at some time or other. Me already, as a tragic poet would say, the voice of fate calls. Soon I must drink the poison; and I think that I had better repair to the bath first, in order that the women may not have the
5 trouble of washing my body after I am dead.

When he had done speaking, Crito said: And have you any commands for us, Socrates—anything to say about your children, or any other matter in which we can serve you?
10
Nothing particular, Crito, he replied: only, as I have always told you, take care of yourselves; that is a service which you may be ever rendering to me and mine and to all of us, whether you promise to do so or not. But if you have no thought for yourselves, and care not to
15 walk according to the rule which I have prescribed for you, not now for the first time, however much you may profess or promise at the moment, it will be of no avail.

We will do our best, said Crito: And in what way shall we bury
20 you?

In any way that you like; but you must get hold of me, and take care that I do not run away from you. Then he turned to us, and added with a smile:—I cannot make Crito believe that I am the same
25 Socrates who have been talking and conducting the argument; he

fancies that I am the other Socrates whom he will soon see, a dead
body—and he asks, How shall he bury me? And though I have spoken
many words, in the endeavor to show that when I have drunk the
poison I shall leave you and go to the joys of the blessed,—these
30 words of mine, with which I was comforting you and myself, have
had, as I perceive, no effect upon Crito. And therefore I want you to
be surety for me to him now, as at the trial he was surety to the
judges for me: but let the promise be of another sort; for he was
surety for me to the judges that I would remain, and you must be my
35 surety to him that I shall not remain, but go away and depart; and
then he will suffer less at my death, and not be grieved when he sees
my body being burned or buried. I would not have him sorrow at my
hard lot, or say at the burial, Thus we lay out Socrates, or, Thus we
follow him to the grave or bury him; for false words are not only evil
40 in themselves, but they infect the soul with evil. Be of good cheer
then, my dear Crito, and say that you are burying my body only, and
do with that whatever is usual, and what you think best.

When he had spoken these words, he arose and went into a
45 chamber to bathe; Crito followed him and told us to wait. So we
remained behind, talking and thinking of the subject of discourse,
and also of the greatness of our sorrow; he was like a father of whom
we were being bereaved, and we were about to pass the rest of our
lives as orphans. When he had taken the bath his children were
50 brought to him—(he had two young sons and an elder one); and the
women of his family also came, and he talked to them and gave them
a few directions in the presence of Crito; then he dismissed them and
returned to us.

55 Now the hour of sunset was near, for a good deal of time had
passed while he was within. When he came out, he sat down with us
again after his bath, but not much was said. Soon the jailer, who was
the servant of the Eleven, entered and stood by him, saying:—To you,
Socrates, whom I know to be the noblest and gentlest and best of all
60 who ever came to this place, I will not impute the angry feelings of
other men, who rage and swear at me, when, in obedience to the
authorities, I bid them drink the poison—indeed, I am sure that you
will not be angry with me; for others, as you are aware, and not I, are

to blame. And so fare you well, and try to bear lightly what must
65 needs be—you know my errand. Then bursting into tears he turned
away and went out.

Socrates looked at him and said: I return your good wishes, and
will do as you bid. Then turning to us, he said, How charming the
70 man is: since I have been in prison he has always been coming to see
me, and at times he would talk to me, and was as good to me as could
be, and now see how generously he sorrows on my account. We must
do as he says, Crito; and therefore let the cup be brought, if the
poison is prepared: if not, let the attendant prepare some.
75   Yet, said Crito, the sun is still upon the hill-tops, and I know that
many a one has taken the draught late, and after the announcement
has been made to him, he has eaten and drunk, and enjoyed the
society of his beloved; do not hurry—there is time enough.

80   Socrates said: Yes, Crito, and they of whom you speak are right in
so acting, for they think that they will be gainers by the delay; but I
am right in not following their example, for I do not think that I
should gain anything by drinking the poison a little later; I should
only be ridiculous in my own eyes for sparing and saving a life which
85 is already forfeit. Please then to do as I say, and not to refuse me.

Crito made a sign to the servant, who was standing by; and he
went out, and having been absent for some time, returned with the
jailer carrying the cup of poison. Socrates said: You, my good friend,
90 who are experienced in these matters, shall give me directions how I
am to proceed. The man answered: You have only to walk about until
your legs are heavy, and then to lie down, and the poison will act. At
the same time he handed the cup to Socrates, who in the easiest and
gentlest manner, without the least fear or change of color or feature,
95 looking at the man with all his eyes, Echecrates, as his manner was,
took the cup and said: What do you say about making a libation out of
this cup to any god? May I, or not? The man answered: We only
prepare, Socrates, just so much as we deem enough. I understand, he
said: but I may and must ask the gods to prosper my journey from
100 this to the other world—even so—and so be it according to my prayer.
Then raising the cup to his lips, quite readily and cheerfully he drank

off the poison. And hitherto most of us had been able to control our sorrow; but now when we saw him drinking, and saw too that he had finished the drought, we could no longer forbear, and in spite of

105 myself my own tears were flowing fast; so that I covered my face and wept, not for him, but at the thought of my own calamity in having to part from such a friend. Nor was I the first; for Crito, when he found himself unable to restrain his tears, had got up, and I followed; and at that moment, Apollodorus, who had been weeping all the time, broke

110 out in a loud and passionate cry which made cowards of us all. Socrates alone retained his calmness: What is this strange outcry? he said. I sent away the women mainly in order that they might not misbehave in this way, for I have been told that a man should die in peace. Be quiet then, and have patience. When we heard his words we

115 were ashamed, and refrained our tears; and he walked about until, as he said, his legs began to fail, and then he lay on his back, according to the directions, and the man who gave him the poison now and then looked at his feet and legs; and after a while he pressed his foot hard, and asked him if he could feel; and he said, No; and then his leg, and

120 so upwards and upwards, and showed us that he was cold and stiff. And he felt them himself, and said: When the poison reaches the heart, that will be the end. He was beginning to grow cold about the groin, when he uncovered his face, for he had covered himself up, and said—they were his last words—he said: Crito, I owe a cock to

125 Asclepius[1]; will you remember to pay the debt? The debt shall be paid, said Crito; is there anything else? There was no answer to this question; but in a minute or two a movement was heard, and the attendants uncovered him; his eyes were set, and Crito closed his eyes and mouth.

130   Such was the end, Echecrates, of our friend; concerning whom I may truly say, that of all the men of his time whom I have known, he was the wisest and most just and best.

---

[1]   An offering was made to Asclepius by one who was recovering from an illness.

Thomas Aquinas

Summa Theologiae

First Part, Question 75

Article One: Whether the soul is a body?

OBJ 1: It would seem that the soul is a body. For the soul is the moving principle of the body. Nor does it move unless moved. First, because seemingly nothing can move unless it is itself moved, since
5 nothing gives what it has not; for instance, what is not hot does not give heat. Secondly, because if there be anything that moves and is not moved, it must be the cause of eternal, unchanging movement, as we find proved in the <u>Physics</u> viii, 6; and this does not appear to be the case in the movement of an animal, which is caused by the soul.
10 Therefore the soul is a mover moved. But every mover moved is a body. Therefore the soul is a body.

OBJ 2: Further, all knowledge is caused by means of a likeness. But there can be no likeness of a body to an incorporeal thing. If, therefore, the soul were not a body, it could not have knowledge of
15 corporeal things.

OBJ 3: Further, between the mover and the moved there must be contact. But contact is only between bodies. Since, therefore, the soul moves the body, it seems that the soul must be a body.

On the contrary, Augustine says (<u>On the Trinity</u> vi, 6) that the
20 soul "is simple in comparison with the body, inasmuch as it does not occupy space by its bulk."

I answer that, To seek the nature of the soul, we must premise that the soul is defined as the first principle of life of those things which live: for we call living things **animate**, i.e. having a soul, and
25 those things which have no life, **inanimate**. Now life is shown principally by two actions, knowledge and movement. The philosophers of old, not being able to rise above their imagination, supposed that the principle of these actions was something corporeal:

for they asserted that only bodies were real things; and that what is
30   not corporeal is nothing: hence they maintained that the soul is
something corporeal. This opinion can be proved to be false in many
ways; but we shall make use of only one proof, based on universal and
certain principles, which shows clearly that the soul is not a body.

It is manifest that not every principle of vital action is a soul, for
35   then the eye would be a soul, as it is a principle of vision; and the
same might be applied to the other instruments of the soul: but it is
the **first principle of life**, which we call **the soul**. Now, though a
body may be a principle of life, or to be a living thing, as the heart is a
principle of life in an animal, yet nothing corporeal can be the first
40   principle of life. For it is clear that to be a principle of life, or to be a
living thing, does not belong to a body as such; since, if that were the
case, every body would be a living thing, or a principle of life.
Therefore a body is competent to be a living thing or even a principle
of life, as "such" a body. Now that it is actually such a body, it owes to
45   some principle which is called its act. Therefore the soul, which is the
first principle of life, is not a body, but the act of a body; thus heat,
which is the principle of calefaction, is not a body, but an act of a
body.

Reply OBJ 1: As everything which is in motion must be moved by
50   something else, a process which cannot be prolonged indefinitely, we
must allow that not every mover is moved. For, since to be moved is
to pass from potentiality to actuality, the mover gives what it has to
the thing moved, inasmuch as it causes it to be in act. But, as is
shown in the <u>Physics</u> viii, 6, there is a mover which is altogether
55   immovable, and not moved either essentially, or accidentally; and
such a mover can cause an invariable movement. There is, however,
another kind of mover, which, though not moved essentially, is moved
accidentally; and for this reason it does not cause an invariable
movement; such a mover, is the soul. There is, again, another mover,
60   which is moved essentially—namely, the body. And because the
philosophers of old believed that nothing existed but bodies, they
maintained that every mover is moved; and that the soul is moved
directly, and is a body.

Reply OBJ 2: The likeness of a thing known is not of necessity
65   actually in the nature of the knower; but given a thing which knows
potentially, and afterwards knows actually, the likeness of the thing

known must be in the nature of the knower, not actually, but only potentially; thus color is not actually in the pupil of the eye, but only potentially. Hence it is necessary, not that the likeness of corporeal
70 things should be actually in the nature of the soul, but that there be a potentiality in the soul for such a likeness. But the ancient philosophers omitted to distinguish between actuality and potentiality; and so they held that the soul must be a body in order to have knowledge of a body; and that it must be composed of the
75 principles of which all bodies are formed in order to know all bodies.

Reply OBJ 3: There are two kinds of contact; of **quantity**, and of **power**. By the former a body can be touched only by a body; by the latter a body can be touched by an incorporeal thing, which moves that body.

Article Two: Whether the human soul is something subsistent?

(subsistent ≈ what exists in its own right)

OBJ 1: It would seem that the human soul is not something subsistent. For that which subsists is said to be "this particular thing." Now "this particular thing" is said not of the soul, but of that which is composed of soul and body. Therefore the soul is not
5 something subsistent.

OBJ 2: Further, everything subsistent operates. But the soul does not operate; for, as the Philosopher says (<u>On the Soul</u> i, 4), "to say that the soul feels or understands is like saying that the soul weaves or builds." Therefore the soul is not subsistent.

10 OBJ 3: Further, if the soul were subsistent, it would have some operation apart from the body. But it has no operation apart from the body, not even that of understanding: for the act of understanding does not take place without a phantasm, which cannot exist apart from the body. Therefore the human soul is not something subsistent.

15 On the contrary, Augustine says (<u>On the Trinity</u> x, 7): "Who understands that the nature of the soul is that of a substance and not that of a body, will see that those who maintain the corporeal nature of the soul, are led astray through associating with the soul those things without which they are unable to think of any nature—i.e.
20 imaginary pictures of corporeal things." Therefore the nature of the

human intellect is not only incorporeal, but it is also a substance, that is, something subsistent.

I answer that, It must necessarily be allowed that the principle of intellectual operation which we call the soul, is a principle both
25 incorporeal and subsistent. For it is clear that by means of the intellect man can have knowledge of all corporeal things. Now whatever knows certain things cannot have any of them in its own nature; because that which is in it naturally would impede the knowledge of anything else. Thus we observe that a sick man's tongue
30 being vitiated by a feverish and bitter humor, is insensible to anything sweet, and everything seems bitter to it. Therefore, if the intellectual principle contained the nature of a body it would be unable to know all bodies. Now every body has its own determinate nature. Therefore it is impossible for the intellectual principle to be a
35 body. It is likewise impossible for it to understand by means of a bodily organ; since the determinate nature of that organ would impede knowledge of all bodies; as when a certain determinate color is not only in the pupil of the eye, but also in a glass vase, the liquid in the vase seems to be of that same color.

40   Therefore the intellectual principle which we call the mind or the intellect has an operation per se apart from the body. Now only that which subsists can have an operation per se. For nothing can operate but what is actual: for which reason we do not say that heat imparts heat, but that what is hot gives heat. We must conclude, therefore,
45 that the human soul, which is called the intellect or the mind, is something incorporeal and subsistent.

Reply OBJ 1: "This particular thing" can be taken in two senses. Firstly, for anything subsistent; secondly, for that which subsists, and is complete in a specific nature. The former sense excludes the
50 inherence of an accident or of a material form; the latter excludes also the imperfection of the part, so that a hand can be called "this particular thing" in the first sense, but not in the second. Therefore, as the human soul is a part of human nature, it can indeed be called "this particular thing," in the first sense, as being something
55 subsistent; but not in the second, for in this sense, what is composed of body and soul is said to be "this particular thing."

Reply OBJ 2: Aristotle wrote those words as expressing not his own opinion, but the opinion of those who said that to understand is

to be moved, as is clear from the context. Or we may reply that to
60 operate per se belongs to what exists per se. But for a thing to exist
per se, it suffices sometimes that it be not inherent, as an accident or
a material form; even though it be part of something. Nevertheless,
that is rightly said to subsist per se, which is neither inherent in the
above sense, nor part of anything else. In this sense, the eye or the
65 hand cannot be said to subsist per se; nor can it for that reason be
said to operate per se. Hence the operation of the parts is through
each part attributed to the whole. For we say that man sees with the
eye, and feels with the hand, and not in the same sense as when we
say that what is hot gives heat by its heat; for heat, strictly speaking,
70 does not give heat. We may therefore say that the soul understands,
as the eye sees; but it is more correct to say that man understands
through the soul.

Reply OBJ 3: The body is necessary for the action of the intellect,
not as its origin of action, but on the part of the object; for the
75 phantasm is to the intellect what color is to the sight. Neither does
such a dependence on the body prove the intellect to be non-
subsistent; otherwise it would follow that an animal is non-
subsistent, since it requires external objects of the senses in order to
perform its act of perception.

Article Three: Whether the souls of brute animals are subsistent?

OBJ 1: It would seem that the souls of brute animals are
subsistent. For man is of the same genus as other animals; and, as we
have just shown (A2), the soul of man is subsistent. Therefore the
souls of other animals are subsistent.
5 OBJ 2: Further, the relation of the sensitive faculty to sensible
objects is like the relation of the intellectual faculty to intelligible
objects. But the intellect, apart from the body, apprehends intelligible
objects. Therefore the sensitive faculty, apart from the body, perceives
sensible objects. Therefore, since the souls of brute animals are
10 sensitive, it follows that they are subsistent; just as the human
intellectual soul is subsistent.
OBJ 3: Further, the soul of brute animals moves the body. But
the body is not a mover, but is moved. Therefore the soul of brute
animals has an operation apart from the body.

15   On the contrary, Is what is written in the book *On the Teachings of the Church* xvi, xvii: "Man alone we believe to have a subsistent soul: whereas the souls of animals are not subsistent."

        I answer that, The ancient philosophers made no distinction between sense and intellect, and referred both a corporeal principle,
20   as has been said (A1). Plato, however, drew a distinction between intellect and sense; yet he referred both to an incorporeal principle, maintaining that sensing, just as understanding, belongs to the soul as such. From this it follows that even the souls of brute animals are subsistent. But Aristotle held that of the operations of the soul,
25   understanding alone is performed without a corporeal organ. On the other hand, sensation and the consequent operations of the sensitive soul are evidently accompanied with change in the body; thus in the act of vision, the pupil of the eye is affected by a reflection of color: and so with the other senses. Hence it is clear that the sensitive soul
30   has no per se operation of its own, and that every operation of the sensitive soul belongs to the composite. Wherefore we conclude that as the souls of brute animals have no per se operations they are not subsistent. For the operation of anything follows the mode of its being.
35   Reply OBJ 1: Although man is of the same "genus" as other animals, he is of a different "species." Specific difference is derived from the difference of form; nor does every difference of form necessarily imply a diversity of "genus."

        Reply OBJ 2: The relation of the sensitive faculty to the sensible
40   object is in one way the same as that of the intellectual faculty to the intelligible object, in so far as each is in potentiality to its object. But in another way their relations differ, inasmuch as the impression of the object on the sense is accompanied with change in the body; so that excessive strength of the sensible corrupts sense; a thing that
45   never occurs in the case of the intellect. For an intellect that understands the highest of intelligible objects is more able afterwards to understand those that are lower. If, however, in the process of intellectual operation the body is weary, this result is accidental, inasmuch as the intellect requires the operation of the sensitive
50   powers in the production of the phantasms.

        Reply OBJ 3: Motive power is of two kinds. One, the appetitive power, commands motion. The operation of this power in the sensitive

soul is not apart from the body; for anger, joy, and passions of a like nature are accompanied by a change in the body. The other motive
55 power is that which executes motion in adapting the members for obeying the appetite; and the act of this power does not consist in moving, but in being moved. Whence it is clear that to move is not an act of the sensitive soul without the body.

Article Six: Whether the human soul is incorruptible?

OBJ 3: Further, nothing is without its own proper operation. But the operation proper to the soul, which is to understand through a phantasm, cannot be without the body. For the soul understands nothing without a phantasm; and there is no phantasm without the
5 body as the Philosopher says (On the Soul i, 1). Therefore the soul cannot survive the dissolution of the body.

On the contrary, Dionysius says (On the Divine Names iv) that human souls owe to Divine goodness that they are "intellectual," and that they have "an incorruptible substantial life."
10 I answer that, We must assert that the intellectual principle which we call the human soul is incorruptible. For a thing may be corrupted in two ways—**per se (essentially)**, and **accidentally**. Now it is impossible for any substance to be generated or corrupted accidentally, that is, by the generation or corruption of something else. For generation and corruption belong to a thing, just as
15 existence belongs to it, which is acquired by generation and lost by corruption. Therefore, whatever has existence per se cannot be generated or corrupted except per se; while things which do not subsist, such as accidents and material forms, acquire existence or
20 lost it through the generation or corruption of composite things. Now it was shown above (AA2, 3) that the souls of brutes are not self-subsistent, whereas the human soul is; so that the souls of brutes are corrupted, when their bodies are corrupted; while the human soul could not be corrupted unless it were corrupted per se. This, indeed,
25 is impossible, not only as regards the human soul, but also as regards anything subsistent that is a form alone. For it is clear that what belongs to a thing by virtue of itself is inseparable from it; but existence belongs to a form, which is an act, by virtue of itself. Wherefore matter acquires actual existence as it acquires the form;
30 while it is corrupted so far as the form is separated from it. But it is

impossible for a form to be separated from itself; and therefore it is impossible for a subsistent form to cease to exist.

Granted even that the soul is composed of matter and form, as some pretend, we should nevertheless have to maintain that it is
35 incorruptible. For corruption is found only where there is contrariety; since generation and corruption are from contraries and into contraries. Wherefore the heavenly bodies, since they have no matter subject to contrariety, are incorruptible. Now there can be no contrariety in the intellectual soul; for it receives according to the
40 manner of its existence, and those things which it receives are without contrariety; for the notions even of contraries are not themselves contrary, since contraries belong to the same knowledge. Therefore it is impossible for the intellectual soul to be corruptible. Moreover we may take a sign of this from the fact that everything
45 naturally aspires to existence after its own manner. Now, in things that have knowledge, desire ensues upon knowledge. The senses indeed do not know existence, except under the conditions of **here** and **now**, whereas the intellect apprehends existence absolutely, and for all time; so that everything that has an intellect naturally desires
50 always to exist. But a natural desire cannot be in vain. Therefore every intellectual substance is incorruptible.

Reply OBJ 3: To understand through a phantasm is the proper operation of the soul by virtue of its union with the body. After separation from the body it will have another mode of understanding,
55 similar to other substances separated from bodies, as will appear later on (Q89,A1).

III. GOD

We have selected passages from the writings of materialism, Platonic formalism, and the Aristotelian and Thomistic account, to see the implications a certain explanation of nature may have for matters which go beyond the natural order of things. We have chosen God, and in particular the existence of God, as a matter which finds itself near the absolute limit of philosophical thought.

What would a materialist have to tell us about God, and whether God exists or not? Lucretius himself, in *On the Nature of Things*, expresses his view and defends it. Once again, he is taken to represent the Pre-Socratic materialistic account of the natural world. Similarly with the Platonic account. Is there any special way of considering this question which Plato's formalism may shed some light on? We have taken passages from a lesser-known dialogue, *the Laws*, to give an indication of what Plato himself would say.

Finally, what do Aristotle and Thomas Aquinas have to say about the existence of God—once more, it must be emphasized, from a *philosophical* perspective, that is, from the perspective of reason alone, and not from the privileged viewpoint of Faith (recall that Aquinas was a Catholic theologian as well as a philosopher.) Does the account of nature we have learned from these men allow them to deal consistently with God and, perhaps, even provide arguments for His very existence?

Lucretius

On the Nature of Things

Selections from Book V

The order of my design has now brought me to this point, where I must proceed to show that the world is formed of a mortal body and at the same time had birth; to show too in what way that union of matter founded earth, heaven, sea, stars, sun, and the ball of the
5 moon; also what living creatures sprang out of the earth, as well as those which never at any time were born; in what way too mankind began to use with one another varied speech by the names conferred on things; and also in what ways the fear of the gods gained an entry into men's breasts, and now throughout the world maintains as holy
10 temples, lakes, groves, altars, and idols of the gods. Furthermore I shall make clear by what force piloting nature guides the courses of the sun and the wanderings of the moon; lest perhaps we imagine that these of their own free will between heaven and earth traverse their everlasting orbits, graciously furthering the increase of crops
15 and living creatures, or we think they roll on by any forethought of the gods. For they who have been rightly taught that the gods lead a life without care, if nevertheless they wonder by what plan all things can be carried on, above all in regard to those things which are seen overhead in the ethereal borders, are carried back again into their old
20 religious scruples and take to themselves hard taskmasters, whom they, poor wretches, believe to be almighty, not knowing what can, what cannot be, in short by what system each thing has its powers defined, its deep-set boundary mark.

Well then not to detain you any longer by mere promises, look
25 before all on seas and lands and heaven: their threefold nature, their three bodies, Memmius, three forms so unlike, three such wondrous textures a single day shall give over to destruction; and the mass and fabric of the world upheld for many years shall tumble to ruin. Nor can I fail to perceive with what a novel and strange effect it falls upon
30 the mind, this destruction of heaven and earth that is to be, and how

hard it is for me to produce a full conviction of it by words; as is the case when you bring to the ears a thing as yet without example, and yet you cannot submit it to the eyesight nor put it into the hands; through which the straightest highway of belief leads into the human
35 breast and quarters of the mind. But yet I will speak out: it well may be that the reality itself will bring credit to my words and that you will see earthquakes arise and all things grievously shattered to pieces in short time. But this may pilot fortune guide far away from us, and may reason rather than the reality convince that all things
40 may be overpowered and tumble in with a frightful crash.

But before I shall begin on this question to pour forth decrees of fate with more sanctity and much more certainty than the Pythia who speaks out from the tripod and laurel of Phoebus, I will clearly set forth to you many comforting topics in learned language; lest held
45 in the yoke of religion you might suppose that earth and sun and heaven, sea, stars, and moon must last for ever with divine body; and therefore think it right that they after the fashion of the giants should all suffer punishment for their monstrous guilt, who by their reasoning displace the walls of the world and seek to quench the
50 glorious sun of heaven, branding immortal things in mortal speech; though in truth these things are so far from possessing divinity and are so unworthy of being reckoned in the number of gods, that they may be thought to afford a notable instance of what is quite without vital motion and sense. For it is quite impossible to suppose that the
55 nature and judgment of the mind can exist with just any body whatever; even as a tree cannot exist in the ether nor clouds in the salt sea, nor can fishes live in the fields nor blood exist in woods nor sap in stones. Where each thing can grow and abide is fixed and ordained. Thus the nature of the mind cannot come into being alone
60 without the body nor exist far away from the sinews and blood. But if (for this would be much more likely to happen than that) the force itself of the mind might be in the head or shoulders or heels or might be born in any other part of the body, it would after all be wont to abide in one and the same man or vessel. But since in our body even
65 it is fixed and seen to be ordained where the soul and the mind can severally be and grow, it must still more strenuously be denied that it can abide out of the body and the living place altogether in crumbling clods of earth or in the fire of the sun or in water or in the high

borders of ether. These things therefore are not possessed of divine
70   sense, since they cannot be quickened with the vital feeling.

This too you cannot possibly believe, that the holy seats of the
gods exist in any parts of the world: the fine nature of the gods far
withdrawn from our senses is hardly seen by the thought of the mind;
and since it has ever eluded the touch and stroke of the hands, it
75   must touch nothing which is tangible for us; for that cannot touch
which does not admit of being touched in turn. And therefore their
seats as well must be unlike our seats, fine, even as their bodies are
fine. All which I will prove to you later in copious argument. To say
again that for the sake of men they have willed to set in order the
80   glorious nature of the world and therefore it is right to praise the
work of the gods, calling as it does for all praise, and to believe that it
will be eternal and immortal, and that it is an unholy thing ever to
shake by any force from its fixed seats that which by the forethought
of the gods in ancient days has been established on everlasting
85   foundations for mankind, or to assail it by speech and utterly
overturn it from top to bottom; and to invent and add other figments
of the kind, Memmius, is all sheer folly. For what advantage can our
gratitude bestow on immortal and blessed beings, that for our sakes
they should take in hand to administer anything? And what novel
90   incident should have induced them at rest so long up to now to desire
to change their former life? For it seems natural he should rejoice in a
new state of things, whom old things annoy; but for him whom no ill
has befallen in times gone by, when he passed a pleasant existence,
what could have kindled in such a one a love of change? Did life lie
95   groveling in darkness and sorrow, until the first dawn of the birth of
things? Or what evil had it been for us never to have been born?
Whoever has been born must want to continue in life, so long as fond
pleasure shall keep him; but for him who has never tasted the love,
never been on the lists, of life, what harm not to have been born?
100   Whence again was first implanted in the gods a pattern for begetting
things in general as well as the preconception of what men are, so
that they knew and saw in mind what they wanted to make? And in
what way was the power of first-beginnings ever ascertained, and
what they could effect by a change in their mutual arrangements,
105   unless nature herself gave the model for making things? For in this
way the first-beginnings of things many in number in many ways

impelled by blows for infinite ages back and kept in motion by their own weights have been carried along and to unite in all manner of ways and thoroughly test every kind of production possible by their
110 mutual combinations; that it is not strange if they have also fallen into arrangements and have come into patterns like to those out of which this sum of things is now carried on by constant renewing.

But if I did not know what the first-beginnings of things are, yet this judging by the very arrangements of heaven I would venture to
115 affirm, and led by many other facts to maintain, that the nature of things has by no means been made for us by divine power: so great are the defects with which it is encumbered. In the first place of all the space which the vast reach of heaven covers, a portion greedy mountains and forests of wild beasts have occupied, rocks and
120 wasteful pools take up and the sea which holds wide apart the coasts of different lands. Next of nearly two thirds burning heat and the constant fall of frost rob mortals. What is left for tillage, even that nature by its power would overrun with thorns, unless the force of man made head against it, accustomed for the sake of a livelihood to
125 groan beneath the strong hoe and to cut through the earth by pressing down the plough. Unless by turning up the fruitful clods with the share and laboring the soil of the earth we stimulate things to rise, they could not spontaneously come up into the clear air; and even then sometimes when things earned with great toil now put
130 forth their leaves over the lands and are all in blossom, either the ethereal sun burns them up with excessive heats or sudden rains and cold frosts cut them off, and the blasts of the winds waste them by a furious hurricane. Again why does nature give food and increase to the frightful race of wild beasts dangerous to mankind both by sea
135 and land? Why do the seasons of the year bring diseases in their train? Why stalks abroad untimely death? Then too the baby, like to a sailor cast away by the cruel waves, lies naked on the ground, speechless, wanting every furtherance of life, soon as nature by the throes of birth has shed him forth from his mother's womb into the
140 borders of light: he fills the room with a rueful wailing, as well he may whose destiny it is to go through in life so many ills. But the different flocks, herds, and wild beasts grow up; they want no rattles; to none of them need be addressed the fond broken accents of the fostering nurse; they ask not different dresses according to the

145 season; no nor do they want arms or lofty walls whereby to protect their own, the earth itself and nature manifold in her works producing in plenty all things for all.

First of all, since the body of the earth and water and the light breath of air and burning heats, out of which this sum of things is
150 seen to be formed, do all consist of a body that had a birth and is mortal, the whole nature of the world must be reckoned of a like body. For those things whose parts and members we see to be of a body that had a birth and of forms that are mortal, we perceive to be likewise without exception mortal, and at the same time to have had a birth.
155 Since therefore I see that the principal members and parts of the world are destroyed and begotten anew, I may be sure that for heaven and earth as well there has been a time of beginning and there will be a time of destruction.

Again if there was no birth-time of earth and heaven and they
160 have been from everlasting, why before the Theban war and the destruction of Troy have not other poets as well sung other themes? Whither have so many deeds of men so often passed away, why live they nowhere embodied in lasting records of fame? The truth, I think, is that the sum has but a recent date and the nature of the world is
165 new and has but lately had its commencement. Wherefore even now some arts are receiving their last polish, some are even in course of growth: just now many improvements have been made in ships; only yesterday musicians have given birth to tuneful melodies; then too this nature or system of things has been discovered lately, and I the
170 very first of all have only now been found able to transfer it into native words. But if you happen to believe that before this all things have existed just the same, but that the generations of men have perished by burning heat, or that cities have fallen by some great concussion of the world, or that after constant rains devouring rivers
175 have gone forth over the earth and have destroyed towns, so much the more you must yield and admit that there will be entire destruction too of earth and heaven; for when things were tried by so great distempers and so great dangers, at that time had a more disastrous cause pressed upon them, they would far and wide have
180 gone to destruction and mighty ruin. And in no other way are we proved to be mortals, except because we all alike in turn fall sick of

the same diseases which those had whom nature has withdrawn from life.

But in what ways the concourse of matter founded earth and
185 heaven and the deeps of the sea, the courses of the sun and moon, I
will next in order describe. For verily not by design did the first-
beginnings of things station themselves each in its right place by
keen intelligence, nor did they bargain to say what motions each
should assume, but because the first-beginnings of things many in
190 number in many ways impelled by blows for infinite ages back and
kept in motion by their own weights have been carried along and to
unite in all manner of ways and thoroughly to test every kind of
production possible by their mutual combinations, therefore it is that
spread abroad through great time after trying unions and motions of
195 every kind they at length meet together in those masses which
suddenly brought together become often the rudiments of great
things, of earth, sea, and heaven and the race of living things.

Plato

The Laws

Book X, 884-896

Athenian. And now having spoken of assaults, let us sum up all acts of violence under a single law, which shall be as follows:—No one shall take or carry away any of his neighbor's goods, neither shall he use anything which is his neighbor's without the consent of the
5 owner; for these are the offenses which are and have been, and will ever be, the source of all the aforesaid evils. The greatest of them are excesses and insolences of youth, and are offenses against the greatest when they are done against religion; and especially great when in violation of public and holy rites, or of the partly-common
10 rites in which tribes and phratries share; and in the second degree great when they are committed against private rites and sepulchers, and in the third degree (not to repeat the acts formerly mentioned), when insults are offered to parents; the fourth kind of violence is when any one, regardless of the authority of the rulers, takes or
15 carries away or makes use of anything which belongs to them, not having their consent; and the fifth kind is when the violation of the civil rights of an individual demands reparation. There should be a common law embracing all these cases. For we have already said in general terms what shall be the punishment of the sacrilege, whether
20 fraudulent or violent, and now we have to determine what is to be the punishment of those who speak or act insolently toward the Gods. But first we must give them an admonition which may be in the following terms:—No one who in obedience to the laws believed that there were Gods, ever intentionally do any unholy act, or uttered any
25 unlawful word; but he who did must have supposed one of three things,—either that they did not exist,—which is the first possibility, or secondly, that, if they did, they took no care of man, or thirdly, that they were easily appeased and turned aside from their purpose by sacrifices and prayers.
30   Cleinias.   What shall we say or do to these persons?

227

Athenian. My good friend, let us first hear the jests which I suspect that they in their superiority will utter against us.

Cleinias.   What jests?

Athenian. They will make some irreverent speech of this
35 sort:—'O inhabitants of Athens, and Sparta, and Cnosus,' they will reply, 'in that you speak truly; for some of us deny the very existence of the Gods, while others, as you say, are of opinion that they do not care about us; and others that they are turned from their course by gifts. Now we have a right to claim, as you yourself allowed, in the
40 matter of laws, that before you are hard upon us and threaten us, you should argue with us and convince us—you should first attempt to teach and persuade us that there are Gods by reasonable evidences, and also that they are too good to be unrighteous, or to be propitiated, or turned from their course by gifts. For when we hear such things
45 said of them by those who are esteemed to be the best of poets, and orators, and prophets, and priests, and by innumerable others, the thoughts of most of us are not set upon abstaining from unrighteous acts, but upon doing them and atoning for them. When lawgivers profess that they are gentle and not stern, we think that they should
50 first of all use persuasion to us, and show us the existence of Gods, if not in a better manner than other men, at any rate in a truer; and who knows but that we shall hearken to you? If then our request is a fair one, please to accept our challenge.'

Cleinias.   But is there any difficulty in proving the existence of
55 the Gods?

Athenian.   How would you prove it?

Cleinias.   How? In the first place, the earth and the sun, and the stars and the universe, and the fair order of the seasons, and the division of them into years and months, furnish proofs of their
60 existence; and also there is the fact that all Hellenes and barbarians believe in them.

Athenian. I fear, my sweet friend, though I will not say that I much regard, the contempt with which the profane will be likely to assail us. For you do not understand the nature of their complaint,
65 and you fancy that they rush into impiety only from a love of sensual pleasure.

Cleinias.   Why, Stranger, what other reason is there?

Athenian. One which you who live in a different atmosphere would never guess.

70 Cleinias. What is it?

Athenian. A very grievous sort of ignorance which is imagined to be the greatest wisdom.

Cleinias. What do you mean?

Athenian. At Athens there are tales preserved in writing which
75 the virtue of your state, as I am informed, refuses to admit. They speak of the Gods in prose as well as verse, and the oldest of them tell of the origins of the heavens and of the world, and not far from the beginning of their story they proceed to narrate the birth of the Gods, and how after they were born they behaved to one another. Whether
80 these stories have in other ways a good or a bad influence, I should not like to be severe upon them, because they are ancient; but, looking at them with reference to the duties of children to their parents, I cannot praise them, or think that they are useful, or at all true. Of the words of the ancients I have nothing more to say; and I
85 should wish to say of them only what is pleasing to the Gods. But as to our younger generation and their wisdom, I cannot let them off when they do mischief. For do but mark the effect of their words: when you and I argue for the existence of the Gods, and produce the sun, moon, stars, and earth, claiming for them a divine being, if we
90 would listen to the aforesaid philosophers we should say that they are earth and stones only, which can have no care at all of human affairs, and that all religion is a cooking up of words and a make-believe. ...

Cleinias. What a dreadful picture, Stranger, have you given, and how great is the injury which is thus inflicted on young men to
95 the ruin both of states and families!

Athenian. True, Cleinias; but then what should the lawgiver do when this evil is of long standing? should he only rise up in the state and threaten all mankind, proclaiming that if they will not say and think that the Gods are such as the law ordains (and this may be
100 extended generally to the honorable, the just, and to all the highest things, and to all that relates to virtue and vice), and if they will not make their actions conform to the copy which the law gives them, then he who refuses to obey the law shall die, or suffer stripes and

bonds, or privation of citizenship, or in some cases be punished by
105 loss of property and exile? Should he not rather, when he is making
laws for men, at the same time infuse the spirit of persuasion into his
words, and mitigate the severity of them as far as he can?

Cleinias.   Why, Stranger, if such persuasion be at all possible,
then a legislator who has anything in him ought never to weary of
110 persuading men; he ought to leave nothing unsaid in support of the
ancient opinion that there are Gods, and of all those other truths
which you were just now mentioning; he ought to support the law and
also art, and acknowledge that both alike exist by nature, and no less
than nature, if they are the creations of mind in accordance with
115 right reason, as you appear to me to maintain, and I am disposed to
agree with you in thinking.

Athenian. Yes, my enthusiastic Cleinias; but are not these
things when spoken to a multitude hard to be understood, not to
mention that they take up a dismal length of time?

120 Cleinias.   Why, Stranger, shall we, whose patience failed not
when drinking or music were the themes of discourse, weary now of
discoursing about the Gods, and about Divine things? And the
greatest help to rational legislation is that the laws when once
written down are always at rest; they can be put to the test at any
125 future time, and therefore, if on first hearing they seem difficult,
there is no reason for apprehension about them, because any man
however dull can go over them and consider them again and again;
nor if they are tedious but useful, is there any reason or religion, as it
seems to me, in any man refusing to maintain the principles of them
130 to the utmost of his power.

Megillus   Stranger, I like what Cleinias is saying.

Athenian. Yes, Megillus, and we should do as he proposes; for if
impious discourses were not scattered, as I may say, throughout the
world, there would have been no need for any vindication of the
135 existence of the Gods—but seeing that they are spread far and wide,
such arguments are needed; and who should come to the rescue of the
greatest laws, when they are being undermined by bad men, but the
legislator himself?

Megillus   There is no more proper champion of them.

140 Athenian. Well, then, tell me, Cleinias,—for I must ask you to be
my partner,—does not he who talks in this way conceive fire and

water and earth and air to be the first elements of all things? these he calls nature, and out of these he supposes the soul to be formed afterwards; and this is not a mere conjecture of ours about his
145 meaning, but is what he really means.

Cleinias.   Very true.

Athenian.   Then, by Heaven, we have discovered the source of this vain opinion of all those physical investigators; and I would have you examine their arguments with the utmost care, for their impiety
150 is a very serious matter; they not only make a bad and mistaken use of argument, but they lead away the minds of others: that is my opinion of them.

Cleinias.   You are right, but I should like to know how this happens.
155 Athenian.   I fear that the argument may seem singular.

Cleinias.   Do not hesitate, Stranger; I see that you are afraid of such a discussion carrying you beyond the limits of legislation. But if there be no other way of showing our agreement in the belief that there are Gods, of whom the law is said now to approve, let us take
160 this way, my good sir.

Athenian.   Then I suppose that I must repeat the singular argument of those who manufacture the soul according to their own impious notions; they affirm that which is the first cause of the generation and destruction of all things, to be not first, but last, and
165 that which is last to be first, and hence they have fallen into error about the true nature of the Gods.

Cleinias.   Still I do not understand you.

Athenian.   Nearly all of them, my friends, seem to be ignorant of the nature and power of the soul, especially in what relates to her
170 origin: they do not know that she is among the first of things, and before all bodies, and is the chief author of their changes and transpositions. And if this is true, and if the soul is older than the body, must not the things which are of the soul's kindred be of necessity prior to those which appertain to the body?
175 Cleinias.   Certainly.

Athenian.   Then thought and attention and mind and art and law will be prior to that which is hard and soft and heavy and light; and the great and primitive works and actions will be works of art; they will be the first, and after them will come nature and works of nature,

180 which however is a wrong term for men to apply to them; these will
follow, and will be under the government of art and mind.

Cleinias.   But why is the word 'nature' wrong?

Athenian.   Because those who use the term mean to say that
nature is the first creative power; but if the soul turned out to be the
185 first primeval element, and not fire or air, then in the truest sense
and beyond other things the soul may be said to exist by nature; and
this would be true if you proved that the soul is older than the body,
but not otherwise.

Cleinias.   You are quite right.

190 Athenian.   Shall we, then, take this as the next point to which
our attention should be directed?

Cleinias.   By all means.

Athenian.   Come, then, and if ever we are to call upon the Gods,
let us call upon them now in all seriousness to come to the
195 demonstration of their own existence. And so holding fast to the rope
we will venture upon the depths of the argument. When questions of
this sort are asked of me, my safest answer would appear to be as
follows:—Some one says to me, 'O Stranger, are all things at rest and
nothing in motion, or is the exact opposite of this true, or are some
200 things in motion and others at rest?'—To this I shall reply that some
things are in motion and others at rest.

Everything which is thus changing and moving is in process of
generation; only when at rest has it real existence, but when passing
into another state it is destroyed utterly. Have we not mentioned all
205 motions that there are, and comprehended them under their kinds
and numbered them with the exception, my friends, of two?

Cleinias.   Which are they?

Athenian.   Just the two, with which our present inquiry is
concerned.

210 Cleinias.   Speak plainer.

Athenian.   I suppose that our inquiry has reference to the soul?

Cleinias.   Very true.

Athenian.   Let us assume that there is a motion able to move
other things, but not to move itself;—that is one kind; and there is
215 another kind which can move itself as well as other things, working

in composition and decomposition, by increase and diminution and generation and destruction,—that is also one of the many kinds of motion.

Cleinias. Granted.

220 Athenian. And we will assume that which is moved by other, and is changed by other, to be the ninth, and that which changes itself and others, and is coincident with every action and every passion, and is the true principle of change and motion in all that is,—that we shall be inclined to call the tenth.

225 Cleinias. Certainly.

Athenian. And which of these ten motions ought we to prefer as being the mightiest and most efficient?

Cleinias. I must say that the motion which is able to move itself is ten thousand times superior to all the others.

230 Athenian. Very good; but may I make one or two corrections in what I have been saying?

Cleinias. What are they?

Athenian. When I spoke of the tenth sort of motion, that was not quite correct.

235 Cleinias. What was the error?

Athenian. According to the true order, the tenth was really the first in generation and power; then follows the second, which was strangely enough termed the ninth by us.

Cleinias. What do you mean?

240 Athenian. I mean this: when one thing changes another, and that another, of such will there be any primary changing element? How can a thing which is moved by another ever be the beginning of change? Impossible. But when the self-moved changes another, and that again another, and thus thousands upon tens of thousands of 245 bodies are set in motion, must not the principle of all this motion be the change of the self-moving principle?

Cleinias. Very true, and I quite agree.

Athenian. Or, to put the question in another way, making answer to ourselves:—If, as most of these philosophers have the 250 audacity to affirm, all things were at rest in one mass, which of the above-mentioned principles of motion would first spring up among them?

Cleinias.   Clearly, the self-moving; for there could be no change
in them arising out of any external cause; the change must first take
255 place in themselves.

Athenian.   Then we must say that self-motion being the origin of
all motions, and the first which arises among things at rest as well as
among things in motion, is the eldest and mightiest principle of
change, and that which is changed by another and yet moves another
260 is second.

Aristotle

Physics VII

Chapter 1

Everything which is moved must be moved by something: for if it does not have its own principle of motion, it is clear that it is moved by another (for the mover will be another thing:) but if [the principle of its motion] is in itself, let AB be that which is moved *per se*, and not
5 by this, that some part of it is moved. First, then, the assumption that AB is moved by itself because the whole is moved by nothing outside of it is just as if, with KL moving LM and itself being moved, someone were to say that KM is not moved by something because it is not clear whether it is a mover or whether it is moved: further, it is not
10 necessary that what is being moved (but not by something) stops because some other thing has come to rest, but if something which is moved rests because some other thing has stopped, it is necessary that the former is moved by something. Given this, everything which is moved must be moved by something. For since we assumed that AB
15 is moved, it is necessary that it is divisible: for everything which is moved is divisible. Let [AB] be divided at C. Now if CB is not moved then AB will not be moved: for if it were moved, it is clear that AC would move while CB was at rest, so that [AB] would not be moved *per se* and first. Therefore it is necessary that while CB is not moved
20 AB is at rest. But it was agreed that whatever is at rest while some [other] thing is not moved is moved by something, so that everything which is moved is necessarily moved by something: for that which is moved will be continuously divisible, and while a part is not being moved the whole must be at rest.
25 Since, then, everything which is moved must be moved by something, if something is moved according to motion in place by another which is moved, and again the mover is moved by another which is moved, and that one by another, always in this way, it is necessary that there be a first mover, and that it not proceed into the
30 infinite: for let it be not so, but let it be made infinite. And let A be

moved by B, and B by C, and C by D, and always what is next by what is beyond that. Now since it is given that the mover moves what is moved, and the motion of what is moved and that of the mover must occur at the same time (for the mover moves [what is moved]

35 and what is moved is moved at the same time)—then it is clear that the motion of A and of B and of C and of each of the movers and things which are moved will be simultaneous. Let there be the motion of each, and let that of A be E, that of B be F, and those of C and D be G and H. For even though each is always moved by each, we may

40 take the motion of each in this way as one in number: for every motion is from something to something, and it is not infinite with respect to its extremes. Now I call 'one in number' a motion which proceeds from something one and the same in number to something one in number in a time one and the same in number. For motion

45 may be the same in kind and in species and in number: in kind, on the one hand, that which is of the same category, as of substance or of quality, in species, that which is from something the same in species to something the same in species, as from white to black or from a good to an evil not differing in species, and in number, that which is

50 from what is one in number to what is one in number in the same time, as from this white to this black, or from this place to that place, in this time: for if it is in another [time,] the motion will not be one in number but in species. We have spoken of these things already.

Let us assume the time in which A moved according to its motion,
55 and let it be K. Now when the motion of A is completed the time will also be completed. And since the movers and the things which are moved are infinite, the motion EFGH, that of the whole, will also be infinite: for it may be assumed that A and B and the others are equal to each other, or it may be assumed that they are greater than the

60 others, so that if they are either equal to or greater than the others, in either case the whole is infinite: for we assume what is possible. But since A and each of the others moves [another] at the same time, the whole motion will be in the same time as that of A: but that of A was in a completed [time:] so that the infinite [will move] in a finite

65 [time;] but this is impossible. ...for it was assumed that an infinite motion [occurred] in a finite time, not of one thing, but of many. Whence it happens also with these things: for each is moved according to its motion, but that any things are moved at the same

time is not impossible. But if that which is first moving is [moving]
70 according to place, and it is a bodily motion, it is necessary that it is
either touching or continuous with what is being moved, just as we
see with all [the movers and things which are moved,] it is necessary
that the things which are moved and the movers be either touching or
continuous with one another, so that there is a certain one [made up]
75 of all of them. Now this [one] is either finite or infinite; it makes no
difference for the moment: for the motion will be wholly infinite,
being of things which are in finite, for it was assumed that they are
either equal to or greater than each other: for what is possible we
may take as being so.

80   Now whether ABCD is something finite or infinite, the motion
EFGH moves in time K, which in finite, and infinite happens to be
traversed in a finite time, whether this [traversing] is finite or
infinite. And each is impossible: so that it is necessary to make a
stand and [say] that there is something which is a first mover and
85 something which is first being moved: for it makes no difference that
the impossible comes about from a hypothesis: for the hypothesis
assumed was possible, and nothing impossible should come about
from a possible assumption.

Thomas Aquinas

Summa Contra Gentiles

Book I, Chapter 13

First, then, we shall set forth the arguments whereby Aristotle proceeds to prove that God exists; he intends to prove this from motion in two ways.

The first way is as follows: Everything which is moved is moved
5 by another thing. And it is apparent to our senses that something is moved, for example, the sun; and therefore something is moved by another, which is moving it. Either, then, that mover is itself moved, or not. If it is not moved, therefore we have proved that it is necessary to posit some unmoved mover, and we call this God. But if it is itself
10 moved, therefore it is moved by another, which moves it. Either, then, we shall go on ad infinitum, or we must arrive at some unmoved mover. But it is not possible to go on ad infinitum, and therefore it is necessary to posit some first unmoved mover.

Now in this proof there are two propositions which must
15 themselves be proved, namely, that everything which is moved is moved by another, and that among movers and things which are moved one cannot go on ad infinitum.

The first of these the Philosopher proves in three ways.

[We omit the first two proofs.]
20 Thirdly, he proves it in this way: No one thing is both in potency and in act with respect to the same thing at the same time. But everything which is moved, in that respect, is in potency, since motion is the act of what exists in potency insofar as it is such. But everything which moves [another], as such, is in act, since everything
25 acts only to the extent that it is itself in act. Therefore, nothing is both a mover and what is moved with respect to the same thing, and so nothing can move itself.

And the other proposition, that among movers and things which are moved one cannot go on ad infinitum, he proves in three ways.
30 [We omit the first proof.]

The second argument proving the same point is this: among movers and things which are moved in an order, one of which is moved by another in order, it is found that, if the first mover be removed, or stop moving, none of the others will move or be moved, 35 since the first is the cause of the others' moving. Yet if there are movers and things which are moved in order ad infinitum, there will not be a first mover, rather, all will be intermediate movers. Therefore, none of the others will be able to be moved, and so nothing will be moved in the world.

40 The third arguments comes to the same, except that it has a reversed order, beginning with the superior. And it is this: That which moves [another] as an instrument cannot do so unless there be some other which moves principally. But if one were to go on ad infinitum among movers and things which are moved, then all [the 45 movers] will be like instrumental movers, since they were assumed to be moved movers. But then there would be no principal mover, and therefore nothing would be moved [at all].

And so the proof of each of the propositions which was assumed in the first way of demonstration by which Aristotle showed that there 50 is a first unmoved mover is clear.

Thomas Aquinas

Summa Theologiae

First Part, Question 2, Article 3

Whether God exists?

OBJ 1: It seems that God does not exist; because if one of two contraries be infinite, the other would be altogether destroyed. But the word *God* means that He is infinite goodness. If, therefore, God
5 existed, there would be no evil discoverable; but there is evil in the world. Therefore God does not exist.

OBJ 2: Further, it is superfluous to suppose that what can be accounted for by a few principles has been produced by many. But it seems that everything we see in the world can be accounted for by
10 other principles, supposing God did not exist. For all natural things can be reduced to one principle which is nature; and all voluntary things can be reduced to one principle which is human reason, or will. Therefore there is no need to suppose God's existence.

On the contrary, It is said in the person of God: "I am Who am."
15 (Exodus 3:14)

I answer that, The existence of God can be proved in five ways.

The first and more manifest way is the argument from motion. It is certain, and evident to our senses, that in the world some things are in motion. Now whatever is in motion is put in motion by another,
20 for nothing can be in motion except it is in potentiality to that towards which it is in motion; whereas a thing moves inasmuch as it is in act. For motion is nothing else than the reduction of something from potentiality to actuality. But nothing can be reduced from potentiality to actuality, except by something in a state of actuality.
25 Thus that which is actually hot, as fire, makes wood, which is potentially hot, to be actually hot, and thereby moves and changes it. Now it is not possible that the same thing should be at once in actuality and potentiality in the same respect, but only in different respects. For what is actually hot cannot simultaneously be

30   potentially hot; but it is simultaneously potentially cold. It is
      therefore impossible that in the same respect and in the same way a
      thing should be both mover and moved, i.e. that it should move itself.
      Therefore, whatever is in motion must be put in motion by another. If
      that by which it is put in motion be itself put in motion, then this also
35   must needs be put in motion by another, and that by another again.
      But this cannot go on to infinity, because then there would be no first
      mover, and, consequently, no other mover; seeing that subsequent
      movers move only inasmuch as they are put in motion by the first
      mover; as the staff moves only because it is put in motion by the
40   hand. Therefore it is necessary to arrive at a first mover, put in
      motion by no other; and this everyone understands to be God.

      The second way is from the nature of the efficient cause. In the
      world of sense we find there is an order of efficient causes. There is no
      case known (neither is it, indeed, possible) in which a thing is found
45   to be the efficient cause of itself; for so it would be prior to itself,
      which is impossible. Now in efficient causes it is not possible to go on
      to infinity, because in all efficient causes following in order, the first
      is the cause of the intermediate cause, and the intermediate is the
      cause of the ultimate cause, whether the intermediate cause be
50   several, or only one. Now to take away the cause is to take away the
      effect. Therefore, if there be no first cause among efficient causes,
      there will be no ultimate, nor any intermediate cause. But if in
      efficient causes it is possible to go on to infinity, there will be no first
      efficient cause, neither will there be an ultimate effect, nor any
55   intermediate efficient causes; all of which is plainly false. Therefore it
      is necessary to admit a first efficient cause, to which everyone gives
      the name of God.

      The third way is taken from possibility and necessity, and runs
      thus. We find in nature things that are possible to be and not to be,
60   since they are found to be generated, and to corrupt, and
      consequently, they are possible to be and not to be. But it is
      impossible for these always to exist, for that which is possible not to
      be at some time is not. Therefore, if everything is possible not to be,
      then at one time there could have been nothing in existence. Now if
65   this were true, even now there would be nothing in existence, because
      that which does not exist only begins to exist by something already
      existing. Therefore, if at one time nothing was in existence, it would

have been impossible for anything to have begun to exist; and thus even now nothing would be in existence—which is absurd. Therefore,

70 not all beings are merely possible, but there must exist something the existence of which is necessary. But every necessary thing either has its necessity caused by another, or not. Now it is impossible to go on to infinity in necessary things which have their necessity caused by another, as has been already proved in regard to efficient causes.

75 Therefore we cannot but postulate the existence of some being having of itself its own necessity, and not receiving it from another, but rather causing in others their necessity. This all men speak of as God.

The fourth way is taken from the gradation to be found in things. Among beings there are some more and some less good, true, noble

80 and the like. But "more" and "less" are predicated of different things, according as they resemble in their different ways something which is the maximum, as a thing is said to be hotter according as it more nearly resembles that which is hottest; so that there is something which is truest, something best, something noblest and, consequently,

85 something which is uttermost being; for those things that are greatest in truth are greatest in being, as it is written in <u>De Metaphysica</u> ii. Now the maximum in any genus is the cause of all in that genus; as fire, which is the maximum heat, is the cause of all hot things. Therefore there must also be something which is to all beings the

90 cause of their being, goodness, and every other perfection; and this we call God.

The fifth way is taken from the governance of the world. We see that things which lack intelligence, such as natural bodies, act for an end, and this is evident from their acting always, or nearly always, in

95 the same way, so as to obtain the best result. Hence it is plain that not fortuitously, but designedly, do they achieve their end. Now whatever lacks intelligence cannot move towards an end, unless it be directed by some being endowed with knowledge and intelligence; as the arrow is shot to its mark by the archer. Therefore some intelligent

100 being exists by whom all natural things are directed to their end; and this being we call God.

Reply OBJ 1: As Augustine says (<u>Enchiridion</u> 11): "Since God is the highest good, He would not allow any evil to exist in His works, unless His omnipotence and goodness were such as to bring good even

105 out of evil." This is part of the infinite goodness of God, that He should allow evil to exist, and out of it produce good.

Reply OBJ 2: Since nature works for a determinate end under the direction of a higher agent, whatever is done by nature must needs be traced back to God, as to its first cause. So also whatever is done

110 voluntarily must also be traced back to some higher cause other than human reason or will, since these can change or fail; for all things that are changeable and capable of defect must be traced back to an immovable and self-necessary first principle, as was shown in the body of the Article.

Anselm of Canterbury

Anselm of Canterbury was a tenth-century philosopher and theologian. Probably best-known for his pursuit of philosophy as "faith seeking understanding", his most famous philosophical work is the *Proslogium*, in which he attempts to formulate arguments for the existence and attributes of God. This selection contains the basic argument for God's existence, sometimes called the *ontological* argument.

Proslogium, Chapter 2

Therefore, Lord, you who give understanding to faith, give to me as much as you think is useful, that I may understand that you are as we believe and what we believe [you to be]. And we believe, in fact, that you are something than which nothing greater can be thought.
5 Or, rather, is there no such nature, because "the fool said in his heart: there is no God" (Psalms xiv 1)? But certainly this very fool, when he hears what I say: 'something than which nothing greater can be thought', understands what he hears; and what he understands is in his intellect, even if he does not know that it exists. For it is one thing
10 for something to be in the intellect, another that something is understood to be [exist]. For when a painter first considers what is going to be made, he has this thing in his intellect, yet he does not know that the thing, which he has not yet made, exists. But when he has painted it, he both has it in his intellect and understands that
15 what he has made exists. And so even the fool has become convinced that something than which nothing greater can be thought is in the intellect, because he understands this when he hears it, and whatever is understood is in the intellect. And certainly that than which a greater cannot be thought cannot be in the intellect alone. For if it is
20 in the intellect alone, it can be thought also [to be] in reality, which is greater. If, then, that than which a greater cannot be thought is in the intellect alone, that than which a greater cannot be thought is that than which a greater can be thought. But clearly this cannot be.

Therefore there is no doubt that something than which a greater
25   cannot be thought exists, both in the intellect and in reality.

René Descartes

René Descartes was a seventeenth-century French mathematician and philosopher. In philosophy he is undoubtedly best known for claiming <u>cogito ergo sum</u> ("I think, therefore I am") as the ultimate basis of human knowledge. This selection, taken from his *Meditations on First Philosophy*, contains the basic argument he gives for the existence of God, another example of an *ontological* argument.

Meditations on First Philosophy, V

Now, if from the very fact that I can derive from my thoughts the idea of something, it follows that all that I clearly and distinctly recognize as characteristic of this thing does in reality characterize it, can I not derive from this an argument which will prove the existence
5 of God? It is certain that I find in my mind the idea of God, of a supremely perfect Being, no less than that of any shape or number whatsoever; and I recognize that an eternal existence belongs to his nature no less clearly and distinctly than I recognize that all I can demonstrate about some figure or number actually belongs to the
10 nature of that figure or number. Thus, even if everything that I concluded in the preceding Meditations were (by chance) not true, the existence of God should pass in my mind as at least as certain as I have hitherto considered all the mathematical truths.

And this is true even though I must admit that it does not at first
15 appear entirely obvious, but seems to have some appearance of sophistry. For since in all other matters I have become accustomed to make a distinction between existence and essence, I am easily convinced that the existence of God can be separated from his essence, and that thus I can conceive of God as not actually existing.
20 Nevertheless, when I consider this with more attention, I find it manifest that we can no more separate the existence of God from his essence than we can separate from the essence of a triangle the fact that the size of its three angles equals two right angles, or from the idea of a mountain the idea of a valley. Thus it is no less self-

25 contradictory to conceive of a God, a supremely perfect Being, who
lacks existence—that is, who lacks some perfection—than it is to
conceive of a mountain for which there is no valley.

But even though in fact I cannot conceive of a God without
existence, any more than of a mountain without a valley,
30 nevertheless, just as from the mere fact that I conceive a mountain
with a valley, it does not follow that any mountain exists in the world,
so likewise, though I conceive of God as existing, it does not seem to
follow for this reason that God exists. For my thought does not
impose any necessity upon things; and just as I can at my pleasure
35 imagine a winged horse, even though no horse has wings, so I could
perhaps attribute existence to God, even though no God existed.

It is here that there is sophistry hidden. For from the fact that I
cannot conceive a mountain without a valley it does not follow that
there is a mountain or a valley anywhere, but only that the mountain
40 and the valley, whether they exist or not, are inseparable from each
other. From the fact alone that I cannot conceive God except as
existing, it follows that existence is inseparable from him, and
consequently that he does, in truth, exist. Not that my though can
bring about this result or that it imposes any necessity on things; on
45 the contrary, the necessity which is in the thing itself—that is, the
necessity of the existence of God—determines me to have this
thought. For it is not in my power to conceive of a God without
existence—that is to say, of a supremely perfect Being without a
supreme perfection—as it is in my power to imagine a horse either
50 with or without wings.

John Locke

John Locke was a seventeenth-century British philosopher. He is perhaps best-known for his *Second Treatise on Government*, which came to have a tremendous impact upon the Founding Fathers and the writers of the U.S. Constitution. His interests ranged far beyond political philosophy, however, and we have included his argument for the existence of God taken from the *Essay Concerning Human Understanding*.

Essay Concerning Human Understanding

Book IV, Chapter 10: Of Our Knowledge of the Existence of a God

1. We are capable of knowing certainly that there is a God. Though God has given us no innate ideas of himself; though he has stamped no original characters on our minds, wherein we may read his being; yet having furnished us with those faculties our minds are
5 endowed with, he hath not left himself without witness: since we have sense, perception, and reason, and cannot want a clear proof of him, as long as we carry ourselves about us. Nor can we justly complain of our ignorance in this great point; since he has so plentifully provided us with the means to discover and know him; so
10 far as is necessary to the end of our being, and the great concernment of our happiness. But, though this be the most obvious truth that reason discovers, and though its evidence be (if I mistake not) equal to mathematical certainty: yet it requires thought and attention; and the mind must apply itself to a regular deduction of it from some part
15 of our intuitive knowledge, or else we shall be as uncertain and ignorant of this as of other propositions, which are in themselves capable of clear demonstration. To show, therefore, that we are capable of knowing, i.e. being certain that there is a God, and how we may come by this certainty, I think we need go no further than
20 ourselves, and that undoubted knowledge we have of our own existence.

2. For man knows that he himself exists. I think it is beyond question, that man has a clear idea of his own being; he knows certainly he exists, and that he is something. He that can doubt
25 whether he be anything or no, I speak not to; no more than I would argue with pure nothing, or endeavor to convince nonentity that it were something. If any one pretends to be so skeptical as to deny his own existence, (for really to doubt of it is manifestly impossible,) let him for me enjoy his beloved happiness of being nothing, until hunger
30 or some other pain convince him of the contrary. This, then, I think I may take for a truth, which every one's certain knowledge assures him of, beyond the liberty of doubting, viz. that he is something that actually exists.

3 He knows also that nothing cannot produce a being; therefore
35 something must have existed from eternity. In the next place, man knows, by an intuitive certainty, that bare nothing can no more produce any real being, than it can be equal to two right angles. If a man knows not that nonentity, or the absence of all being, cannot be equal to two right angles, it is impossible he should know any
40 demonstration in Euclid. If, therefore, we know there is some real being, and that nonentity cannot produce any real being, it is an evident demonstration, that from eternity there has been something; since what was not from eternity had a beginning; and what had a beginning must be produced by something else.

45 4. And that eternal Being must be most powerful. Next, it is evident, that what had its being and beginning from another, must also have all that which is in and belongs to its being from another too. All the powers it has must be owing to and received from the same source. This eternal source, then, of all being must also be the
50 source and original of all power; and so this eternal Being must be also the most powerful.

5. And most knowing. Again, a man finds in himself perception and knowledge. We have then got one step further; and we are certain now that there is not only some being, but some knowing,
55 intelligent being in the world. There was a time, then, when there was no knowing being, and when knowledge began to be; or else there has been also a knowing being from eternity. If it be said, there was a time when no being had any knowledge, when that eternal being was void of all understanding; I reply, that then it was impossible there

60 should ever have been any knowledge: it being as impossible that things wholly void of knowledge, and operating blindly, and without any perception, should produce a knowing being, as it is impossible that a triangle should make itself three angles bigger than two right ones. For it is as repugnant to the idea of senseless matter, that it

65 should put into itself sense, perception, and knowledge, as it is repugnant to the idea of a triangle, that it should put into itself greater angles than two right ones.

6. And therefore God. Thus, from the consideration of ourselves, and what we infallibly find in our own constitutions, our reason leads

70 us to the knowledge of this certain and evident truth,- That there is an eternal, most powerful, and most knowing Being; which whether any one will please to call God, it matters not. The thing is evident; and from this idea duly considered, will easily be deduced all those other attributes, which we ought to ascribe to this eternal Being. If,

75 nevertheless, any one should be found so senselessly arrogant, as to suppose man alone knowing and wise, but yet the product of mere ignorance and chance; and that all the rest of the universe acted only by that blind haphazard; I shall leave with him that very rational and emphatical rebuke of Tully (I. ii. De Leg.), to be considered at his

80 leisure: "What can be more sillily arrogant and misbecoming, than for a man to think that he has a mind and understanding in him, but yet in all the universe beside there is no such thing? Or that those things, which with the utmost stretch of his reason he can scarce comprehend, should be moved and managed without any reason at

85 all?" *Quid est enim verius, quam neminem esse oportere tam stulte arrogantem, ut in se mentem et rationem putet inesse, in caelo mundoque non putet? Aut ea quae vix summa ingenii ratione comprehendat, nulla ratione moveri putet?*

From what has been said, it is plain to me we have a more certain

90 knowledge of the existence of a God, than of anything our senses have not immediately discovered to us. Nay, I presume I may say, that we more certainly know that there is a God, than that there is anything else without us. When I say we know, I mean there is such a knowledge within our reach which we cannot miss, if we will but

95 apply our minds to that, as we do to several other inquiries.

Appendix

I   Univocal, Equivocal, and Analogous Words

Most commonly, when we use a single word to signify two concepts, or two things, we use the word in a *univocal* way (from the Latin, *univoce, with a single voice*). For example, when we use the word *bear* to describe both a polar bear and a grizzly, we use the word univocally. Both are bears, and the word *bear* has the same meaning (the single voice of the Latin word univocal) in each case. This is not to say that a polar bear and a grizzly bear are the same—only that they are both bears. Examples could be multiplied: isosceles triangle and equilateral triangle are equally triangles, oak and aspen are both trees, salesman and accountant are both occupations, and so on. This is the most common way in which we use words.

We use words in an equivocal way (from the Latin, *equivoce, with an equal voice*) when the same word is used to signify two entirely different concepts. This is quite possible. Since we give words their meanings (which is to say, we use vocal or written signs to bring to mind whatever concepts we choose, as a group, to bring out,) it can very well happen (and it does) that the same sign is used to bring to mind very different concepts.

When we used the word *bear* above in a univocal way, we used it to describe two different species of animal. The word *bear*, in that context, had the same meaning, or signification. We can use the word *bear*, however, to signify things in an equivocal way as well—different context, different manner of signifying. For example, *bear* as describing an animal and *bear* as describing the act of carrying a load do not mean the same thing. Same word, differently used.

We cannot overemphasize the importance of seeing these distinctions as *distinctions in the way we use words*. There is no such thing as a univocal word, as such. A word may be *used* univocally; but it may then be *used* equivocally, or analogously. The simple fact is that words do have many different meanings, and coming to realize this is one of the most important beginnings one can make in philosophy.

One might think at this point that the distinctions in the way in which we use words have been made. Either we use words with the same meaning, or not. If they have the same meaning, we use them univocally, otherwise they are being used equivocally. But there is still another distinction to be made. For we can see, in our usage of words, that we sometimes use words with different meanings, but consciously maintain some connection between one of the two meanings and another. Thus, when using the same word with different meanings, we can recognize that the meanings can be entirely different, or they can be related.

Words that are used analogously have meanings which differ, to be sure, but which retain a reasonable connection to one another none the less. In fact, usually there is a first meaning, to which an extended meaning is then related. The first meaning is called the *prime analogate*.

For example, one might use the word *tree* to describe, in a univocal manner, any number of species of certain types of plant. Oak, aspen, maple, birch, yew—all are trees. One might also use the word *tree* to describe an action taken by a hound dog when chasing a possum or other prey. Here, *tree* is a verb. The two meanings differ: a plant is not an action; yet the meanings are consciously related to one another. However much the action of *treeing* a possum has to do with cornering it, one crucial aspect of treeing is where it occurs: in a tree. The word *tree*, used to describe both the plant and the action, then, is being used in an analogous manner.

II   Essential vs. Non-essential

There are only a few ways in which a *predicate* (some descriptive term) can describe a subject. These *ways of describing* or *ways of predicating* (technically called *predicables*) fall out into two groups. Some are essential, others are non-essential.

Alpacas are mammals is an example of *essential* predication. What this simply means is that we are referring to some part of the *essence* of the thing. Essential predicates provide a direct answer to the question *what is it*. What is an alpaca? *An alpaca is a mammal.* The response supplies at least part of the answer to one of the most basic questions we ask: what is that thing? In sum, then, essential predicates give a direct (though perhaps not complete) answer to the question *what is it*.

We know that Pomeranians and Great Danes are types of dog, but are they *essentially* the same animal? Pomeranians and Great Danes *do* differ greatly from one another, so much so that one might think they are essentially different things. But even great and significant differences between things do not make them essentially different. Not all differences are essential: that is, not all differences serve to tell us *what something is*. The simple fact that Pomeranians are small dogs and Great Danes are large dogs is not enough to distinguish them from one another in an essential way. We would say, rather, that such differences in size are *accidental*, not *essential*. In sum, then, non-essential predicates, however true, do not give a direct answer to the question *what is it*.

III   The Categories

Speaking universally, the things we *predicate* (the things we use *to describe other things*, whether essentially or accidentally) fall out into ten classes, or groups, which are called the *predicaments* or *categories*.[1] The first and most fundamental distinction among the categories is rooted in the way they exist.

First, *to exist in a subject* means to be incapable of existing apart from that subject. For example, the quality of a thing which we call *red* is incapable of existence apart from some subject. Red does not have existence in its own right. It must exist in some thing in order to exist at all. Such things are called *accidents*.

At first glance, it might seem that everything exists in other things; but, upon reflection, we see that this could not possibly be so—for if there were no subjects for things to exist in, nothing would exist! Things which exist in their own right in this way, which do not rely upon another thing in which to exist, are called *substances*. Of course substances do depend upon other things for their existence in *certain* ways. How could living things survive without other substances to eat, for instance? The point we wish to make, however, is that some things exist *in* others, they depend upon them, not for survival, but for being there in the first place.

The first of the categories, then, is *substance*. As we just noted, substances do not exist in other things, but they are themselves the basis for the existence of all else. Remember also that we are speaking here of substance as a category, as something which can be predicated, and hence of substance as a universal. Examples of substances abound, since all living and natural things are substances.

The second category is *quantity*. Within this category are contained such things as we normally associate with quantity, such as numbers and measures. But quantity is of two different sorts, corresponding to two different questions we ask concerning the quantity of a thing: for we ask both *how much* and *how many*. And just as it would be incorrect to ask concerning the number of people in a room how much are in the room?, so it would be incorrect to ask

---

1   *Predicaments* comes from a Latin word meaning *what is predicated*, while *categories* comes from a Greek word meaning the same thing.

concerning a continuous quantity, such as a length, how many is it? The distinction between the questions is an indication of an underlying difference in the types of quantity: there are *discrete* quantities and *continuous* quantities. Discrete quantities are the how many of parts which are actually distinct from one another, while continuous quantities are the basis for the how much question we ask of parts which are not actually distinct.

The third category is *quality*. Less well-defined than the previous two categories, a direct translation of the Greek word Aristotle uses to name it, το ποιον, might be *of what sort*. What quality signifies is best seen in the four types into which it is immediately divided.

Some qualities are habits, or dispositions, such as the quality of being a *smoker* or an *artist*, others are abilities, or inabilities, such as *sighted* or *blind*, still others are sense qualities, such as *sweet* or *white*, and, finally, others are the shapes of substances, such as *triangular* or *spherical*.

Next is the category of *relation*, or *reference to another*. Relations occur only between two things. Examples are *greater* and *smaller*, *parent* and *child*, *identical* and *similar*. In each case, note that the relation entails a connection between one thing and another.

The fifth category is *action, the doing of something to another*. So, we are not speaking of all actions, but only of transitive actions (you will find the grammatical distinction between *transitive* and *intransitive* verbs of use here). Further, since this sort of action is the doing of something to another, the category of action is associated with the category of relation (as well as with the category of being passive, which we take up now.)

The sixth category, *being passive*, necessarily implies that there is something which is acting, which is doing something. So, we have action, the doing of something to another, being passive, receiving the action done, and the relation established between the two. (Keep in mind that not all relations depend upon the categories of action and being passive; some depend upon quantity, such as greater and taller.) An example of things which are connected as action, being passive, and relation is: *cutting*, the action, *being cut*, the being passive, and *cutter*, the relation between them.

Next come the two categories of *when* and *where*. Things are contained in these groupings which answer the questions *where is it* and *when is it.* Do not confuse when and where with the quantities of place and time. *A minute* is a quantity: it tells us how much with respect to duration. *In a minute* tells us when something will occur. Similarly, *an acre* is a quantity: it tells us how much with respect to size. *On that acre,* on the other hand, tells us where something is, and so it would be contained in the category of where.

The ninth category is *position,* that is, the order that the parts of a thing have. This is not position in the sense of location (for example, we might say someone's position is twenty miles west of town,) since that reduces to the category of where, but in the sense of the arrangement of bodily parts. Examples of positions are *kneeling, laying down, upside-down,* and so on. Note also that, in this context, verb-forms can express position and not action. *To kneel upon* is an action (*to be knelt upon* would be the being passive,) while the verb-form derived from it describes the posture, or position, of kneeling.

Last among the categories is *habit.* (Note that we listed habit among the types of quality above. Here, we use the word in a different sense.) Though English usage frowns upon it, *habit* here means something like *the having of something.* This type of accident is peculiar to humans, insofar as only we can have things through acquisition.

In some sense, animals do have things: birds have feathers and mammals have fur, but these things are parts of their substances. Only humans have possessions which they acquire through reason and art. Thus, corresponding to the protection afforded a bird by feathers and a mammal by fur is clothing, which humans acquire through the arts of weaving and sewing. What animals have by nature humans possess by means of a special category, which is called habit. Examples of habits, then, are *being clothed, armed* (*having weapons*), *wearing glasses,* and so on.

IV   Simple Opposition

At the very heart of human knowledge is our basic ability to see that *this is not that*—to distinguish one thing from another.

This recognition (that one thing is not another) is seen more clearly when we consider simple opposition. For when we try to understand the world around us, we often discover an opposition between the thing in question and other things. (This is not to say that all things are opposed to one another—some things are merely *other*.) There are a number of different ways in which one simple expression (we are not speaking of statements here) can be opposed to another. We will address three of them.

First, two simple expressions can be opposed by way of *contradictory* opposition. When such expressions contradict one another, one of them simply and entirely takes away what the other says. Contradictory opposition is based upon the absolute opposition between being and non-being. The contradictory opposite of *alpaca* would be that which says everything which alpaca does not say—the absolute opposite. In this case that would be *non-alpaca*, everything which is not an alpaca. This is the clearest and most complete type of opposition. Here there is no middle ground, as is sometimes found with other types of opposition. Every conceivable thing is either an alpaca or a non-alpaca. This, then, is characteristic of contradictory opposition: it divides all things into two in this absolute way. Such a division is sometimes called a *dichotomy*, from the Greek, meaning *cut in two*.

The next type of opposition is not as absolute. It is called privative opposition. While contradictory opposition is absolute, the opposition of being and non-being, this type of opposition is qualified: it is the opposition between being and non-being *in a certain thing*. While it seems obvious that there are beings which belong only to certain types of subjects (for example, only mammals have mammary glands,) what does it mean to speak of a *non-being* as restricted to a certain type of subject?

Actually, there are countless examples of such things, though we tend not to bring them to mind as examples of non-being.

Take, for instance, the sense of sight. Not all things are sighted, and it is obvious that sight can only exist in something which has eyes. So much, then, for a being which exists in some determinate subject. What is the opposite of *sighted?* Well, we should ask, what type of opposite are we interested in? Its contradictory would be *non-sighted.* Is there anything which represents the non-being of sight in things which have sight? Such a question at first sounds contradictory, but there is such a thing.

Let us consider a human being and a stone. A stone has no sight. Yet we do not, on that account, say that it is *blind.* Blindness cannot apply to a stone. Why is this? Because blindness is conceived as the lack of sight in a thing which has the natural ability to see. *Blindness* is conceptually different from *not seeing.* A stone does not see. Neither does a person who is blind. Yet we do not say of both that they are blind. Blindness is that peculiar type of non-being which we call a *privation.* It is the non-being of a thing in a determinate subject. Blindness is the non-being of sight, not absolutely (that is simply non-sighted,) but in a thing which naturally has the ability to see. Illiteracy is the non-being of the ability to read, not in just anything (we would not call a tree illiterate, even though it cannot read,) but in something which has the natural ability to read. And so privative opposition, though like contradictory opposition insofar as we speak of being and non-being, is still a limited type of opposition. Its limitation is exactly *where it can be found.* Blindness and sight are not found everywhere, while non-sighted and sighted together encompass all possible things. There can be nothing which is neither sighted nor non-seeing; many things, however, are neither sighted nor blind.

The third sort of opposition is even more limited than the previous two. Both contradictory and privative opposition entail *being versus non-being.* The third type, contrary opposition, is an opposition between *one being and another being.* Contraries are conceptually inseparable. For example, *hot* is conceptually inseparable from *cold.* As extremes with respect to temperature, each is necessary for the understanding of the other. One cannot conceive of hot, as such, without also conceiving of cold, as such.

It might seem, at this point, that these things are not opposites at all—in fact, they seem to rely upon one another. But their opposition is not in whether one can be *understood* without the other (for, as we just said, they cannot,) but in whether one can *exist* along with the other, *at the same time, and in the same place.* And here we see the distinct type of opposition which contrary opposition expresses: it is *an opposition between one being and another in the same thing, but not at the same time.*

The same thing cannot be both hot and cold simultaneously. (This is not to say that different parts cannot be hot and cold at the same time, but that *the same part* cannot.) Note that hot and cold are at the extremes within a class, that is, that hot and cold have something in common: they belong to the same genus, namely, temperature. This is another characteristic of contraries. One could say that contraries are extremes within a genus, were it not for the existence of contraries which are not extremes. Certainly many of the familiar types of contrary opposition are extremes within a common genus: hot and cold, black and white, sweet and sour, rough and smooth. Even and odd are also contraries, however, yet they cannot be called extremes, since there is no intermediate state between them. In many cases, then, but not in all, contraries are extremes within a genus, such that there are intermediate states between them.

The very possibility of intermediate states distinguishes contrary opposition from the previous two types also. For, in contradictory opposition, something either is an alpaca or it is not, and, given that we are speaking of things which have the natural ability to see, something is either sighted or blind. Yet this is not so with all contraries. Given that we are speaking of temperature, it is not the case that something is either hot or cold, for there is an infinite number of temperatures between these extremes. The only characteristic of opposition which remains for contraries is that the same thing cannot be both of them at the same time—it is possible that it is neither.

V   Contraries vs. Contradictories

Propositional Quality

The most fundamental way in which statements can differ has to do with what is called their *quality*. A statement (or proposition) claims either that some predicate belongs to some subject, or that it does not. Propositions of the first sort are said to be *affirmative*, while propositions of the second sort are *negative*.

In the abstract, taking *s* as any subject whatsoever and *p* as any predicate, the form of an affirmative proposition is:

s is p

while the form of a negative proposition is:

s is not p.

Bear in mind that the quality of a proposition depends upon whether one is joining or separating the predicate and subject. Is the statement *no maple is an oak tree* affirmative, then, or negative? We need simply ask whether the predicate of the proposition given, *oak tree*, is being associated with, or distinguished from, the subject, *maple*. Clearly, a separation between the two is being expression. Therefore this proposition is negative.

Propositional Quantity

The second characteristic of a proposition is its *quantity*. The quantity of a proposition as a whole is based upon the quantity of its subject. Though there are four types of quantity a subject can have, we are directly concerned only with two: *universal* and *particular*.

The proposition:

every dog is a four-legged animal

is a *universal* proposition (or a proposition with *universal* quantity). This not only means that it is referring to more than a single individual, but also that it is referring to each and every individual signified by the word *dog*. In this case, the quantifier *every* is what signifies the proposition's universal quantity.

Now consider the proposition:

no dog is a cat.

This is also a universal proposition. Why? Because the quantity of a proposition is based solely upon the quantity of a subject. If we are referring to each and every dog in the proposition, then it must have universal quantity. In this case, the quantifier *no* indicates universality. Now, the word no, we just saw, is also a sign that this proposition has negative quality: in this case, this word serves two functions, indicating both its quality and the quantity of the proposition as a whole.

Particular quantity is usually indicated by the quantifier *some*, whether we are speaking affirmatively or negatively. For example:

some dogs have fleas

is a common affirmative form, while:

some dogs do not have fleas

is a common form of the particular negative proposition.

Propositional Type

The *type* of a proposition comes down to a combination of its quantity and its quality. Given our summary of quality and quantity above, then, four sorts of propositional type are possible. This can be easily seen by making reference to the following grid:

	affirmative	negative
universal	A	E
particular	I	O

(The letters A, E, I, and O come from the two first vowels of each of the Latin words *affirmo, I affirm,* and *nego, I deny.*)

Opposition

Let us now use these distinctions to speak of two of the ways in which propositions can be *opposed* to one another. For purposes of clarification, we can represent these four propositions on a square, with the universals at the top and the affirmatives at the left:

This device is called *the square of opposition.*

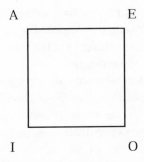

First, assume that the four propositions represented on the square have the same subject and predicate; thus, they are all talking about the same thing. To find opposed propositions, then, we need only look for pairs of affirmative and negative propositions.

The first such pair we will discuss is *A* and *E*. Putting these in terms of a common subject and predicate, we would be considering the relation between *all s is p* and *no s is p,* where *s* and *p* can refer to anything whatsoever, as long as it is the same thing in the case of each proposition.

All s is p and *no s is p,* then, are opposites. This is more than to say that they are saying different things, although they certainly are. It is to say that a person claiming that *all s is p* and a person claiming that *no s is p* are *disagreeing* with one another, in the strict sense of the word.

This sort of disagreement, or opposition, is called *contrary* opposition, and the propositions *all s is p* and *no s is p* are called *contraries.* It is the opposition between universal propositions, one affirmative, the other negative.

We have seen contrary opposition before, not as an opposition between propositions, but as an opposition between simple expressions. Earlier, we spoke of hot and cold as being opposed in this way, as contraries. At that point, we defined such opposition as being between extremes within the same group, or class. Thus, hot and cold are contraries because they are at extremes within the class of temperatures. We also pointed out that, though it is not necessary that things have one or the other of these contraries at any given time, nevertheless, it is impossible for both to be present simultaneously. With contraries, as opposed to contradictories, it is possible to have neither one, but impossible to have both at the same time. (The exact same thing cannot be both hot and cold simultaneously, but it can be neither one.)

There is a good reason why we call the opposition between type *A* and type *E* contrary opposition also. Type *A* and type *E* can be seen as extremes with respect to the those propositions which make claims about the same subject and predicate. Let us take a concrete example.

With respect to the color of swans, one person might make the claim that *every swan is white*. This is a *logically* extreme claim. (Note that a *logically* extreme claim need not be false; it is extreme not in the common sense where we use it to mean *unreasonable*, but only in a logical sense.) Type *A* is extreme here because it is the *most* one can say affirmatively of swans and whiteness. One can say no more, in an affirmative way, about swans being white, and it makes no sense to say *more than every swan is white*.

With respect to denying whiteness of swans, the most one can say is *no swans are white*. Again, it makes no sense to say *even fewer than none of the swans are white*.

It makes sense, then, to speak of the opposition between type *A* and type *E* as contrary opposition, since it is very much like the opposition between simple expressions of which we have already spoken.

The next type of opposition which concerns us is that between a universal and a particular proposition, one of which is affirmative, the other negative. There are two instances of this opposition represented on the square, namely, the opposition between type *A* and type *O*, and the opposition between type *E* and type *I*. This type is called *contradictory* opposition, and it is the greatest opposition two propositions can have to one another. In other words, *two people cannot disagree more than when they contradict one another.*

We also saw this type of opposition earlier. There also it was taken as the strictest type of opposition which can occur: in that case, it was between two *simple expressions.* Here, it is between two *propositions.*

When we considered contradictory opposition earlier, we saw that everything must be either one of the opposites, or the other. For example, everything must be either *hot* or *non-hot.* This either-or characteristic also applies to contradictory propositions, as we will shortly see.

Rules For Truth and Falsity

What remains is to look at the rules for the truth and falsity of contraries and contradictories.

The rule for contradictories is immediately seen and simple: in fact, this rule is one of the basic truths upon which all human thought is based.. Simply put, **one of two contradictory propositions must be true, the other false; they cannot both be true, and they cannot both be false**. Here we can see the reason why this opposition is called *contradictory,* since it is very much like contradictory opposition among simple expressions. Among simple expressions, as we saw, something must be either one of two contradictories or the other—there is no third alternative, and it cannot be both. (For instance, something must be either *hot* or *non-hot.* It cannot be both at the same time, nor can it be neither one nor the other, since, between them, they encompass all things.)

Though we depend upon the truth of this rule for all our reasoning, it can be made manifest through examples. Suppose it were false that all swans were white. What, at the very least, must be true? That no swans are white? No, what we can be certain is true is that some swans are not white. It does not follow from saying *it is false that all swans are white* that *no swans are white* is true. All that necessarily follows is that some are not white. Now suppose that every swan was in fact white. The proposition *some swans are not white* would necessarily be false. (How could any swan not be white if it were true that all swans are white?) The same can be easily seen using examples of the opposition between types *E* and *I*.

What does this rule imply? Consider the situation where persons are *disagreeing* in this way: *they are contradicting one another. Apart from the truth of the matter,* we do know one thing: one of them must be right and the other wrong. Contradictories cannot both be true, nor can they both be false. Of course, this logical truth does not settle the important matter of who is right and who is wrong. Nevertheless, we do know so much about the situation.

The rule for the truth and falsity of contraries is what one would expect, given what we have said of contrary terms already. Though both propositions cannot be true, they can both be false; and there are *intermediates* between these contraries (namely, the particular affirmative and the particular negative proposition).

Though it is not possible that *every swan is white and* that *no swan is white*, it is possible that both are false, in which case the intermediates *some swan is white* and *some swan is not white* would be true.

While one can tell from a true or a false proposition whether its contradictory is true or false, that is not the case with contraries. If the first of two contraries is true, then the other is false; but if the first is false, the other could be true, but it could also be false. Logically, we say that the other contrary is *undecided* (or *unknown*), which is merely to say that we do not know whether it is true or false. (Obviously, it *must* be one or the other, but we cannot tell *which* using logic alone.) **Contraries cannot both be true, though they can both be false.**

VI   Necessary vs. Contingent

One thing which some descriptive terms (or predicates) have in common is that each is *necessary* to the subject of which it is predicated, which is to say that it *must* belong to that thing. For example, *humans are animals, triangles are three-sided* and *potential is needed for change* are all necessary propositions.

Other predicates, however, are not related to the subject in this way; in fact, some things are decidedly *unnecessary* to the subjects to which they belong. For example, it is not necessary that *humans are tall*, or that *triangles are blue* or that *things change slowly*. This second sort of proposition is called *contingent*, contingent being the opposite of necessary. While necessary things must belong to their subjects, contingent things may or may not belong. Every true proposition, then, is possible on account of either a necessary or a contingent connection between the subject and the predicate.

VII   Inference Signs, Validity, and Soundness

In every argument, one is *going from one thing to another*. This process of going from one to another is what distinguishes argumentation (formulating arguments) from mere predication (making propositions.) The part of an argument one is going *from* is generally called a *premise* (arguments will generally have two premises). The part of an argument one is going *to* is called the *conclusion*.

Suppose, for example, we were given the following argument:

Could these be common porpoises? Stanton asked. They sure had the look of the breed. But since common porpoises are found exclusively in the southern latitudes and these animals had been with him for many miles as he journeyed south across the equator, they could not be common porpoises. They must be a similar species.

An *argument* is being made here; a *simple* argument, but an argument none the less. Can we identify which parts are the premises and which is the conclusion? The keys to doing this are what are called *inference signs*. Inference signs are certain words we use to indicate to our listeners or readers how propositions in our arguments are to be taken. The use of such signs arose from the necessity of distinguishing the different parts of arguments in order that they be understood. Consider these three propositions:

human is mortal
animal is mortal
human is animal.

Without inference signs, it is impossible to decide whether this person is trying to conclude that humans are animals or that animals are mortal or that humans are mortal—in fact, there is no indication here of whether an argument is *even being made*. These could be three simple statements which the speaker intends to be taken separately. But consider this way of expressing the same three statements:

since every human is an animal, every human is mortal, for
every animal is mortal.

Several things become clear upon reflection, the first of which is
that this speaker is definitely making an argument. The use of the
words *since* and *for* makes this clear. That is because *since* and *for*
can be used as inference signs. Here, they are meant to point out that
the propositions *every human is an animal* and *every animal is
mortal* are to be taken as the *premises* of the argument. The
proposition *every human is mortal* is seen to be the conclusion by
process of elimination.

Returning to the example we gave above:

Could these be common porpoises? Stanton asked. They sure
had the look of the breed. But since common porpoises are
found exclusively in the southern latitudes and these animals
had been with him for many miles as he journeyed south
across the equator, they could not be common porpoises. They
must be a similar species.

We can now see that the proposition *common porpoises are found
exclusively in the southern latitudes* is being taken as a premise of the
argument. The same is true for the proposition which follows it, *these
animals had been with him for many miles as he journeyed south
across the equator*, since it is preceded by the conjunction *and* (as if
one were to say *since this is so and [since] that is so...*). The
conclusion is *they [the animals he is looking at] could not be common
porpoises*.

Inference signs[2] are crucial for the study of philosophy, since
philosophers present arguments for the positions that they hold.
Words like *since* and *therefore* enable us to distinguish between the
point the author is trying to make (his conclusion) and the *reasons*
(premises) he uses to justify his view.

When its process of reasoning is good (logical, reasonable,) then
an argument are said to be *valid*. When propositions correspond to

---

2   Common signs of inference include *since, for,* and *because,* for premises and
     therefore, thus, so, and *it follows that,* for conclusions.

the way things are, then those propositions are said to be *true*. Though there is something distinctly *right* about both truth and validity, they are also different from one another. In fact, an argument can be valid even though the propositions it contains are false, and invalid even though the propositions it contains are true. Consider this example.

	every fish is a mammal	(The symbol ∴ is an
	every whale is a fish	abbreviation for
∴	every whale is a mammal	*therefore*.)

Notice that the first two propositions (which are where the argument is going *from*, the part of an argument we call the *premises*) are false while the third proposition (which is where the argument is going *to*, the part of an argument we call the *conclusion*) is true. One might think that false propositions could not lead us to a true conclusion; nevertheless, this argument *is valid*, as can be shown using this diagram.

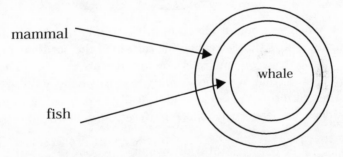

So, clearly, the validity (*logical correctness*) of the process of reasoning contained in an argument is independent of the truth of the propositions it contains; in other words, *how* it goes (that is, *well* or *poorly*) from the premises to the conclusion has nothing to do with whether the premises and conclusion are true or not.

This is an example of an *invalid* argument which contains true propositions.

every car is a vehicle
every station wagon is a vehicle
∴   every station wagon is a car

Here, the problem is not to be found in *what* is being claimed (for, in fact, all these statements are true,) but in the *way* the argument tries to go from one part to another. The following series of diagrams make it clear that one cannot get from the first two statements to the third in a logical manner.

We would first diagram *every car is a vehicle* in this way:

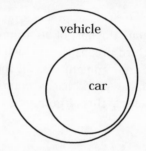

Yet, when we come to diagram *every station wagon is a vehicle*, we quickly realize that we cannot be certain of the position of the one term, *station wagon* in relation to the other, *car*. The only requirement is that we place *station wagon* wholly within *vehicle*. Since there are three possible (and logically *incompatible*) ways to do this, it does not necessarily follow that *every station wagon is a car.*

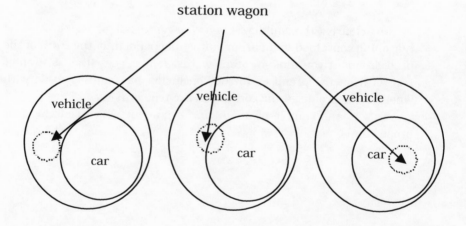

This should suffice to show that the truth or falsity of propositions is something very different from the validity or invalidity of arguments.

Soundness is the goal of argumentation. One might ask *what do we expect from our arguments, truth, or validity?* The answer, of course, is *both*. Valid arguments, though correct in one respect, are of little value if one is proceeding from a false antecedent. Similarly, true propositions lead nowhere if one's reasoning is not correct. *We want to reason 1) in a correct way 2) about true things.* This is to say that we want our arguments to be *sound*. An argument is *unsound*, then, if it is invalid, or if it has a false premise, or both.

VIII   Enthymemes

An *enthymeme* is an argument with a missing (or unstated) premise. It is not, strictly speaking, a different form of reasoning at all, but a different way in which to *present* an argument.

There are several reasons why someone may choose to leave a premise unstated. Perhaps it is obvious, as in the example: *all kangaroos are marsupials because they carry their young in a pouch.* The missing premise is that *all animals which carry their young in a pouch are marsupials*—an obvious enough fact, and so one which does not need to be explicitly stated. The motivation for leaving a premise unstated in this case is efficiency and brevity—it is much more wordy to bring out explicitly what is obvious to everyone anyway, and which (incidentally) everyone automatically supplies in their own mind when they see that the argument is valid.

There are other, less praiseworthy, reasons for leaving a premise unstated. One might leave it out because it is either false or highly questionable. For example, one might say: *of course the current administration is dishonest:: they're politicians, aren't they?* Of course, the unstated claim is that *all politicians are dishonest*, which is either false or highly questionable.[3]

Regardless of the *reason* for leaving a premise unstated, however, no argument can conclude validly without it; in fact, enthymemes are conclusive only to the extent that the person who hears them *can supply mentally* the premise which is left unstated.[4] In any other case, someone may be *persuaded* by an enthymeme to accept the conclusion (as in the example just given,) but they have not accepted it because they have seen it proved. Such a use (or, better, *misuse*) of enthymemes for rhetorical purposes is quite common, especially in the political, social, and ethical realms, where persuasion oftentimes leads directly to action, with relatively little time allowed for one to reflect upon the soundness of arguments presented. An enthymeme

---

3   Keep in mind that the missing premise is not *some politicians are dishonest* but the much stronger claim that *all politicians are dishonest.*

4   In fact, it is the hope of persons who use enthymemes to mask a false or questionable premise that their listeners will *not* make mentally explicit the missing premise, otherwise they will not end up being persuaded of the conclusion, which is the intention of such persons in the first place.

279

in, say, mathematics, on the other hand, will soon be discovered, since there is ample time to reflect upon whether the arguments provided are or are not sound. Since an argument cannot reach a valid conclusion without its premises, it is the function of logic to supply what is missing in enthymemes.

IX   Conditional Arguments

The main premise in a conditional argument (technically called a *conditional syllogism*) is a conditional (if... then) proposition. Conditional propositions have two main parts: the portion following the *if*, which is called the *antecedent*, and the portion following the *then* (or the other portion if the *then* is omitted), which is called the *consequent*. This distinction ought to borne in mind, both for understanding what a conditional syllogism is and for deciding whether it is or is not valid.

The other premise in a conditional syllogism is a statement with one of four possible functions: it can either affirm or deny the antecedent of the main premise, or it can affirm or deny the consequent of the main premise. It is very important to realize that *to affirm* here does not mean *to make an affirmative proposition*, nor does *to deny* mean *to make a negative statement*. This is best seen in an example:

> if it is raining then something is getting wet;
> it is raining.

In this case, the minor premise *affirms* the antecedent contained in the major premise. This is not to say that it affirms the antecedent because it is an affirmative proposition, (which it happens to be), but because it re-states what the antecedent is claiming. The following is also an example of a minor premise affirming the antecedent of the major premise:

> if it is not raining then nothing is getting wet;
> it is not raining.

Even though the minor premise has negative quality, it still affirms the antecedent because the antecedent is also negative—one re-states a negative only in a negative. Here is an instance in which the minor premise denies the antecedent:

if it is raining then something is getting wet;
it is not raining.

Here are two examples in which the consequent is affirmed and denied, respectively:

if it is raining then something is getting wet;
something is getting wet

if it is raining then something is getting wet;
nothing is getting wet.

These, then, are the four possible forms of the conditional syllogism. It is one of the simpler forms of argumentation. The rules for the validity of conditional syllogisms are also quite simple, and we will derive them here. Let us take the first form, in which the minor premise affirms the antecedent contained in the major premise.

if it is raining then something is getting wet;
it is raining.

In this instance, one can intuitively see that a valid conclusion can be drawn from these premises. One might ask: does anything necessarily follow from the premises given? Clearly:

if it is raining then something is getting wet;
it is raining;
∴ something is getting wet.

This valid form of reasoning, in which the minor premise affirms the antecedent and the conclusion affirms the consequent, simply makes explicit the already-existing connection between antecedent and consequent in the major premise.

This valid argument form is called *modus ponens* (*modus ponens* is Latin for *the method of setting something down as so.*) We can explicitly give the conditions for *modus ponens* as follows:

when one affirms the antecedent of a conditional proposition as a premise, one can validly affirm the consequent as a conclusion.

Let us turn to the second possible conditional form of argument, in which the minor premise *denies* the antecedent:

> if it is raining then something is getting wet;
> it is not raining.

In this instance, one might be led to conclude that nothing is getting wet—it certainly sounds like that ought to be the conclusion. Yet this conclusion does not follow, as can be easily seen by asking whether something might not be getting wet on account of something other than the rain—sprinklers, for example. It simply does not follow that nothing is getting wet from the simple fact that it is not raining. This very common logical mistake is called *the fallacy of denying the antecedent* (for obvious reasons). The truth is that this second form of conditional reasoning has no valid conclusion.

The third form we mentioned was an argument in which the minor premise affirms the consequent contained in the major premise.

> if it is raining then something is getting wet;
> something is getting wet.

As in the last case, it is fairly easy to see, upon reflection, that nothing follows from this combination of premises. The fact that something happens to be getting wet is no proof that it must be raining: it could from an altogether different source. This logical mistake, which is also very common, is called *the fallacy of affirming the consequent*, again, for obvious reasons.

The last form of conditional argument had the minor premise denying the consequent contained in the major premise.

> if it is raining then something is getting wet;
> nothing is getting wet.

In this instance, it is not as clear whether something follows of necessity, or not. One might think it possible to conclude that it is not raining—and this does follow, in fact.

> if it is raining then something is getting wet;
> nothing is getting wet;
> ∴   it is not raining.

Nevertheless, it is not as clear as in the case of modus ponens exactly why it follows. There is a way to prove that this argument form, which is called modus tollens (*modus tollens* is Latin for *the method of taking something away,*) is in fact valid: and the argument uses *modus ponens* to do so.

Let us suppose that the conclusion does not follow: it would then be possible for the premises to be true and the conclusion false. So, if it is raining then something is getting wet and nothing is getting wet, is it possible that it is raining? No—because if it were raining, then something would be getting wet. We know this already, through the argument called *modus ponens*. In this indirect way, then, we can prove that *modus tollens* is also a valid form of conditional reasoning. We can explicitly give the conditions for *modus tollens* as follows:

> when one denies the consequent of a conditional proposition as a premise, one can validly deny the antecedent as a conclusion.

Of the four possible forms of conditional reasoning, then, two are valid and two are invalid. It is very important to distinguish among them, both because the fallacies associated with the invalid forms are very common (some mistakes are easier to make than others,) and because conditional arguments *in general* are used often in our everyday speaking and writing.